# THE REVOLUTION BETRAYED

## What is the Soviet Union and Where is it Going?

AAKAR BOOKS CLASSICS

# THE REVOLUTION BETRAYED

## What is the Soviet Union and Where is it Going?

Leon Trotsky

*Edited by*
Saurobijay Sarkar

THE REVOLUTION BETRAYED
What is the Soviet Union and Where is it Going?
Leon Trotsky



Indian Edition 2006
Reprinted 2009
Reprinted 2014
**Reprinted 2021**

ISBN 978-81-87879-74-9



*Published by*
**AAKAR BOOKS**
28 E Pocket IV, Mayur Vihar Phase I, Delhi 110 091
Phone : 011 2279 5505 Telefax : 011 2279 5641
aakarbooks@gmail.com; www.aakarbooks.com

*Printed at*
Sapra Brothers, Noida.

ACKNOWLEDGEMENTS

I am grateful to all the contributors who have consistently encouraged me towards the publication of the Indian edition of this book. I would like to acknowledge the efforts and encouragement of the comrades in the Indian Institute of Marxist Studies (Kolkata Chapter) and the 'Other Voice' publication. Thanks to Mr. K.K. Saxena and others in Aakar Books. Without their committed endeavours, the project could not have been successfully completed, in such a short time and with such perfection. This edition of the book is dedicated to late comrade Harry Magdoff and comrade Paul. M. Sweezy as homage to their contribution towards Marxist thoughts.

# CONTENTS

# FOREWORD TO THE INDIAN EDITION

*—Saurobijay Sarkar*

The collapse of the Soviet Union and the Eastern Europe has ushered in a sea change in the arena of international politics. Not only did the capitalist elements throughout the world celebrate the phenomenon of the collapse of existing 'socialism', it also produced lots of frustration and confusion in the leadership and the rank- and- file militants of the international communist movement. The collapse of Soviet Russia and the adoption of open economy policy by China's 'Communist' rulers have naturally given birth lots of fundamental questions like:

> **'If socialism, which is altogether a different mode of production as compared with capitalism, 'collapsed' with the return of capitalism, can it (socialism) be really a viable alternative to capitalism?'**
>
> **'What were the economic foundations of the societies in Soviet Russia, Eastern Europe, China, Cuba and other 'socialist' states?'**
>
> **'Whether dictatorship of the proletariat is really viable or is it equivalent to the Communist party dictatorship?'**

It could really be a noteworthy thing, if communists throughout the world honestly and wholeheartedly tried to find the answers from the Marxist—Leninist orientation and engage in polemics with each other. Instead, a significant portion is swayed away by the phenomenon of the collapse of existing 'socialism' and has adopted the lines of Eurocommunism, etc.

by negating the fundamentals of Marxism. Alongside these trends, there are the Social democrats of various other shades throughout the world. In India this treacherous Social Democratic trend can be found in the parties like CPI (M), CPI, etc., which had the Stalinist background, and also in the parties like RSP, which had its origin deeply rooted in Anti-Stalinism. Although these parties officially still don't endorse social democracy fully, they in practice collaborate wholeheartedly with the capitalist parties and execute the same capitalist policies in the states, where they are in power. Communist Party of India (Marxist) (CPI (M)), with the objective of justifying it's own position, clarifies today's China as a socialist one adopting open economy. Along with these trends, trends of exactly opposite nature can be found in the Indian and the international Communist movements. These trends either in the name of 'Maoism' by CPI (Maoist) in India or by some sectarian Fourth Internationalist groupings in some parts of the world, fail to understand the importance of organizing the debate regarding this issue within the rank-and-file militants of the left parties and their mass organizations and are thus confined to their own circles. In essence, from this perspective they are the two sides of the same coin. Instead of engaging themselves into polemics they simply like to curse others as either 'Trotskyite' or 'Stalinist' or by some other terminology. Although the politics of CPI (Maoist) and other like-minded ultra left outfits differs a lot from that of the sectarian Fourth Internationalist groupings, essentially both the trends suffer from the same disease of sectarianism and dogmatism.

Needless to say, the problem of sectarianism leads to the lack of a democratic environment within the communist camps- not only among different factions, but inside the communist party also. The lack of inner party democracy and the democratic attitude as a whole, affects the entire communist movement. In the name of ideological struggle, personal attacks are frequently used as a weapon to ambush the opponent. This not only dilutes the ideological struggle, but hampers the unified mass movement also. Some people point out the formation of the Communist party itself as the root cause of the birth of sectarianism. The fundamental theme of their criticism is that the principle of 'democratic centralism' itself is devoid of any sort of democracy. The history of the Bolshevik Party, at least in its early days, is in sharp contrast with this type of analysis. The inner party democracy inside the Bolshevik Party was sharply manifested through the open debates in Iskra, Pravda, etc. Lenin himself engaged in polemics with prominent Bolshevik personalities like Trotsky, Bukharin, etc., at the same time still considered them as honest Bolsheviks. The democratic culture was not only confined to the Bolshevik Party, Lenin and the Bolshevik Party acknowledged the presence of other honest Communists outside the Bolshevik Party also. The best example of this can be found in the case of Leon Trotsky, who joined the Bolshevik Party only in the year of 1917. There were differences over certain issues among Trotsky, his small independent group and the Bolsheviks. Occasionally Lenin and Trotsky used bitter words against each other as a part of political debate, but that did not prevent Trotsky from joining the Bolshevik Party afterwards and becoming one of the closest followers of Lenin.

The bourgeois world wholeheartedly and deliberately attempts to portray the 'Communist rule' and the Communist rulers as ruthless and intolerant of any sort of criticism. Bourgeois scholars as a proof of lack of democracy indicate the existence 'one party rulings' in the post-revolutionary society and want to conclude that the bourgeois democracy, which is a multi party democracy (***in reality the democracy of the capitalist class and its servant parties!***) is superior to the democracy in the post-revolutionary society. Again if we cite the example of Soviet Russia in its early days, we can see that even before 1921, the Mensheviks and the Socialist Revolutionaries had significant representations in the Soviets along with the Bolsheviks. Only in the year of 1921, due to the exceptional circumstances of the civil war, when the leadership of the Mensheviks and the Socialist Revolutionaries turned into open counter-revolution, all other parties and factions were banned. Lenin and Trotsky categorically termed this banning as temporary, but unfortunately this became permanent in the later period. After the death of Lenin in April 1923, Trotsky fought for the right to organize the faction or separate organization, but his fight went in vain. Some people within the 'Marxist' camp pointed out that the 1921 phenomenon or the incident of the crushing of the rebellion of Kronstadt sailors by the Bolsheviks was the starting point of the curtailment of democracy. Posing the question of democracy in this manner is utterly wrong. The question of socialism and democracy needs to be judged only in the plane of class struggle. Kronstadt rebellion was a rebellion against the Bolsheviks and the Soviets; the rebels joined hands with the whiteguards to crush the world's first workers' state and raised the slogan: 'Soviets without Bolsheviks', which was truly undemocratic in principle and counter-revolutionary in essence. Kronstadt was an example, but the key point is that any political analysis needs to be based upon the concrete objective conditions. The bourgeois world and the imperialist camp with their own objectives, attempt to portray the Kronstadt phenomenon and the crushing of the uprising in Hungary in 1956 or in Czechoslovakia in 1968 by the Soviet army in the same mirror. Unfortunately some left groups or intellectuals, failing to understand the essence of each phenomenon, commit the same error. To them democracy is the primary thing, class struggle is secondary. This approach, no doubt leads to dilution. But this sort of analysis needs to be fought ideologically instead of simply using terminology like 'counter-revolutionary',' agents', 'provocateurs' etc. To elaborate further, the words like 'revisionist', 'counter-revolutionary', 'Fascist' were often used in the communist movement with an objective to isolate the political opponent and this trend still continues.

As a result of this kind of sectarianism, the Indian communist movement and the International Communist movement underwent a series of unjustified splits. Although splits are the manifestations of the social crisis, sometimes those occurred quiet irrationally based on petty issues and simple slogan-mongering. The objective of the Marxists cannot simply be splitting based on petty issues, or unification for the sake of unification, but to decide on the fundamental points of class struggle based on concrete reality, i.e. concrete objective conditions. These fundamental points of class struggle, in turn will decide the pivotal points of unification or disintegration. The best example of this can be traced back in the formation of Third International when the treachery of 2nd International leaders was exposed. The leaders of the 2nd International took a class collaborationist line of serving the bourgeoisie of their own nations in the First World War. The objective conditions demanded the split and the formation of the revolutionary international. Had it not been formed, had the split not occurred, the fate of the Russian Revolution would be in the graveyard. That was the highest point of ideological struggle, where splitting was essential.

In contrast to this phenomenon, a number of splits occurred in the international Communist movement along with the Indian Communist movement, which may be termed as 'unjustified'. The existence of numerous 'Maoist' groups and 'Trotskyist' groups in many countries are the best examples of this phenomenon. The notable thing is that except in few cases there is essentially no fundamental difference between different groupings. Sectarianism, lack of democratic environment and the inability to decide on the fundamental points of class struggle based on present objective conditions were the key points behind these splits. The task of the genuine Marxists would therefore be to create a sphere of discussion and debate instead of simply labeling others as 'Stalinist', 'Trotskyite', 'Maoist', etc. It is true that the Stalin–Trotsky debate or Mao's own assertion about Stalin still have relevance today, but to put forward these debates properly in an organized manner and relate those debates to today's objective conditions, Marxists need to be tolerant and non-sectarian. The seeds of sectarianism are rooted in the trends of the International Communist movement, but the ultimate manifestation of intolerance could be visualized, when two groups term each other as 'counter-revolutionary' and engage in the annihilation of the forces of each other. The leadership of the Chinese Communist Party today and the CPI (M) in India becoming capitalist servants, their 'democracy' plays in the hands of reaction. But the ultra-left outfits in India like Peoples war (PW) and Maoist Communist Center (MCC) in the past were heavily engaged in ambushing each other. The inner contradiction among different CPI (ML) groups and its crude manifestation in the 1970s, 1980s and afterwards was and is an obstacle to the path of class struggle in the Indian subcontinent. Herein the task lies both in India and abroad, to put democratic centralism and true Marxist culture in practice and organize debates and discussions over crucial issues to fight sectarianism and opportunism.

The Indian communist movement also has undergone splits in the past. The formation of CPI (M) from CPI and the formation of CPI (ML) from CPI (M) are the best examples of this. In both the cases the ideological differences based on concrete objective conditions play the key role. Nevertheless, in those cases also and as a whole in the Indian Communist movement the tendency of ambushing the opponent artificially has come to the forefront. Naxalites were termed as 'Trotskyites', 'Counter-revolutionary', 'CIA Agents', etc. by CPI (M) leadership. The same tendency can be found within the CPI (ML) camps also. Even in the undivided Communist Party of India, there was a tendency of branding political opponents as 'Trotskyite' (for example, the Randive line during the peasant's struggle in Telengana was condemned as 'Trotskyite'), whereas none of the organizations or individuals endorsed either the program of 'Permanent Revolution' nor agreed with Trotsky's characterization of Soviet Russia as a 'degenerated workers' state'. None of the organizations ever felt the need to go scientifically through the thesis of Trotsky, Rosa Luxemburg, Gramsci or others, who were rejected by the official Communist movement. It is admitted that after the collapse of Soviet Russia and the 'Socialist' regime of East Europe, the thirst for Marxist ideas has taken a new dimension. **Venezuelan President Hugo Chavez**, while saying 'Capitalism must be transcended', declared openly in the World Forum of intellectuals and artists in Venezuela, in December 2004 that there is a need to study the original principle of socialism and its errors. He referred to the importance of early 20th Century **Russian revolutionary Leon Trotsky's** ideas, embodied in **"The Permanent Revolution"** and how it explains that there are no national solutions to global problems, referring to the need for a global effort to deal with today's challenges. **(Reference: venezuelaanalysis.com - a news group in Venezuela).** Although his statement carries lots of significance, it will be rather premature and foolish to predict the fate of the Venezuelan movement from a single statement. **There were, of course, some elements in Chavez's speech, which Marxists would disagree with.** He defended Brazilian President Luis "Lula" Da Silva, who has been sharply criticized by the Latin American left, and who was booed during his speech at the World Social Forum. Apart from the natural reluctance of a guest to criticize his host, Chavez naturally sees leaders like Lula in Brazil or Kirchner in Argentina, or the new leaders of Uruguay as potential allies in the fight against US imperialism. This also explains his favorable reference to President Putin of Russia.

**Equally important is the article of Celia Hart, a member of the Cuban Communist Party, in TRIcontinental, on May 10, 2004.** Celia Hart comes from a family of veteran Cuban revolutionaries who fought against the Batista dictatorship together with **Fidel Castro** and **Che Guevara.** When Batista was finally overthrown, her father Armando was made the first Minister of Education of the Revolution and her mother Hayd Santamar was made President of La Casa de las Amcas (the House of the Americas), which she in effect founded. However, in Tricontinental, in the article titled **"Socialism in one country and the Cuban Revolution"**, she has written that

> **"Everything Trotsky foresaw in The Revolution Betrayed was furthered considerably."**

She further wrote that

> **"...Fidel Castro, Cuban president for more than 40 years, rarely takes off his guerrilla uniform; he has never cut a deal with**

> **the enemy and his words always resonate with internationalism. Chavez, in the midst of his political crisis, does not stop calling for the unity of Latin America and the Caribbean. They are two authentic internationalist leaders.**
>
> **Then, why Trotsky? In the first place, because it is politically necessary. Yes. The experience of the old fighter is vital to save time and effort for the new movements. No one is preaching that people should become Trotsky fanatics. But he should be studied with the same care that we devote to Gramsci or Mariategui."**

One need not agree fully with her assessment regarding Fidel Castro, Chavez or even Trotsky, but the most important thing to be noted here is that this is the first time in history that a magazine published from a 'Socialist' state, openly publishes an article, which overwhelmingly defends the political and revolutionary heritage of Leon Trotsky along with Lenin. Needless to say, the article of Celia Hart provoked an intense debate on the question of Trotsky internationally.

It is true that the declarations of Chavez or Celia Hart does not necessarily prove the correctness of the theoretical positions of Trotsky, but it surely indicates that the orthodoxy and regimentation in the official Communist movement has been diminished a lot. In India the best of this example can be found in the tendency of **CPIML (liberation)**.

While basing itself on the principle of democratic centralism as opposed to the RSDLP-like party structure by some CPI (ML) groups, **CPIML(liberation)** is trying to give space for the debates over the fundamental issues of Marxism-Leninism. This is manifested very sharply in their declaration of the 5th Congress, where they declare that the party's fundamental principle is **Marxism, Leninism and Mao Zedong thought**, as opposed to the earlier declarations of **Marxism-Leninism-Mao Zedong** thought. This shows that as opposed to the concept of 'Maoism', which declares that Maoism is the only and one pure continuation of Marxism Leninism, **CPIML (liberation)** clearly recognizes that thoughts of other variants like Gramsci, Trotsky, etc., needs to be studied and discussions and debates needs to be organized in every circle.

This work, by a leader of the Bolshevik Party and an

architect of the Russian Revolution along with Lenin—**Leon Trotsky**, while attempting to focus on the economic foundations of Soviet society in the 1930s, characterized the Soviet state as a **'degenerated workers' state'**, whose ultimate fate would be towards capitalism in the absence of a political revolution. Trotsky does not limit the explanation of major historical developments to the "cult of the personality" but rather probes and dissects the very essence of bureaucracy, which usurped power in the world's first workers' state. This approach was in sharp contrast with that followed by Nikita Khrushchev in the Twentieth Congress of the CPUSSR, where in the name of 'de-Stalinization' personal attacks were launched against Stalin as a weapon to hide the root cause of the degeneration of the Soviet society. One may not agree with the formulations advocated by Trotsky and subsequently his followers, but it is admittable that his approach at least attempted to focus on some key aspects in post-revolutionary society and throw some fundamental questions like 'What will be the fate of this post-revolutionary society?' or whether 'Socialism can be victorious within the periphery of a single country?' It is noteworthy that Trotsky's critique was done not as a post-mortem, but a priori to determine the fate of the revolution and socialism. Although Official Communist parties in Soviet Russia, Eastern Europe, China and elsewhere assured everyone regarding the 'victory of socialism', questions began to pop up even in the trends or once admirers of official communism apart from those of 'Trotskyism'. Notable Marxist scholars like **Paul M. Sweezy** or **Charles Bettelheim** devoted a lot to this aspect. Although their formulations differ from each other and essentially with that of Trotsky, they in the later period no longer upheld the view that victory of Socialism was achieved in the USSR. **Paul M. Sweezy,** founder of the independent Marxist magazine ***Monthly Review,*** in his famous book **'Post Revolutionary Society',** in the chapter 'Is There a Ruling Class in the USSR?' commented that

> "Now, I have no doubt that those who control the Soviet state are to be found among the privileged layers of the society, but I fail to see what sense it makes to lump together all these hetero-

> geneous groups-undoubtedly riddled with conflicts of interest over sharing the privileges—into a collectivity called the "bureaucracy"...". (pp. 111)

Sweezy drew a conclusion that the Soviet Russia during the 1930s and afterwards could no longer be termed as socialist, rather a new class is formed among the privileged layers of society. Sweezy engaged in sharp polemics with Trotsky's point of view that it is not the ruling class but the bureaucracy comprised of trade union leadership, military generals, etc. through the ruling party controlled the state, which was still based on the property relation that was formed after the October revolution. Like Trotsky in 'The Revolution Betrayed', Sweezy, who was influenced by Mao's ideology, at least tried sincerely to find the economic foundations of soviet society and the class nature of Soviet state, although he was not in agreement with the analysis put forward by Trotsky. Herein lies the task of the Marxists, to draw an insight on the property relations, distribution pattern, surplus generation, the consumption pattern and as a whole economic foundations in the then Soviet Union, Eastern Europe, past and present China along with the nature of the political formations in those states, and highlight the debate scientifically, not just emphatically.

Marxism is neither determinist nor voluntarist; or in other words both determinist and voluntarist. "Men make their own history," Marx wrote in the second paragraph of ***The Eighteenth Brumaire of Louis Bonaparte,*** "but they do not make it just as they please; they do not make it under circumstances chosen by themselves, but under circumstances directly encountered, given and transmitted from the past." The objective of the Marxists therefore is to focus on the objective conditions in the past and present in order to initiate the debate, instead of becoming blind followers of Lenin, Stalin, Mao, Trotsky or others.

The objective of this work is to promote debates and discussions within the best elements of the Communist movement and highlight the principle of 'democratic centralism', i.e. Communist Party is neither a closed, rigid circle nor a loose association of individuals. This trend, which has been initiated by **CPIML (liberation)** to some extent, needs to be carried forward in the Indian and the International Communist movement. **CPIML (liberation)** although doesn't agree with lots of Trotsky's formulations, nevertheless tries to come out of the attitude of the sectarian slogan-mongering. This new edition, a tribute to the heroic sacrifices of the Indian communists including the martyrs of **Naxalbari**, has the objective of reorienting the programmatic debate within the Indian and the International communist movement.

# INTRODUCTION

## The Purpose of the Present Work

The bourgeois world at first tried to pretend not to notice the economic successes of the Soviet regime—the experimental proof, that is, of the practicability of socialist methods. The learned economists of capital still often try to maintain a deeply cogitative silence about the unprecedented tempo of Russia's industrial development, or confine themselves to remarks about an extreme "exploitation of the peasantry". They are missing a wonderful opportunity to explain why the brutal exploitation of the peasants in China, for instance, or Japan, or India, never produced an industrial tempo remotely approaching that of the Soviet Union.

Facts win out, however, in the end. The bookstalls of all civilized countries are now loaded with books about the Soviet Union. It is no wonder; such prodigies are rare. The literature dictated by blind reactionary hatred is fast dwindling. A noticeable proportion of the newest works on the Soviet Union adopt a favorable, if not even a rapturous, tone. As a sign of the improving international reputation of the parvenu state, this abundance of pro-Soviet literature can only be welcomed. Moreover, it is incomparably better to idealize the Soviet Union than fascist Italy. The reader, however, would seek in vain in the pages of this literature a scientific appraisal of what is actually taking place in the land of the October Revolution.

The writings of the "friends of the Soviet Union" fall into three principal categories:

> A dilettante journalism, reportage with a more or less "left" slant, makes up the principal mass of their articles and books.
>
> Alongside it, although more pretentious, stand the productions of a humanitarian, lyric and pacifistical "communism
>
> Third comes economic schematization, in the spirit of the old-German *Katheder-Sozializmus*.

Louis Fischer and Duranty are sufficiently well-known representatives of the first type. The late Barbusse and Romain Rolland represent the category of "humanitarian" friends. It is not accidental that before ever coming over to Stalin the former wrote a life of Christ and the latter a biography of Gandhi. And finally, the conservatively pedantic socialism has found its most authoritative representation in the indefatigable Fabian couple, Beatrice and Sidney Webb.

What unites these three categories, despite their differences, is a kowtowing before accomplished fact, and a partiality for sedative generalizations. To revolt against their own capitalism was beyond these writers. They are the more ready, therefore, to take their stand upon a foreign revolution which has already ebbed back into its channels. Before the October Revolution, and for a number of years after, not one of these people, nor any of their spiritual forebears, gave a thought to the question how socialism would arrive in the world. That makes it easy for them to recognize as socialism what we have in the Soviet Union. This gives them not only the aspect of progressive men, in step with the epoch, but even a certain moral stability. And at the same time it commits them to absolutely nothing. This kind of contemplative, optimistic, and anything but destructive, literature, which sees all unpleasantness in the past, has a very quieting effect on the nerves of the reader and therefore finds a ready market. Thus there is quietly coming into being an international school, which might be described as *Bolshevism for the Cultured Bourgeoisie*, or more concisely, *Socialism for the Radical Tourists*.

We shall not enter into a polemic with the productions of this school, since they offer no serious grounds for polemic. Questions end for them where they really only begin. The purpose of the present investigation is to estimate correctly what is, in order to better understand what is coming to be. We shall dwell upon the past only so far as that helps us to see the future. Our book will be critical. Whoever worships the accomplished fact is incapable of preparing the future.

The process of economic and cultural development in the Soviet Union has already passed through several stages, but has by no means arrived at an inner equilibrium. If you remember that the task of socialism is to create a classless society based upon solidarity and the harmonious satisfaction of all needs, there is not yet, in this fundamental sense, a hint of socialism in the Soviet Union. To be sure, the contradictions of Soviet society are deeply different from the contradictions of capitalism. But they are nevertheless very tense. They find their expression in material and cultural inequalities, governmental repressions, political groupings, and the struggle of factions. Police repression hushes up and distorts a political struggle, but does not eliminate it. The thoughts, which are forbidden, exercise an influence on the governmental policy at every step, fertilizing or blocking it. In these circumstances, an analysis of the development of the Soviet Union cannot for a minute neglect to consider those ideas and slogans under which a stifled but passionate political struggle is being waged throughout the country. History here merges directly with living politics.

The safe-and-sane "left" philistines love to tell us that in criticizing the Soviet Union we must be extremely cautious lest we injure the process of socialist construction. We, for our part, are far from regarding the Soviet state as so shaky a structure. The enemies of the Soviet Union are far better informed about it than its real friends, the workers of all countries. In the general staffs of the imperialist governments an accurate account is kept of the pluses and minuses of the Soviet Union, and not only on the basis of public reports. The enemy can, unfortunately, take advantage of the weak side of the workers' state, but never of a criticism of those tendencies, which they themselves consider its favourable features. The hostility to criticism of the majority of the official "friends" really conceals a fear not of the fragility of the Soviet Union, but of the fragility of their own sympathy with it. We shall tranquilly disregard all fears and warnings of this kind. It is facts and not illusions that decide. We intend the face and not the mask.

August 4, 1936

# POSTSCRIPT

*This book was completed and sent to the publishers before the "terrorist" conspiracy trial of Moscow was announced. Naturally, therefore, the proceedings at the trial could not be evaluated in its pages. Its indication of the historic logic of this "terrorist" trial, and its advance exposure of the fact that its mystery is deliberate mystification, is so much the more significant.*

September 1936

## *Chapter 1*

# WHAT HAS BEEN ACHIEVED

### 1. The Principal Indices of Industrial Growth

Owing to the insignificance of the Russian bourgeoisie, the democratic tasks of backward Russia—such as liquidation of the monarchy and the semi-feudal slavery of the peasants—could be achieved only through a dictatorship of the proletariat. The proletariat, however, having seized the power at the head of the peasant masses, could not stop at the achievement of these democratic tasks. The bourgeois revolution was directly bound with the first stages of a socialist revolution. That fact was not accidental. The history of recent decades very clearly shows that, in the conditions of capitalist decline, backward countries are unable to attain that level which the old centres of capitalism have attained. Having themselves arrived in a blind alley, the highly civilized nations block the road of proletarian revolution, not because her economy was the first to become ripe for a socialist change, but because she could not develop further on a capitalist basis. Socialization of the means of production had become a necessary condition for bringing the country out of barbarism. That is the *law of combined development* for backward countries. Entering upon the socialist revolution as "the weakest link in the capitalist chain" (Lenin), the former empire of the tzars is even now, in the 19th year after the revolution, still confronted with the task of "catching up with and outstripping"—consequently in the first place catching up with—Europe and America. She has, that is, to solve those problems of technique and productivity, which were long ago solved by capitalism in the advanced countries.

Could it indeed be otherwise? The overthrow of the old ruling classes did not achieve, but only completely revealed, the task: to rise from barbarism to culture. At the same time, by concentrating the means of production in the hands of the state, the revolution made it possible to apply new and incomparably more effective industrial methods. Only thanks to a planned directive was it possible in so brief a span to restore what had been destroyed by the imperialist and civil wars, to create gigantic new enterprises, to introduce new kinds of production and establish new branches of industry.

The extraordinary tardiness in the development of the international revolution, upon whose prompt aid the leaders of the Bolshevik party had counted, created immense difficulties for the Soviet Union, but also revealed its inner powers and resources. However, a correct appraisal of the results achieved—their grandeur as well as their inadequacy—is possible only with the help of an international scale of measurement. This book will be a historic and sociological interpretation of the process, not a piling up of statistical illustrations. Nevertheless, in the interests of the further discussion, it is necessary to take as a point of departure certain important mathematical data.

The vast scope of industrialization in the Soviet Union, as against a background of stagnation and decline in almost the whole capitalist world, appears unanswerably in the following gross indices. Industrial production in Germany, thanks solely to feverish war preparations, is now returning to the level of 1929. Production in Great Britain, holding to the apron strings of protectionism, has raised itself 3 or 4 per cent during these six years. Industrial production in the United States has declined approximately 25 per cent; in France, more than 30 per cent. First place among capitalist countries is occupied by Japan, who is furiously arming herself and robbing her neighbours. Her production has risen almost 40 per cent! But even this exceptional index fades before the dynamic of development in the Soviet Union. Her industrial production has increased during this same period approximately 3½ times, or 250 per cent. The heavy industries have increased their production during the last decade (1925 to 1935) more than 10 times. In the first year of the Five-Year Plan (1928 to 1929), capital investments amounted to 5.4 billion rubles; for 1936, 32 billion are indicated.

If in view of the instability of the ruble as a unit of measurement, we lay aside money estimates; we arrive at another unit, which is absolutely unquestionable. In December 1913, the Don basin produced 2,275,000 tons of coal; in December 1935, 7,125,000 tons. During the last three years the production of iron has doubled. The production of steel and of the rolling mills has increased almost 2½ times. The output of oil, coal and iron has increased from 3 to 3½ times the pre-war figure. In 1920, when the first plan of electrification was drawn up, there were 10 district power stations in the country with a total power production of 253,000 kilowatts. In 1935, there were already 95 of these stations with a total power of 4,345,000 kilowatts. In 1925, the Soviet Union stood 11th in the production of electro-energy; in 1935, it was second only to Germany and the United States. In the production of coal, the Soviet Union has moved forward from 10th to 4th place. In steel, from 6th to 3rd place. In the production of tractors, to the first place in the world. This also is true of the production of sugar.

Gigantic achievement in industry, enormously promising beginnings in agriculture, an extraordinary growth of the old industrial cities and a building of new ones, a rapid increase of the numbers of workers, a rise in cultural level and cultural demands—such are the indubitable results of the October revolution, in which the prophets of the old world tried to see the grave of human civilization. With the bourgeois economists we have no longer anything to quarrel over. Socialism has demonstrated its right to victory, not on the pages of *Das Kapital*, but in an industrial arena comprising a sixth part of the earth's surface—not in the language of dialectics, but in the language of steel, cement and electricity. Even if the Soviet Union, as a result of internal difficulties, external blows and the mistakes of leadership, were to collapse—which we firmly hope will not happen—there would remain an earnest of the future this indestructible fact, that thanks solely to a proletarian revolution a backward country has achieved in less than 10 years successes unexampled in history.

This also ends the quarrel with the reformists in the workers' movement. Can we compare for one moment their mouselike fussing with the titanic work accomplished by this people aroused to a new life by revolution? If in 1918 the Social-Democrats of Germany had employed the power imposed upon them by the workers for a socialist revolution, and not for the rescue of capitalism, it is easy to see on the basis of the Russian experience what unconquerable economic power would be possessed today by a socialist bloc of Central and Eastern Europe and a considerable part of Asia. The peoples of the world will pay for the historic crime of reformism with new wars and revolutions.

## 2. Comparative Estimate of these Achievements

The dynamic coefficients of Soviet industry are unexampled. But they are still far from decisive. The Soviet Union is uplifting itself from a terribly low level, while the capitalist countries are slipping down from a very high one. The correlation of forces at the present moment is determined not by the rate of growth, but by contrasting the entire power of the two camps as expressed in material accumulations, technique, culture and, above all, the productivity of human labour. When we approach the matter from this statistical point of view, the situation changes at once, and to the extreme disadvantage of the Soviet Union.

The question formulated by Lenin—Who shall prevail? —is a question of the correlation of forces between the Soviet Union and the world revolutionary proletariat on the one hand, and on the other international capital and the hostile forces within the Union. The economic successes of the Soviet Union make it possible for her to fortify herself, advance, arm herself, and, when necessary, retreat and wait—in a word, hold out. But in its essence the question, who shall prevail—not only as a military, but still more as an economic question—confronts the Soviet Union on a world scale. Military intervention is a danger. The intervention of cheap goods in the baggage trains of a capitalist army would be an incomparably greater one. The victory of the proletariat in one of the Western countries would, of course, immediately and radically alter the correlation of forces. But so long as the Soviet Union remains isolated, and, worse than that, so long as the European proletariat suffers reverses and continues to fall back, the strength of the Soviet structure is measured in the last analysis by the productivity of labour. And that, under a market economy, expresses itself in production costs and prices. The difference between domestic prices and prices in the world market is one of the chief means of measuring this correlation of forces. The Soviet statisticians, however, are forbidden even to approach that question. The reason is that, notwithstanding its condition of stagnation and rot, capitalism is still far ahead in the matter of technique, organization and labour skill.

The traditional backwardness of agriculture in the Soviet Union is well enough known. In no branch of it has progress been made that can in the remotest degree bear comparison with the progress in industry.

"We are still way behind the capitalist countries in the beet crop," complains Molotov, for example, at the end of 1935. "In 1934 we reaped from one hectare [approximately 2½ acres] 82 hundredweight; in 1935, in the Ukraine with an extraordinary harvest 131 hundredweight. In Czechoslovakia and Germany, they reap about 250 hundredweight, in France, over 300 per hectare."

Molotov's complaint could be extended to every branch of agriculture—textile as well as grain growing, and especially to stockbreeding. The proper rotation of crops, selection of seeds, fertilization, the tractors, combines, blooded stock farms—all these are preparing a truly gigantic revolution in socialized agriculture. But it is just in this most conservative realm that the revolution demands time. Meanwhile, notwithstanding collectivization, the problem still is to approach the higher models of the capitalist West, handicapped though it is with the small-farm system.

The struggle to raise the productivity of labour in industry runs in two channels: adoption of an advanced technique and better use of labour power. What made it possible to establish gigantic factories of the most modern type in the space of a few years was, on the one hand, the existence in the West of a high capitalist technique, on the other, the domestic regime of planned economy. In this sphere foreign achievements are in process of assimilation. The fact that Soviet industry, as also the equipping of the Red Army, has developed at a forced tempo, contains enormous potential advantages. The industries had not been compelled to drag along an antiquated implementation as in England and France. The army has not been condemned to carry old-fashioned equipment. But this same feverish growth has also had its negative side. There is no correspondence between the different elements of industry; men lag behind technique; the leadership is not equal to its tasks. Altogether this expresses itself in extremely high production costs and poor quality of product.

"Our works," writes the head of the oil industry, "possess the same equipment as the American. But the organization of the drilling lags; the men are not sufficiently skilled." The numerous breakdowns, he explains are a result of "carelessness, lack of skill and lack of technical supervision".

Molotov complains: "We are extremely backward in organization of the building industry.... It is carried on for the most part in old ways with an abominable use of tools and mechanisms." Such confessions are scattered throughout the Soviet press. The new technique is still far from giving the results produced in its capitalist fatherlands.

The wholesale success of the heavy industries is a gigantic conquest. On that foundation alone it is possible to build. However, the test of modern industry is the production of delicate mechanisms, which demand both technical and general culture. In this sphere the backwardness of the Soviet Union is still great.

Undoubtedly the most important successes, both quantitative and qualitative, have been achieved in the war industries. The army and fleet are the most influential clients, and the most fastidious customers. Nevertheless, in a series of their public speeches the heads of the War Department, among them Voroshilov, complain unceasingly: "We are not always fully satisfied with the quality of the products which you give us for the Red Army." It is not hard to sense the anxiety which these cautious words conceal.

The products of machine manufacture, says the head of the heavy industries in an official report, "must be good quality and unfortunately are not". And again: "machines with us are expensive." As always, the speaker refrains from giving accurate comparative data in relation to world production.

The tractor is the pride of Soviet industry. But the coefficient of effective use of the tractors is very low. During the previous industrial year, it was necessary to subject 18 per cent of the tractors to capital repairs. A considerable number, moreover, were out of order again at the very height of the tilling season. According to certain calculations, the machine and tractor stations will cover expenses only with a harvest of 20 to 22 hundredweight of grain per hectare. At present, when the average harvest is less than half of that, the state is compelled to disburse billions to meet the deficit.

Things are worse still in the sphere of auto transport. In America a truck travels 60 to 80, or even 100,000 km a year; in the Soviet Union only 20,000—that is, a third or a fourth as much. Out of every 100 machines, only 55 are working; the rest are undergoing repairs or awaiting them. The cost of repairs is double the cost of all the new machines put out. It is no wonder that the state accounting office reports: "Auto transport is nothing but a heavy burden on the cost of production."

The increase of carrying power of the railroads is accompanied, according to the president of the Council of Peoples Commissars, "by innumerable wrecks and breakdowns". The fundamental cause is the same: low skill of labour inherited from the past. The struggle to keep the switches in neat condition is becoming a heroic exploit, about which prize switchgirls make reports in the Kremlin to the highest circles of power. Water transport, notwithstanding the progress of recent years, is far behind that of the railroads. Periodically the newspapers are speckled with communications about "the abominable operation of marine transport", "extremely low quality of ship repairs", etc.

In the light industries, conditions are even less favourable than in the heavy. A unique law of Soviet industry may be formulated thus: commodities are, as a general rule, worse the nearer they stand to the mass consumer. In the textile industry, according to *Pravda,* "there is a shamefully large percentage of defective goods, poverty of selection, predominance of low grades". Complaints of the poor quality of articles of wide consumption appear periodically in the press: "clumsy ironware"; "ugly furniture, badly put together and carelessly finished"; "you cant find decent buttons"; "the system of social food supply works absolutely unsatisfactorily". And so on, endlessly.

To characterize industrial progress by quantitative indices alone, without considering quality, is almost like describing a man's physique by his height and disregarding his chest measurements. Moreover, to judge correctly the dynamic of Soviet industry, it is necessary, along with qualitative corrections, to have always in mind the fact that swift progress in some branches is accompanied by backwardness in others. The creation of gigantic automobile factories is paid for in the scarcity and bad maintenance of the highways. "The dilapidation of our roads is extraordinary. On our most important highway—Moscow to Yaroslavl—automobiles can make only 10 kilometers [6 miles] an hour" (Izvestia). The president of the State Planning Commission asserts that the country still maintains "the tradition of pristine roadlessness".

Municipal economy is in a similar condition. New industrial towns arise in a brief span; at the same time dozens of old towns are running to seed. The capitals and industrial centres are growing and adorning themselves; expensive theatres and clubs are springing up in various parts of the country; but the dearth of living quarters is unbearable. Dwelling houses remains as a rule uncared for. "We build badly and at great expense. Our houses are being used up and not restored. We repair little and badly" (Izvestia).

The entire Soviet economy consists of such disproportions. Within certain limits they are inevitable, since it had been and remains necessary to begin the advance with the most important branches. Nevertheless the backwardness of certain branches greatly decreases the useful operation operation of others. From the standpoint of an ideal planning directive, which would guarantee not the maximum tempo in separate branches, but the optimum result in economy as a whole, the statistical coefficient of growth would be lower in the first period, but economy as a whole, and particularly the consumer, would gain. In the long run the general industrial dynamic would also gain.

In the official statistics, the production and repair of automobiles is added to the total of industrial production. From the standpoint of economic efficiency, it would be proper to subtract, not add. This observation applies to many other branches of industry. For that reason, all total estimates in rubles have only a relative value. It is not certain what a ruble is. It is not always certain what hides behind it—the construction of a machine, or its premature breakdown. If, according to an estimate in "stable" rubles, the total production of the big industries has increased by comparison with the pre-war level 6 times, the actual output of oil, coal and iron measured in tons will have increased 3 to 3½ times. The fundamental cause of this divergence of indices lies in the fact that Soviet industry has created a series of new branches unknown to tzarist Russia, but a supplementary cause is to be found in the tendentious manipulation of statistics. It is well known that every bureaucracy has an organic need to doll-up the facts.

### 3. Production Per Capita of the Population

The average individual productivity of labour in the Soviet Union is still very low. In the *best* metal foundry, according to the acknowledgement of its director, the output of iron and steel per individual worker is a third as much as the *average* output of American foundries. A comparison of average figures in both countries would probably give a ratio of 1 to 5, or worse. In these circumstances the announcement that blast furnaces are used "better" in the Soviet Union than in capitalist countries remains meaningless. The function of technique is to economize human labour and nothing else. In the timber and building industries things are even less favourable than in the metal industry. To each worker in the quarries in the United States falls 5,000 tons a year, in the Soviet Union 500 tons—that is, 1/10 as much. Such crying differences are explained not only by a lack of skilled workers, but still more by poor organization of the work. The bureaucracy spurs on the workers with all its might, but is unable to make proper use of labour power. In agriculture things are still less favourable, of course, than in industry. To the low productivity of labour corresponds a low national income, and consequently a low standard of life for the masses of the people.

When they assert that in volume of industrial production the Soviet Union in 1936 will occupy first place in Europe—of itself this progress is gigantic!—they leave out of consideration not only the quality and production cost of the goods, but also the size of the population. The general level of development of a country, however, and especially the living standard of the masses can be defined, at least in rough figures, only by dividing the products by the number of consumers. Let us try to carry out this simple arithmetical operation.

The importance of railroad transport for economy, culture and military ends needs no demonstration. The Soviet Union has 83,000 kilometres of railroads, as against 58,000 in Germany, 63,000 in France, and 417,000 in the United States. This means that for every 10,000 people in Germany there are 8.9 kilometres of railroad, in France 15.2, in the United States 33.1, and in the Soviet Union 5.0. Thus, according to railroad indices, the Soviet Union continues to occupy one of the lowest places in the civilized world. The merchant fleet, which has tripled in the last five years, stands now approximately at par with that of Denmark and Spain. To these facts we must add the still extremely low figure for paved highways. In the Soviet Union

0.6 automobiles were put out for every 1,000 inhabitants. In Great Britain, about 8 (in 1934), in France about 4.5, in the United States 23 (as against 36.5 in 1928). At the same time, in the relative number of horses (about 1 horse to each 10 or 11 citizens) the Soviet Union, despite the extreme backwardness of its railroad, water and auto transport, does not surpass either France or the United States, while remaining far behind them in the quality of the stock.

In the sphere of heavy industry, which has attained the most outstanding successes, the comparative indices still remain unfavourable. The coal output in the Soviet Union for 1935 was about 0.7 tons per person; in Great Britain, almost 5 tons; in the United States, almost 3 tons (as against 5.4 tons in 1913); in Germany, about 2 tons. Steel: in the Soviet Union, about 67 kilograms [kg = 2½ lbs. ap.] per person, in the United States about 250 kilograms, etc. About the same proportions in pig and rolled iron. In the Soviet Union, 153 kilowatt hours of electric power were produced per person in 1935, in Great Britain (1934) 443, in France 363, and in Germany 472.

In the light industries, the per capita indices are as a general rule still lower. Of woollen fabric in 1935, less than 1/2 meter per person, or 8 to 10 times less than in the United States or Great Britain. Woollen cloth is accessible only to privileged Soviet citizens. For the masses cotton print, of which about 16 meters per person was manufactured, still has to do for winter clothes. The production of shoes in the Soviet Union now amounts to about one-half pair per person, in Germany more than a pair, in France a pair and a half, in the United States about three pairs. And this leaves aside the quality index, which would still further lower the comparison. We may take it for granted that in bourgeois countries the percentage of people who have several pairs of shoes is considerably higher than in the Soviet Union. Unfortunately the Soviet Union also still stands among the first in percentage of barefoot people.

Approximately the same correlation, in part still less favourable, prevails in the production of foodstuffs. Notwithstanding Russia's indubitable progress in recent years, conserves, sausages, cheese, to say nothing of pastry and confections, are still completely inaccessible to the fundamental mass of the population. Even in the matter of dairy products things are not favourable. In France and the United States, there is approximately one cow for every five people, in Germany one for every six, in the Soviet Union one for every eight. But when it comes to giving milk, two Soviet cows must be counted approximately as one. Only in the production of grainbearing grasses, especially rye, and also in potatoes, does the Soviet Union, computing by population, considerably surpass the majority of European countries and the United States. But rye bread and potatoes as the predominant food of the population—that is the classic symbol of poverty.

The consumption of paper is one of the chief indices of culture. In 1935, the Soviet Union produced less than 4 kg per person, the United States over 34 (as against 48 in 1928), and Germany 47 kg. Whereas the United States consumes 12 pencils a year per inhabitant, the Soviet Union consumers only 4, and those 4 are of such poor quality that their useful work does not exceed that of one good pencil, or at the outside two. The newspapers frequently complain that the lack of primers, paper, and pencils paralyzes the work of the schools. It is no wonder that the liquidation of illiteracy, indicated for the 10th anniversary of the October Revolution, is still far from accomplished.

The problem can be similarly illumined by starting from more general considerations. The national income per person in the Soviet Union is considerably less than in the West. And since capital investment consumes about 25 to 30 per cent—incomparably more than anywhere else—the total amount consumed by the popular mass cannot but be considerably lower than in the advanced capitalist countries.

To be sure, in the Soviet Union there are no possessing classes, whose extravagance is balanced by an underconsumption of the popular mass. However, the weight of this corrective is not so great as might appear at first glance. The fundamental evil of the capitalist system is not the extravagance of the possessing classes, however disgusting that may be in itself, but the fact that in order to guarantee its right to extravagance the bourgeoisie maintains its private ownership of the means of production, thus condemning the economic system to anarchy and decay. In the matter of luxuries, the bourgeoisie, of course, has a monopoly of consumption. But in things of prime necessity, the toiling masses constitute the overwhelming majority of consumers. We shall see later, moreover, that although the Soviet Union has no possessing class in the proper sense of the word, still she has very privileged commanding strata of the population, who appropriate the lion's share in the sphere of consumption. And so if there is a lower per capita production of things of prime necessity in the Soviet Union than in the advanced capitalist countries, it does mean that the standard of living of the Soviet masses still falls below the capitalist level.

The historic responsibility for this situation lies, of course, upon Russia's black and heavy past, her heritage of darkness and poverty. There was no other way out upon the road of progress except through the overthrow of capitalism. To convince yourself of this, it is only necessary to cast a glance at the Baltic countries and Poland, once the most advanced parts of the tzar's empire, and now hardly emerging from the morass. The undying service of the Soviet regime lies in its intense and successful struggle with Russia's thousand-year-old backwardness. But a correct estimate of what has been attained is the first condition for further progress.

The Soviet regime is passing through a *preparatory* stage, importing, borrowing and appropriating the technical and cultural conquests of the West. The comparative coefficients of production and consumption testify that this preparatory stage is far from finished. Even under the improbable condition of a continuing complete capitalist standstill, it must still occupy a whole historic period. That first is an extremely important conclusion which we shall have need for in our further investigation.

## *Chapter 2*

# ECONOMIC GROWTH AND THE ZIGZAGS OF THE LEADERSHIP

### 1."Military Communism", "The New Economic Policy" (NEP) and the Course toward the Kulak

The line of development of the Soviet economy is far from an uninterrupted and evenly rising curve. In the first 18 years of the new regime you can clearly distinguish several stages marked by sharp crises. A short outline of the economic history of the Soviet Union in connection with the policy of the government is absolutely necessary both for diagnosis and prognosis.

The first three years after the revolution were a period of overt and cruel civil war. Economic life was wholly subjected to the needs of the front. Cultural life lurked in corners and was characterized by a bold range of creative thought, above all the personal thought of Lenin, with an extraordinary scarcity of material means. That was the period of so-called "military communism" (1918–21), which forms a heroic parallel to the "military socialism" of the capitalist countries. The economic problems of the Soviet government in those years came down chiefly to supporting the war industries, and using the scanty resources left from the past for military purposes and to keep the city population alive. Military communism was, in essence, the systematic regimentation of consumption in a besieged fortress.

It is necessary to acknowledge, however, that in its original conception it pursued broader aims. The Soviet government hoped and strove to develop these methods of regimentation directly into a system of planned economy in distribution as well as production. In other words, from "military communism" it hoped gradually, but without destroying the system, to arrive at genuine communism. The programme of the Bolshevik party adopted in March 1919 said:

> "In the sphere of distribution the present task of the Soviet Government is unwaveringly to continue on a planned, organized and state-wide scale to replace trade by the distribution of products."

Reality, however, came into increasing conflict with the programme of "military communism". Production continually declined, and not only because of the quenching of the stimulus of personal interest among the producers. The city demanded grain and raw materials from the rural districts, giving nothing in exchange except vari-coloured pieces of paper, named, according to ancient memory, money. And the muzhik buried his stores in the ground. The government sent out armed workers' detachments for grain. The muzhik cut down his sowings. Industrial production of steel fell from 4.2 million tons to 183,000 tons—that is, to 1/23 of what it had been. The total harvest of grain decreased from 801 million hundredweight to 503 million in 1922. That was a year of terrible hunger. Foreign trade at the same time plunged from 2.9 billion rubles to 30 million. The collapse of the productive forces surpassed anything of the kind that history had ever seen. The country, and the government with it, was at the very edge of the abyss.

The utopian hopes of the epoch of military communism came in later for a cruel, and in many respects just, criticism. The theoretical mistake of the ruling party remains inexplicable, however, only if you leave out of account the fact that all calculations at that time were based on the hope of an early victory of the revolution in the West. It was considered self-evident that the victorious German proletariat would supply Soviet Russia, on credit against future food and raw materials, not only with machines and articles of manufacture, but also with tens of thousands of highly skilled workers, engineers and organizers. And there is no doubt that if the proletarian revolution had triumphed in Germany—a thing that was prevented solely and exclusively by the Social Democrats—the economic development of the Soviet Union as well as of Germany would have advanced with such gigantic strides that the fate of Europe and the world would today have been incomparably more auspicious. It can be said with certainty, however, that even in that happy event it would still have been necessary to renounce the direct state distribution of products in favour of the methods of commerce.

Lenin explained the necessity of restoring the market by the existence in the country of millions of isolated peasant enterprises, unaccustomed to defining their economic relations with the outside world except through trade. Trade circulation would establish a "connection", as it was called, between the peasant and the nationalized industries. The theoretical formula for this "connection" is very simple: industry should supply the rural districts with necessary goods at such prices as would enable the state to forego forcible collection of the products of peasant labour.

To mend economic relations with the rural districts was undoubtedly the most critical and urgent task of the NEP. A brief experiment showed, however, that industry itself, in spite of its socialized character, had need of the methods of money payment worked out by capitalism. A planned economy cannot rest merely on intellectual data. The play of supply and demand remains for a long period a necessary material basis and indispensable corrective.

The market, legalized by the NEP, began, with the help of an organized currency, to do its work. As early as 1923, thanks to an initial stimulus from the rural districts, industry began to revive. Moreover it immediately hit a high tempo. It is sufficient to say that production doubled in 1922 and 1923, and by 1926 had already reached the pre-war level—that is, had grown more than five times its size in 1921. At the same time, although at a much more modest tempo, the harvests were increasing.

Beginning with the critical year 1923, the disagreements

observed earlier in the ruling party on the relation between industry and agriculture began to grow sharp. In a country which had completely exhausted its stores and reserves, industry could not develop except by borrowing grain and raw material from the peasants. Too heavy "forced loans" of products, however, would destroy the stimulus to labour. Not believing in the future prosperity, the peasant would answer the grain expeditions from the city by a sowing strike. Too light collections, on the other hand, threatened a standstill. Not receiving industrial products, the peasants would turn to industrial labour to satisfy their own needs, and revive the old home crafts. The disagreements in the party began about the question how much to take from the villages for industry, in order to hasten the period of dynamic equilibrium between them. The dispute was immediately complicated by the question of the social structure of the village itself.

In the spring of 1923, at a congress of the party, a representative of the "Left Opposition"—not yet, however, known by that name—demonstrated the divergence of industrial and agricultural prices in the form of an ominous diagram. This phenomenon was then first called "the scissors", a term which has since become almost international. If the further lagging of industry—said the speaker—continues to open these scissors, then a break between city and country is inevitable.

The peasants made a sharp distinction between the democratic and agrarian revolution, which the Bolshevik party had carried through, and its policy directed toward laying the foundations of socialism. The expropriation of the landlords and the state lands brought the peasants upwards of half a billion gold rubles a year. In prices of state products, however, the peasants were paying out a much larger sum. So long as the net result of the two revolutions, democratic and socialistic, bound together by the firm snow of October, reduced itself for the peasantry to a loss of hundreds of millions, a union of the two classes remained dubious.

The scattered character of the peasant economy, inherited from the past, was aggravated by the results of the October

Revolution. The number of independent farms rose during the subsequent decade from 16 to 25 million, which naturally strengthened the purely consummatory character of the majority of peasant enterprises. That was one of the causes of the lack of agricultural products.

A small commodity economy inevitably produces exploiters. In proportion as the villages recovered, the differentiation within the peasant mass began to grow. This development fell into the old well-trodden ruts. The growth of the kulak [well-off peasant, employing labour] far outstripped the general growth of agriculture. The policy of the government under the slogan "face to the country" was actually a turning of its face to the kulak. Agricultural taxes fell upon the poor far more heavily than upon the well-to-do, who moreover skimmed the cream of the state credits. The surplus grain, chiefly in possession of the upper strata of the village, was used to enslave the poor and for speculative selling to the bourgeois elements of the cities. Bukharin, the theoretician of the ruling faction at that time, tossed to the peasantry his famous slogan, "Get rich!". In the language of theory that was supposed to mean a gradual growing of the kulaks into socialism. In practice it meant the enrichment of the minority at the expense of the overwhelming majority.

Captive to its own policy, the government was compelled to retreat step by step before the demands of a rural petty bourgeoisie. In 1925 the hiring of labour power and the renting of land were legalized for agriculture. The peasantry was becoming polarized between the small capitalist on one side and the hired hand on the other. At the same time, lacking industrial commodities, the state was crowded out of the rural market. Between the kulak and the petty home craftsman there appeared, as though from under the earth, the middleman. The state enterprises themselves, in search of raw material, were more and more compelled to deal with the private trader. The rising tide of capitalism was visible everywhere. Thinking people saw plainly that a revolution in the forms of property does not solve the problem of socialism, but only raises it.

In 1925, when the course toward the kulak was in full

swing, Stalin began to prepare for the denationalization of the land. To a question asked at his suggestion by a Soviet journalist: "Would it not be expedient in the interest of agriculture to deed over to each peasant for 10 years the parcel of land tilled by him?", Stalin answered: "Yes, and ever for 40 years." The People's Commissar of Agriculture of Georgia, upon Stalin's own initiative, introduced the draft of a law denationalizing the land. The aim was to give the farmer confidence in his own future. While this was going on, in the spring of 1926, almost 60 per cent of the grain destined for sale was in the hands of 6 per cent of the peasant proprietors! The state lacked grain not only for foreign trade, but even for domestic needs. The insignificance of exports made it necessary to forego bringing in articles of manufacture, and cut down to the limit the import of machinery and raw materials.

Retarding industrialization and striking a blow at the general mass of the peasants, this policy of banking on the well-to-do farmer revealed unequivocally inside of two years, 1924–26, its political consequences. It brought about an extraordinary increase of self-consciousness in the petty bourgeoisie of both city and village, a capture by them of many of the lower Soviets, an increase of the power and self-confidence of the bureaucracy, a growing pressure upon the workers, and the complete suppression of party and Soviet democracy. The growth of the kulaks alarmed two eminent members of the ruling group, Zinoviev and Kamenev, who were, significantly, presidents of the Soviets of the two chief proletarian centres, Leningrad and Moscow. But the provinces, and still more the bureaucracy, stood firm for Stalin. The course toward the well-to-do farmer won out. In 1926, Zinoviev and Kamenev with their adherents joined the Opposition of 1923 (the "Trotskyists").

Of course, "in principle" the ruling group did not even then renounce the collectivization of agriculture. They merely put it off a few decades in their perspective. The future People's Commissar of Agriculture, Yakovlev, wrote in 1927 that, although the socialist reconstruction of the village can be accomplished only through collectivization, still "this obviously cannot be done in one, two or three years, and maybe not in one decade". "The collective farms and communes," he continued, "... are now, and will for a long time undoubtedly remain, only small islands in a sea of individual peasant holdings."

And in truth at that period only 8 per cent of the peasant families belonged to the collectives.

The struggle in the party about the so-called "general line", which had come to the surface in 1923, became especially intense and passionate in 1926. In its extended platform, which took up all the problems of industry and economy, the Left Opposition wrote:

> "The party ought to resist and crush all tendencies directed to the annulment or undermining of the nationalization of land, one of the pillars of the proletarian dictatorship."

On that question, the Opposition gained the day; direct attempts against nationalization were abandoned. But the problem, of course, involved more than forms of property in land.

> "To the growth of individual farming [fermerstvo] in the country we must oppose a swifter growth of the collective farms. It is necessary systematically year by year to set aside a considerable sum to aid the poor peasants organized in collectives. The whole work of the co-operatives ought to be imbued with the purpose of converting small production into a vast collectivized production."

But this broad programme of collectivization was stubbornly regarded as utopian for the coming years. During the preparations for the 15th Party Congress, whose task was to expel the Left Opposition, Molotov, the future president of the Soviet of People's Commissars, said repeatedly:

> "We must not slip down (!) into poor peasants illusions about the collectivization of the broad peasant masses. In the present circumstances it is no longer possible."

It was then, according to the calendar, the end of 1927. So far was the ruling group at that time from its own future policy toward the peasants!

Those same years (1923–28) were passed in a struggle of the ruling coalition, Stalin, Molotov, Rykov, Tomsky, Bukharin (Zinoviev and Kamenev went over to the Opposition in the beginning of 1926), against the advocates of "super-industrialization" and planned leadership. The future historian will re-establish with no small surprise the moods of spiteful disbelief in bold economic initiative with which the government of the socialist state was wholly imbued. An acceleration of the tempo of industrialization took place empirically, under impulses from without, with a crude smashing of all calculations and an extraordinary increase of overhead expenses. The demand for a five-year plan, when advanced by the Opposition in 1923, was met with mockery in the spirit of the petty bourgeois who fears "a leap into the unknown". As late as April 1927, Stalin asserted at a plenary meeting of the Central Committee that to attempt to build the Dnieperstroy hydroelectric station would be the same thing for us as for a muzhik to buy a gramophone instead of a cow. This winged aphorism summed up the whole programme. It is worth noting that during those years the bourgeois press of the whole world, and the social-democratic press after it, repeated with sympathy the official attribution to the "Left Opposition" of industrial romanticism.

Amid the noise of party discussions the peasants were replying to the lack of industrial goods with a more and more stubborn strike. They would not take their grain to market, nor increase their sowings. The right wing (Rykov, Tomsky, Bukharin), which was setting the tone at that period, demanded a broader scope for capitalist tendencies in the village through a raising of the price of grain, even at the cost of a lowered tempo in industry. The sole possible way out under such a policy would have been to import articles of manufacture in exchange for exported agricultural raw materials. But this would have meant to form a "connection" not between peasant economy and the socialist industries, but between the kulak and world capitalism. It was not worthwhile to make the October Revolution for that.

"To accelerate industrialization," answered the

representatives of the Opposition at the party conference of 1926, "in particular by way of increased taxation on the kulak, will produce a large mass of goods and lower market prices, and this will be to the advantage both of the worker and of the majority of the peasants... *Face to the village* does not mean turn your back to industry; it means industry to the village. For the 'face' of the state, if it does not include industry, is of no use to the village."

In answer Stalin thundered against the "fantastic plans" of the Opposition. Industry must not "rush ahead, breaking away from agriculture and abandoning the tempo of accumulation in our country". The party decisions continued to repeat these maxims of passive accommodation to the well-off upper circles of the peasantry. The 15th Party Congress, meeting in December 1927 for the final smashing of the "super-industrializes", gave warning of the "danger of a too great involvement of state capital in big construction". The ruling faction at that time still refused to see any other dangers.

In the economic year 1927–28, the so-called restoration period in which industry worked chiefly with pre-revolutionary machinery, and agriculture with the old tools, was coming to an end. For any further advance independent industrial construction on a large scale was necessary. It was impossible to lead any further gropingly and without plan.

The hypothetic possibilities of socialist industrialization had been analyzed by the Opposition as early as 1923–25. Their general conclusion was that, after exhausting the equipment inherited from the bourgeoisie, the Soviet industries might, on the basis of socialist accumulation, achieve a rhythm of growth wholly impossible under capitalism. The leaders of the ruling faction openly ridiculed our cautious coefficients in the vicinity of 15 to 18 per cent as the fantastic music of an unknown future. This constituted at that time the essence of the struggle against "Trotskyism".

The first official draft of the five-year plan, prepared at last in 1927, was completely saturated with the spirit of stingy tinkering. The growth of industrial production was projected with a tempo declining yearly from 9 to 4 per cent.

Consumption per person was to increase during the whole five years by 12 per cent! The incredible timidity of thought in this first plan comes out clearly in the fact that the state budget at the end of the five years was to constitute in all 16 per cent of the national income, whereas the budget of tzarist Russia, which had no intention of creating a socialist society, swallowed 18 per cent! It is perhaps worth adding that the engineers and economists who drew up this plan were some years later severely judged and punished by law as conscious sabotagers acting under the direction of foreign powers. The accused might have answered, had they dared, that their planning work corresponded perfectly with the "general line" of the Politburo at that time and was carried out under its orders.

The struggle of the tendencies was now translated into arithmetical language. "To prevent on the 10th anniversary of the October Revolution such a piddling and completely pessimistic plan," said the platform of the Opposition, "means in reality to work against socialism." A year later, the Politburo adopted a new five-year plan with an average yearly increase of production amounting to 9 per cent. The actual course of the development, however, revealed a stubborn tendency to approach the coefficients of the "super-industrializers". After another year, when the governmental policy had radically changed, the State Planning Commission drew up a third five-year plan, whose rate of growth came far nearer than could have been expected to the hypothetical prognosis made by the Opposition in 1923.

The real history of the economic policy of the Soviet Union, as we thus see, is very different from the official legend. Unfortunately, such pious investigators as the Webbs pay not the slightest attention to this.

## 2. A Sharp Turn: "Five-year Plan in Four Years" and "Complete Collectivization"

Irresoluteness before the individual peasant enterprises, distrust of large plans, defence of a minimum tempo, neglect of international problems—all this taken together formed the essence of the theory of "socialism in one country", first put forward by Stalin in the autumn of 1924 after the defeat of the proletariat in Germany. Not to hurry with industrialization, not to quarrel with the muzhik, not to count on world revolution, and above all to protect the power of the party bureaucracy from criticism! The differentiation of the peasantry was denounced as an intervention of the Opposition. The above-mentioned Yakovlev dismissed the Central Statistical Bureau whose records gave the kulak a greater place than was satisfactory to the authorities, while the leaders tranquilly asserted that the goods famine was out-living itself, that "a peaceful tempo in economic development was at hand", that the grain collections would in the future be carried on more "evenly", etc. The strengthened kulak carried with him the middle peasant and subjected the cities to a grain blockade. In January 1928 the working class stood face-to-face with the shadow of an advancing famine. History knows how to play spiteful jokes. In that very month, when the kulaks were taking the revolution by the throat, the representatives of the Left Opposition were thrown into prison or banished to different parts of Siberia in punishment for their "panic" before the spectre of the kulak.

The government tried to pretend that the grain strike was caused by the naked hostility of the kulak (where did he come from?) to the socialist state—that is, by ordinary political motives. But the kulak is little inclined to that kind of "idealism". If he hid his grain, it was because the bargain offered him was unprofitable. For the very same reason he managed to bring under his influence wide sections of the peasantry. Mere repressions against kulak sabotage were obviously inadequate. It was necessary to change the policy. Even yet, however, no little time was spent in vacillation.

Rykov, then still head of the government, announced in July 1928:

"To develop individual farms is... the chief task of the party."

And Stalin seconded him:

"There are people who think that individual farms have ex-

> hausted their usefulness, that we should not support them.... These people have nothing in common with the line of our party."

Less than a year later, the line of the party had nothing in common with these words. The dawn of "complete collectivization" was on the horizon.

The new orientation was arrived at just as empirically as the preceding, and by way of a hidden struggle within the governmental bloc.

> "The groups of the right and center are united by a general hostility to the Opposition"—thus the platform of the Left gave warning a year before—"and the cutting off of the latter will inevitably accelerate the coming struggle between these two."

And so it happened. The leaders of the disintegrating bloc would not for anything, of course, admit that this prognosis of the left wing, like many others, had come true. As late as the 19th of October, 1928, Stalin announced publicly:

> "It is time to stop gossiping about the existence of a Right deviation and a conciliatory attitude towards it in the Politburo of our Central Committee."

Both groups at that time were feeling out the party machine. The repressed party was living on dark rumours and guesses. But in just a few months the official press, with its usual freedom from embarrassment, announced that the head of the government, Rykov, "had speculated on the economic difficulties of the Soviet power"; that the head of the Communist International, Bukharin, was "a conducting wire of bourgeois-liberal influences"; that Tomsky, president of the all-Russian Central Council of Trade Unions, was nothing but a miserable trade-unionist. All three, Rykov, Bukharin and Tomsky, were members of the Politburo. Whereas the whole preceding struggle against the Left Opposition had taken its weapons from the right groups, Bukharin was now able, without sinning against the truth, to accuse Stalin of using in his struggle with the Right a part of the condemned Left Opposition platform.

In one way or another the change was made. The slogan

"Get rich!", together with the theory of the kulak's growing painlessly into socialism, was belatedly, but all the more decisively, condemned. Industrialization was put upon the order of the day. Self-satisfied quietism was replaced by a panic of haste. The half-forgotten slogan of Lenin, "catch up with and outstrip", was filled out with the words, "in the shortest possible time". The minimalist five-year plan, already confirmed in principle by a congress of the party, gave place to a new plan, the fundamental elements of which were borrowed in toto from the platform of the shattered Left Opposition. Dnieperstroy, only yesterday likened to a gramophone, today occupied the centre of attention.

After the first new successes the slogan was advanced: "Achieve the five-year plan in four years". The startled empires now decided that everything was possible. Opportunism, as has often happened in history, turned into its opposite, adventurism. Whereas from 1923 to 1928 the Politburo had been ready to accept Bukharin's philosophy of a "tortoise tempo", it now lightly jumped from a 20 to a 30 per cent yearly growth, trying to convert every partial and temporary achievement into a norm, and losing sight of the conditioning interrelation of the different branches of industry. The financial holes in the plan were stopped up with printed paper. During the years of the first plan the number of bank notes in circulation rose from 1.7 billion to 5.5, and by the beginning of the second five-year plan had reached 8.4 billion rubles. The bureaucracy not only freed itself from the political control of the masses, upon whom this forced industrialization was laying an unbearable burden, but also from the automatic control exercised by the chervonetz [theoretical par = $5]. The currency system, put on a solid basis at the beginning of the NEP, was now again shaken to its roots.

The chief danger, however, and that not only for the fulfillment of the plan but for the regime itself, appeared from the side of the peasants.

On the 15th of February, 1928, the population of the country learned with surprise from an editorial in *Pravda* that the villages looked not at all the way they had been portrayed up to that moment by the authorities, but on the contrary very much as the expelled Left Opposition had presented them. The press, which only yesterday had been denying the existence of the kulaks, today, on a signal from above, discovered them not only in the villages, but in the party itself. It was revealed that the Communist nuclei were frequently dominated by rich peasants possessing complicated machinery, employing hired labour, concealing from the government hundreds and thousands of poods [1 pood = ap. 36 lbs.] of grain, and implacably denouncing the "Trotskyist" policy. The newspapers vied with each other in printing sensational exposures of how kulaks in the position of local were denying admission to the party to poor peasants and hired hands. All the old criteria were turned upside down; minuses and pluses changed places.

In order to feed the cities, it was necessary immediately to take from the kulak the daily bread. This could be achieved only by force. The expropriation of the grain reserve, and that not only of the kulak but of the middle peasant, was called, in the official language, "extraordinary measures". This phrase is supposed to mean that tomorrow everything will fall back into the old rut. But the peasants did not believe fine words, and they were right. The violent seizures of grain deprived the well-off peasants of their motive to increase sowings. The hired hands and the poor peasant found themselves without work. Agriculture again arrived in a blind alley, and with it the state. It was necessary at any cost to reform the "general line".

Stalin and Molotov, still giving individual farming the chief place, began to emphasize the necessity of a swifter development of the Soviet and collective farms. But since the bitter need of food did not permit a cessation of military expenditures into the country, the programme of promoting individual farms was left hanging in the air. It was necessary to "slip down" to collectivization. The temporary "extraordinary measures" for the collection of grain developed unexpectedly into a programme of "liquidation of the kulaks as a class". From the shower of contradictory commands, more copious than food rations, it became evident that on the peasant question the government had not only no five-year plan, but not even a five months' programme.

According to the new plan, drawn up under the spur of a food crisis, collective farms were at the end of five years to comprise about 20 per cent of the peasant holdings. This programme—whose immensity will be clear when you consider that during the preceding 10 years collectivization had affected less than 1 per cent of the country—was nevertheless by the middle of the five years left far behind. In November 1929, Stalin, abandoning his own vacillations, announced the end of individual farming. The peasants, he said, are entering the collective farms "in whole villages, counties and even provinces". Yakovlev, who two years before had insisted that the collectives would for many years remain only "islands in a sea of peasant holdings", now received an order as People's Commissar of Agriculture to "liquidate the kulaks as a class", and establish complete collectivization at the "earliest possible date". In the year 1929, the proportion of collective farms rose from 1.7 per cent to 3.9 per cent. In 1930 it rose to 23.6, in 1931 to 52.7, in 1932 to 61.5 per cent.

At the present time hardly anybody would be foolish enough to repeat the twaddle of liberals to the effect that collectivization as a whole was accomplished by naked force. In former historic epochs the peasants in their struggle for land have at one time raised an insurrection against the landlords, at another sent a stream of colonizers into untilled regions, at still another rushed into all kinds of sects which promised to reward the muzhik with heaven's vacancies for his narrow quarters on earth. Now, after the expropriation of the great estates and the extreme parcellation of land, the union of these small parcels into big tracts had become a question of life and death for the peasants, for agriculture, and for society as a whole.

The problem, however, is far from settled by these general historic considerations. The real possibilities of collectivization are determined, not by the depth of the impasse in the villages and not by the administrative energy of the government, but primarily by the existing productive resources —that is, the ability of the industries to furnish large-scale agriculture with the requisite machinery. These material conditions were lacking. The collective farms were set up with an equipment suitable in the main only for small-scale farming. In these conditions an exaggeratedly swift collectivization took the character of an economic adventure.

Caught unawares by the radicalism of its own shift of policy, the government did not and could not make even an elementary political preparation for the new course. Not only the peasant masses, but even the local organs of power, were ignorant of what was being demanded of them. The peasants were heated white hot by rumours that their cattle and property were to be seized by the state. This rumour, too, was not so far from the truth. Actually realizing their own former caricature of the Left Opposition, the bureaucracy "robbed the villages". Collectivization appeared to the peasant primarily in the form of an expropriation of all his belongings. They collectivized not only horses, cows, sheep, pigs, but even new-born chickens. They "dekulakized", as one foreign observer wrote, "down to the felt shoes, which they dragged from the feet of little children". As a result there was an epidemic selling of cattle for a song by the peasants, or a slaughter of cattle for meat and hides.

In January 1930, at a Moscow congress, a member of the Central Committee, Andreyev, drew a two-sided picture of collectivization:

> On the one side he asserted that a collective movement powerfully developing throughout the whole country "will now destroy upon its road each and every obstacle"; on the other, a predatory sale by the peasants of their own implements, stock and even seeds before entering the collectives "is assuming positively menacing proportions".

However contradictory those two generalizations may be, they show correctly from opposite sides the epidemic character of collectivization as a measure of despair. "Complete collectivization", wrote the same foreign critic, "plunged the national economy into a condition of ruin almost without precedent, as though a three years' war had passed over."

Twenty-five million isolated peasant egoisms, which yesterday had been the sole motive force of agriculture—weak like an old farmer's nag, but nevertheless forces—the bureaucracy tried to replace at one gesture by the commands of 2,000 collective farm administrative offices, lacking technical equipment, agronomic knowledge and the support of the peasants themselves. The dire consequences of this adventurism soon followed, and they lasted for a number of years. The total harvest of grain, which had risen in 1930 to 835 million hundredweight, fell in the next two years below 700 million. The difference does not seem catastrophic in itself, but it meant a loss of just that quantity of grain needed to keep the towns even at their customary hunger norm. In technical culture, the results were still worse. On the eve of collectivization the production of sugar had reached almost 100 million poods, and at the height of complete collectivization it had fallen, owing to a lack of beets, to 48 million poods—that is, to half what it had been. But the most devastating hurricane hit the animal kingdom. The number of horses fell 55 per cent—from 34.6 million in 1929 to 15.6 million in 1934. The number of horned cattle fell from 30.7 million to 19.5 million—that is, 40 per cent. The number of pigs, 55 per cent; sheep, 66 per cent. The destruction of people—by hunger, cold, epidemics and measures of repression—is unfortunately less accurately tabulated than the slaughter of stock, but it also mounts up to millions. The blame for these sacrifices lies not upon collectivization, but upon the blind, violent, gambling methods with which it was carried through. The bureaucracy foresaw nothing. Even the constitutions of the collectives, which made an attempt to bind the personal interests of the peasants with the welfare of the farm, were not published until after the unhappy villages had thus been cruelly laid waste.

The forced character of this new course arose from the necessity of finding some salvation from the consequences of the policy of 1923–28. But even so, collectivization could and should have assumed a more reasonable tempo and more deliberated forms. Having in its hands both the power and the industries, the bureaucracy could have regulated the process without carrying the nation to the edge of disaster. They could, and should have adopted tempos better corresponding to the material and moral resources of the country. "Under favorable circumstances, internal and external," wrote the émigré organ of the "Left Opposition" in 1930, "the material-technical conditions of agriculture can in the course of some 10 of 15 years be transformed to the bottom, and provide the productive basis for collectivization. However, during the intervening years there would be time to overthrow the Soviet power more than once."

This warning was not exaggerated. Never before had the breath of destruction hung so directly above the territory of the October Revolution, as in the years of complete collectivization. Discontents, distrust, bitterness, were corroding the country. The disturbance of the currency, the mounting up of stable, "conventional", and free market prices, the transition from a simulacrum of *trade* between the state and the peasants to a grain, meat and milk *levy*, the life-and-death struggle with mass plunderings of the collective property and mass concealment of these plunderings, the purely military mobilization of the party for the struggle against kulak sabotage (after the "liquidation" of the kulaks as a class) together with this a return to food cards and hunger rations, and finally a restoration of the passport system—all these measures revived throughout the country the atmosphere of the seemingly so long ended civil war.

The supply to the factories of food and raw materials grew worse from season to season. Unbearable working conditions caused a migration of labour power, malingering, careless work, breakdown of machines, a high percentage of trash products and general low quality. The average productivity of labour declined 11.7 per cent in 1931. According to an incidental acknowledgement of Molotov, printed in the whole Soviet press, industrial production in 1932 rose only 8.5 per cent, instead of the 36 per cent indicated by the year's plan. To be sure, the world was informed soon after this that the five-year plan had been fulfilled in four years and three months. But that means only that the cynicism of the bureaucracy in its manipulations of statistics and public opinion is without limit. That, however, is not the chief thing. Not the fate of the five-year plan, but the fate of the regime was at stake.

The regime survived.

But that is the merit of the regime itself, which had put down deep roots in the popular soil. It is in no less degree due to favourable external circumstances. In those years of economic chaos and civil war in the villages, the Soviet Union was essentially paralyzed in the face of a foreign enemy. The discontent of the peasantry swept through the army. Mistrust and vacillation demoralized the bureaucratic machine, and the commanding cadres. A blow either from the East or West at that period might have had fatal consequences.

Fortunately, the first years of a crisis in trade and industry had created throughout the capitalist world moods of bewildered watchful waiting. Nobody was ready for war; nobody dared attempt it. Moreover, in not one of the hostile countries was there an adequate realization of the acuteness of these social convulsions which where shaking the land of soviets under the roar of the official music in honour of the "general line".

* * *

In spite of its brevity, our historic outline shows, we hope, how far removed the actual development of the workers' state has been from an idyllic picture of the gradual and steady piling up of successes. From the crises of the past we shall later on derive important indications for the future. But, besides that, a historic glance at the economic policy of the Soviet government and its zigzags has seemed to us necessary in order to destroy that artificially inculcated individualistic fetishism which finds the sources of success, both real and pretended, in the extraordinary quality of the leadership, and not in the conditions of socialized property created by the revolution.

The objective superiority of the new social regime reveals itself, too, of course, in the methods of the leaders. But these methods reflect equally the economic and cultural backwardness of the country, and the petty-bourgeois provincial conditions in which the ruling cadres were formed.

It would be the crudest mistake to infer from this that the policy of the Soviet leaders is of third-rate importance. There is no other government in the world in whose hands the fate of the whole country is concentrated to such a degree. The successes and failures of an individual capitalist depend, not wholly of course, but to a very considerable and sometimes decisive degree, upon his personal qualities. *Mutatis mutandis,* the Soviet government occupies in relation to the whole economic system the position, which a capitalist occupies in relation to a single enterprise. The centralized character of the national economy converts the state power into a factor of enormous significance. But for that very reason the policy of the government must be judged, not by summarized results, not by naked statistical data, but by the specific role which conscious foresight and planned leadership have played in achieving these results.

The zigzags of the governmental course have reflected not only the objective contradictions of the situation, but also the inadequate ability of the leaders to understand these contradictions in season and react prophylactically against them. It is not easy to express mistakes of the leadership in bookkeeper's magnitudes, but our schematic exposition of the history of these zigzags permits the conclusion that they have imposed upon the Soviet economy an immense burden of overhead expenses.

It remains of course incomprehensible—at least with a rational approach to history—how and why a faction the least rich of all in ideas, and the most burdened with mistakes, should have gained the upper hand over all other groups, and concentrated an unlimited power in its hands. Our further analysis will give us a key to this problem too. We shall see, at the same time, how the bureaucratic methods of autocratic leadership are coming into sharper and sharper conflict with the demands of economy and culture, and with what inevitable necessity new crises and disturbances arise in the development of the Soviet Union.

However, before taking up the dual role of the "socialist" bureaucracy, we must answer the question: What is the net result of the preceding successes? Is socialism really achieved in the Soviet Union? Or, more cautiously: Do the present economic and cultural achievements constitute a guarantee against the danger of capitalist restoration—just as bourgeois society at a certain stage of its development became insured by its own successes against a restoration of serfdom and feudalism?

# *Chapter 3*

# SOCIALISM AND THE STATE

## 1. The Transitional Regime

Is it true, as the official authorities assert, that socialism is already realized in the Soviet Union? And if not, have the achieved successes at least made sure of its realization within the national boundaries, regardless of the course of events in the rest of the world? The preceding critical appraisal of the chief indices of the Soviet economy ought to give us the point of departure for a correct answer to this question, but we shall require also certain preliminary theoretical points of reference.

Marxism sets out from the development of technique as the fundamental spring of progress, and constructs the communist programme upon the dynamic of the productive forces. If you conceive that some cosmic catastrophe is going to destroy our planet in the fairly near future, then you must, of course, reject the communist perspective along with much else. Except for this as yet problematic danger, however, there is not the slightest scientific ground for setting any limit in advance to our technical productive and cultural possibilities. Marxism is saturated with the optimism of progress, and that alone, by the way, makes it irreconcilably opposed to religion.

The material premise of communism should be so high a development of the economic powers of man that productive labour, having ceased to be a burden, will not require any goading, and the distribution of life's goods, existing in continual abundance, will not demand—as it does not now in any well-off family or "decent" boardinghouse—any control except that of education, habit and social opinion. Speaking frankly, I think it would be pretty dull-witted to consider such a really modest perspective "utopian".

Capitalism prepared the conditions and forces for a social revolution: technique, science and the proletariat. The communist structure cannot, however, immediately replace the bourgeois society. The material and cultural inheritance from the past is wholly inadequate for that. In its first steps the workers' state cannot yet permit everyone to work "according to his abilities"—that is, as much as he can and wishes to—nor can it reward everyone "according to his needs", regardless of the work he does. In order to increase the productive forces, it is necessary to resort to the customary norms of wage payment—that is, to the distribution of life's goods in proportion to the quantity and quality of individual labour.

Marx named this first stage of the new society "the lowest stage of communism", in distinction from the highest, where together with the last phantoms of want material inequality will disappear. In this sense socialism and communism are frequently contrasted as the lower and higher stages of the new society. "We have not yet, of course, *complete* communism," reads the present official Soviet doctrine, "but we have already achieved socialism—that is, the *lowest* stage of communism." In proof of this, they adduce the dominance of the state trusts in industry, the collective farms in agriculture, the state and co-operative enterprises in commerce. At first glance this gives a complete correspondence with the a priori—and therefore hypothetical—scheme of Marx. But it is exactly for the Marxist that this question is not exhausted by a consideration of forms of property regardless of the achieved productivity of labour. By the lowest stage of communism Marx meant, at any rate, a society, which from the very beginning stands higher in its economic development than the most advanced capitalism. Theoretically such a conception is flawless, for taken on a world scale communism, even in its first incipient stage, means a higher level of development that that of bourgeois society. Moreover, Marx expected that the Frenchman would begin the social revolution, the German continue it, the Englishman finish it; and as to the Russian, Marx left him far in the rear. But this conceptual order was upset by the facts. Whoever tries now mechanically to apply the universal historic conception of Marx to the particular case of the Soviet Union at the given stage of its development, will be entangled at once in hopeless contradictions.

Russia was not the strongest, but the weakest link in the chain of capitalism. The present Soviet Union does not stand above the world level of economy, but is only trying to catch up with the capitalist countries. If Marx called that society which was to be formed upon the basis of a socialization of the productive forces of the most advanced capitalism of its epoch, the lowest stage of communism, then this designation obviously does not apply to the Soviet Union, which is still today considerably poorer in technique, culture and the good things of life than the capitalist countries. It would be truer, therefore, to name the present Soviet regime in all its contradictoriness, not a socialist regime, but a preparatory regime transitional from capitalism to socialism.

There is not an ounce of pedantry in this concern for terminological accuracy. The strength and stability of regimes are determined in the long run by the relative productivity of their labour. A socialist economy possessing a technique superior to that of capitalism would really be guaranteed in its socialist development for sure—so to speak, automatically—a thing which unfortunately it is still quite impossible to say about the Soviet economy.

A majority of the vulgar defenders of the Soviet Union as it is are inclined to reason approximately thus: Even though you concede that the present Soviet regime is not yet socialistic, a further development of the productive forces on the present foundations must sooner or later lead to the complete triumph of socialism. Hence only the factor of time is uncertain. And it is worth while making a fuss about that? However triumphant such an argument seems at first glance, it is in fact extremely superficial. Time is by no means a secondary factor when historic processes are in question. It is far more dangerous to confuse the present and the future tenses in politics than in grammar. Evolution is far from consisting, as vulgar evolutionists of the Webb type imagine, in a steady accumulation and continual "improvement" of that which exists. It has its transitions of quantity into quality, its crises, leaps and backward lapses. It is exactly because the Soviet Union is as yet far from having attained the first stage of socialism, as a balanced system of production and distribution that is development does not proceed harmoniously, but in contradictions. Economic contradictions produce social antagonisms, which in turn develop their own logic, not awaiting the further growth of the productive forces. We have just seen how true this was in the case of the kulak who did not wish to "grow" evolutionarily into socialism, and who, to the surprise of the bureaucracy and its ideologues, demanded a new and supplementary revolution. Will the bureaucracy itself, in whose hands the power and wealth are concentrated, wish to grow more peacefully into socialism? As to this, doubts are certainly permissible. In any case, it would be imprudent to take the word of the bureaucracy for it. It is impossible at present to answer finally and irrevocably the question in what direction the economic contradictions and social antagonisms of Soviet society will develop in the course of the next three, five or 10 years. The outcome depends upon a struggle of living social forces— not on a national scale, either, but on an international scale. At every new stage, therefore, a concrete analysis is necessary of actual relations and tendencies in their connection and continual interaction. We shall now see the importance of such an analysis in the case of the state.

## 2. Programme and Reality

Lenin, following Marx and Engels, saw the first distinguishing features of the proletarian revolution in the fact that, having expropriated the exploiters, it would abolish the necessity of a bureaucratic apparatus raised above society— and above all, a police and standing army.

> "The proletariat needs a state—this all the opportunists can tell you," wrote Lenin in 1917, two months before the seizure of

> power, "but they, the opportunists, forget to add that the proletariat needs only a dying state—that is, a state constructed in such a way that it immediately begins to die away and cannot help dying away." (State and Revolution)

This criticism was directed at the time against reformist socialists of the type of the Russian Mensheviks, British Fabians, etc. It now attacks with redoubled force the Soviet idolators with their cult of a bureaucratic state, which has not the slightest intention of "dying away".

The social demand for a bureaucracy arise in all those situations where sharp antagonisms need to be "softened", "adjusted", "regulated" (always in the interests of the privileged, the possessors, and always to the advantage of the bureaucracy itself). Throughout all bourgeois revolutions, therefore, no matter how democratic, there has occurred a reinforcement and perfecting of the bureaucratic apparatus.

> "Officialdom and the standing army—" writes Lenin, "that is a 'parasite' on the body of bourgeois society, a parasite created by the inner contradictions which tear this society, yet nothing but a parasite stopping up the living pores."

Beginning with 1917—that is, from the moment when the conquest of power confronted the party as a practical problem—Lenin was continually occupied with the thought of liquidating this "parasite". After the overthrow of the exploiting classes—he repeats and explains in every chapter of *State and Revolution*—the proletariat will shatter the old bureaucratic machine and create its own apparatus out of employees and workers. And it will take measures against their turning into bureaucrats—

> "measures analyzed in detail by Marx and Engels: (1) not only election but recall at any time; (2) payment no higher than the wages of a worker; (3) immediate transition to a regime in which all will fulfill the functions of control and supervision so that all may for a time become 'bureaucrats', and therefore nobody can become a bureaucrat."

You must not think that Lenin was talking about the problems of a decade. No, this was the first step with which "we should and must begin upon achieving a proletarian revolution".

This same bold view of the state in a proletarian dictatorship found finished expression a year and a half after the conquest of power in the program of the Bolshevik party, including its section on the army. A strong state, but without mandarins; armed power, but without the Samurai! It is not the tasks of defence, which create a military and state bureaucracy, but the class structure of society carried over into the organization of defence. The army is only a copy of the social relations. The struggle against foreign danger necessitates, of course, in the workers' state as in others, a specialized military technical organization, but in no case a privileged officer caste. The party programme demands a replacement of the standing army by an armed people.

The regime of proletarian dictatorship from its very beginning thus ceases to be a "state" in the old sense of the word—a special apparatus, that is, for holding in subjection the majority of the people. The material power, together with the weapons, goes over directly and immediately into the hands of the workers' organizations such as the soviets. The state as a bureaucratic apparatus begins to die away the first day of the proletarian dictatorship. Such is the voice of the party programme—not voided to this day. Strange: it sounds like a spectral voice from the mausoleum.

However you may interpret the nature of the present Soviet state, one thing is indubitable: at the end of its second decade of existence, it has not only not died away, but not begun to "die away." Worse than that, it has grown into a hitherto unheard of apparatus of compulsion. The bureaucracy not only has not disappeared, yielding its place to the masses, but has turned into an uncontrolled force dominating the masses. The army not only has not been replaced by an armed people, but has given birth to a privileged officers' caste, crowned with marshals, while the people, "the armed bearers of the dictatorship", are now forbidden in the Soviet Union to carry even nonexplosive weapons. With the utmost stretch of fancy it would be difficult to imagine a contrast more striking than that which exists between the scheme of the workers' state according to Marx, Engels and Lenin, and the actual state now headed by Stalin. While continuing to publish the works of Lenin (to be sure, with excerpts and distortions by the censor), the present leaders of the Soviet Union and their ideological representatives do not even raise the question of the causes of such a crying divergence between programme and reality. We will try to do this for them.

### 3. The Dual Character of the Workers' State

The proletarian dictatorship is just a bridge between the bourgeois and the socialist society. In its very essence, therefore, it bears a temporary character. An incidental but very essential task of the state, which realizes the dictatorship, consists in preparing for its own dissolution. The degree of the realization of this "incidental" task is, to some extent, a measure of its success in the fulfillment of its fundamental mission: the construction of a society without classes and without material contradictions. Bureaucracy and social harmony are inversely proportional to each other.

In his famous polemic against Duhring, Engels wrote:

> "When, together with class domination and the struggle for individual existence created by the present anarchy in production, those conflicts and excesses which result from this struggle disappear, from that time on there will be nothing to suppress, and there will be no need for a special instrument of suppression, the state."

The philistine considers the gendarme an eternal institution. In reality, the gendarme will bridle mankind only until man shall thoroughly bridle nature. In order that the state shall disappear, "class domination and the struggle for individual existence" must disappear. Engels joins these two conditions together, for in the perspective of changing social regimes a few decades amount to nothing. But the thing looks different to those generations who bear the weight of a revolution. It is true that capitalist anarchy creates the struggle of each against all, but the trouble is that a socialization of the means of production does not yet automatically remove the "struggle for individual existence". That is the nub of the question!

A socialized state even in America, on the basis of the most advanced capitalism, could not immediately provide everyone with as much as he needs, and would therefore be compelled to spur everyone to produce as much as possible. The duty of the stimulator in these circumstances naturally falls to the state, which in its turn cannot but resort, with various changes and mitigations, to the method of labour payment worked out by capitalism. It was in this sense that Marx wrote in 1875:

> "Bourgeois law... is inevitable in the first phase of the communist society, in that form in which it issues after long labor pains from capitalist society. Law can never be higher than the economic structure and the cultural development of society conditioned by that structure."

In explaining these remarkable lines, Lenin adds:

> "Bourgeois law in relation to the distribution of the objects of consumption assumes, of course, inevitably a bourgeois state, for law is nothing without an apparatus capable of compelling observance of its norms. It follows (we are still quoting Lenin) that under Communism not only will bourgeois law survive for a certain time, but also even a bourgeois state without the bourgeoisie!"

This highly significant conclusion, completely ignored by the present official theoreticians, has a decisive significance for the understanding of the nature of the Soviet state—or more accurately, for a first approach to such understanding. Insofar as the state which assumes the task of socialist transformation is compelled to defend inequality—that is, the material privileges of a minority—by methods of compulsion, insofar does it also remain a "bourgeois" state, even though without a bourgeoisie. These words contain neither praise nor blame; they name things with their real name.

The bourgeois norms of distribution, by hastening the growth of material power, ought to serve socialist aims—but only in the last analysis. The state assumes directly and from the very beginning a dual character: socialistic, insofar as it defends social property in the means of production; bourgeois, insofar as the distribution of life's goods is carried out with a capitalistic measure of value and all the consequences ensuing therefrom. Such a contradictory characterization may horrify the dogmatists and scholastics; we can only offer them our condolences.

The final physiognomy of the workers' state ought to be determined by the changing relations between its bourgeois and socialist tendencies. The triumph of the latter ought ipso facto to signify the final liquidation of the gendarme—that is, the dissolving of the state in a self-governing society. From this alone it is sufficiently clear how immeasurably significant is the problem of Soviet bureaucratism, both in itself and as a symptom! It is because Lenin, in accord with his whole intellectual temper, gave an extremely sharpened expression to the conception of Marx, that he revealed the source of the future difficulties, his own among them, although he did not himself succeed in carrying his analysis through to the end. "A bourgeois state without a bourgeoisie" proved inconsistent with genuine Soviet democracy. The dual function of the state could not but affect its structure. Experience revealed what theory was unable clearly to foresee. If for the defence of socialized property against bourgeois counterrevolution a "state of armed workers" was fully adequate, it was a very different matter to regulate inequalities in the sphere of consumption. Those deprived of property are not inclined to create and defend it. The majority cannot concern itself with the privileges of the minority. For the defense of "bourgeois law" the workers' state was compelled to create a "bourgeois" type of instrument—that is, the same old gendarme, although in a new uniform.

We have thus taken the first step toward understanding the fundamental contradictions between Bolshevik programme and Soviet reality. If the state does not die away, but grows more and more despotic, if the plenipotentiaries of the working class become bureaucratized, and the bureaucracy rises above the new society, this is not for some secondary reasons like the psychological relics of the past, etc., but is a result of the iron necessity to give birth to and support a privileged minority so long as it is impossible to guarantee genuine equality.

The tendencies of bureaucratism, which strangle the workers' movement in capitalist countries, would everywhere show themselves even after a proletarian revolution. But it is perfectly obvious that the poorer the society which issues from a revolution, the sterner and more naked would be the expression of this "law", the more crude would be the forms assumed by bureaucratism, and the more dangerous would it become for socialist development. The Soviet state is prevented not only from dying away, but even from freeing itself of the bureaucratic parasite, not by the "relics" of former ruling classes, as declares the naked police doctrine of Stalin, for those relics are powerless in themselves. It is prevented by immeasurably mightier factors, such as material want, cultural backwardness and the resulting dominance of "bourgeois law" in what most immediately and sharply touches every human being, the business of insuring his personal existence.

## 4. "Generalized Want" and the Gendarme

Two years before the Communist Manifesto, young Marx wrote:

> "A development of the productive forces is the absolutely necessary practical premise [of Communism], because without it want is generalized, and with want the struggle for necessities begins again, and that means that all the old crap must revive."

This thought Marx never directly developed, and for no accidental reason: he never foresaw a proletarian revolution in a backward country. Lenin also never dwelt upon it, and this too was not accidental. He did not foresee so prolonged an isolation of the Soviet state. Nevertheless, the citation, merely an abstract construction with Marx, an inference from the opposite, provides an indispensable theoretical key to the wholly concrete difficulties and sicknesses of the Soviet regime. On the historic basis of destitution, aggravated by the destructions of the imperialist and civil wars, the "struggle for individual existence" not only did not disappear the day after the overthrow of the bourgeoisie, and not only did not abate in the succeeding years, but, on the contrary, assumed at times an unheard-of ferocity. Need we recall that certain regions of the country have twice gone to the point of cannibalism?

The distance separating tzarist Russia from the West can really be appreciated only now. In the most favourable conditions—that is, in the absence of inner disturbances and external catastrophes—it would require several more five-year periods before the Soviet Union could fully assimilate those economic and educative achievements upon which the first-born nations of capitalist civilization have expended centuries. The application of socialist methods for the solution of pre-socialist problems—that is the very essence of the present economic and cultural works in the Soviet Union.

The Soviet Union, to be sure, even now excels in productive forces the most advanced countries of the epoch of Marx. But in the first place, in the historic rivalry of two regimes, it is not so much a question of absolutely as of relative levels: the Soviet economy opposes the capitalism of Hitler, Baldwin, and Roosevelt, not Bismarck, Palmerston, or Abraham Lincoln. And in the second place, the very scope of human demands changes fundamentally with the growth of world technique. The contemporaries of Marx knew nothing of automobiles, radios, moving pictures, aeroplanes. A socialist society, however, is unthinkable without the free enjoyment of these goods.

"The lowest stage of Communism", to employ the term of Marx, begins at that level to which the most advanced capitalism has drawn near. The real programme of the coming Soviet five-year plan, however, is to "catch up with Europe and America". The construction of a network of autoroads and asphalt highways in the measureless spaces of the Soviet Union will require much more time and material than to transplant automobile factories from America, or even to acquire their technique. How many years are needed in order to make it possible for every Soviet citizen to use an automobile in any direction he chooses, refilling his gas tank without difficulty en route? In barbarian society the rider and the pedestrian constituted two classes. The automobile differentiates society no less than the saddle horse. So long as even a modest "Ford" remains the privilege of a minority, there survive all the relations and customs proper to a bourgeois society. And together with them there remains the guardian of inequality, the state.

Basing himself wholly upon the Marxian theory of the dictatorship of the proletariat, Lenin did not succeed, as we have said, either in his chief work dedicated to this question (State and Revolution), or in the programme of the party, in drawing all the necessary conclusions as to the character of the state from the economic backwardness and isolatedness of the country. Explaining the revival of bureaucratism by the unfamiliarity of the masses with administration and by the special difficulties resulting from the war, the programme prescribes merely political measures for the overcoming of "bureaucratic distortions": elections and recall at any time of all plenipotentiaries, abolition of material privileges, active control by the masses, etc. It was assumed that along this road the bureaucrat, from being a boss, would turn into a simple and moreover temporary technical agent, and the state would gradually and imperceptibly disappear from the scene.

This obvious underestimation of impending difficulties is explained by the fact that the programme was based wholly upon an international perspective. "The October revolution in Russia has realized the dictatorship of the proletariat.... The era of world proletarian communist revolution has begun." These were the introductory lines of the programme. Their authors not only did not set themselves the aim of constructing "socialism in a single country" —this idea had not entered anybody's head then, and least of all Stalin's —but they also did not touch the question as to what character the Soviet state would assume, if compelled for as long as two decades to solve in isolation those economic and cultural problems which advanced capitalism had solved so long ago.

The post-war revolutionary crisis did not lead to the victory of socialism in Europe. The social democrats rescued the bourgeoisie. That period, which to Lenin and his colleagues looked like a short "breathing spell", has stretched out to a whole historical epoch. The contradictory social structure of the Soviet Union, and the ultra-bureaucratic character of its state, is the direct consequences of this unique and "unforeseen" historical pause, which has at the same time led in the capitalist countries to fascism or the pre-fascist reaction.

While the first attempt to create a state cleansed of bureaucratism fell foul, in the first place, of the unfamiliarity of the masses with self-government, the lack of qualified workers devoted to socialism, etc., it very soon after these immediate difficulties encountered others more profound. That reduction of the state to functions of 'accounting and control", with a continual narrowing of the functions of compulsion, demanded by the party programme, assumed at least a relative condition of general contentment. Just this necessary condition was lacking. No help came from the West. The power of the democratic Soviets proved cramping, even unendurable, when the task of the day was to accommodate those privileged groups whose existence was necessary for defense, for industry, for technique, and science. In this decidedly not "socialistic" operation, taking from 10 and giving to one, these crystallized out and developed a powerful caste of specialists in distribution.

How and why is it, however, that the enormous economic successes of the recent period have led not to a mitigation, but on the contrary to a sharpening, of inequalities, and at the same time to a further growth of bureaucratism, such that from being a "distortion", it has now become a system of administration? Before attempting to answer this question, let us hear how the authoritative leaders of the Soviet bureaucracy look upon their own regime.

### 5. The "Complete Triumph of Socialism" and the "Reinforcement of the Dictatorship"

There have been several announcements during recent years of the "complete triumph" of socialism in the Soviet Union—taking especially categorical forms in connection with the "liquidation of the kulaks as a class." On 30 January, 1931,

*Pravda,* interpreting a speech of Stalin, said: "During the second five-year period, the *last relics* of capitalist elements in our economy will be liquidated." (italics ours) From the point of view of this perspective, the state ought conclusively to die away during the same period, for where the "last relics" of capitalism are liquidated the state has nothing to do.

"The Soviet power," says the programme of the Bolshevik party on this subject, "openly recognizes the inevitability of the class character of every state, so long as the division of society into classes, and therewith all state power, has not completely disappeared."

However, when certain incautious Moscow theoreticians attempted, from the liquidation of the "last relics" of capitalism taken on faith, to infer they dying away of the state, the bureaucracy immediately declared such theories "counterrevolutionary".

Where lies the theoretical mistake of the bureaucracy—in the basic premise or the conclusion? In the one and the other. To the first announcement of "complete triumph", the Left Opposition answered: You must not limit yourself to the socio-juridical form of relations which are unripe, contradictory, in agriculture still very unstable, abstracting from the fundamental criterion: level of the productive forces. Juridical forms themselves have an essentially different social content in dependence upon the height of the technical level. "Law can never be higher than the economic structure and the cultural level conditioned by it" (Marx). Soviet forms of property on a basis of the most modern achievement of American technique transplanted into all branches of economic life—that would indeed be the first stage of socialism. Soviet forms with a low productivity of labour mean only a transitional regime whose destiny history has not yet finally weighed.

"Is it not monstrous?"—we wrote in March 1932. "The country can not get out of a famine of goods. There is a stoppage of supplies at every step. Children lack milk. But the official oracles announce: 'The country has entered into the period of socialism!' Would it be possible more viciously to compromise the name of socialism?" Karl Radek, now a prominent publicist* of the ruling Soviet circles, parried these remarks in the German liberal paper, Berliner Tageblatt, in a special issue devoted to the Soviet Union (May 1932), in the following words which deserve to be immortal:

> "Milk is a product of cows and not of socialism, and you would have actually to confuse socialism with the image of a country where rivers flow milk, in order not to understand that a country can rise for a time to a higher level of development without any considerable rise in the material situation of the popular masses."

These lines were written when a horrible famine was raging in the country.

Socialism is a structure planned to the end of the best satisfaction of human needs; otherwise it does not deserve the name of socialism. If cows are socialized, but there are too few of them, or they have too meagre udders, then conflicts arise out of the inadequate supply of milk—conflicts between city and country, between collectives and individual peasants, between different state of the proletariat, between the whole toiling mass and bureaucracy. It was in fact the socialization of the cows, which led to their mass extermination by the peasants. Social conflicts created by want can in their turn lead to a resurrection of "all the old crap". Such was, in essence, our answer.

The 7th Congress of the Communist International, in a resolution of 29 August, 1935, solemnly affirmed that in the sum total of the successes of the nationalized industries, the achievement of collectivization, the crowding out of capitalist elements and the liquidation of the kulaks as a class, "the final and irrevocable triumph of socialism and the all-sided reinforcement of the state of the proletarian dictatorship, is achieved in the Soviet Union". With all its categorical tone, this testimony of the Communist International is wholly self-contradictory. If socialism has "finally and irrevocably"

---

* Written before the arrest of Karl Radek in August 1936 on charges of a terrorist conspiracy against the Soviet leaders.

triumphed, not as a principle but as a living social regime, then a renewed "reinforcement" of the dictatorship is obvious nonsense. And on the contrary, if the reinforcement of the dictatorship is evoked by the real demands of the regime, which means that the triumph of socialism is still remote. Not only a Marxist, but any realistic political thinker, ought to understand that the very necessity of "reinforcing" the dictatorship—that is, governmental repression—testifies not to the triumph of a classless harmony, but to the growth of new social antagonisms. What lies at the bottom of all this? Lack of the means of subsistence from the low productivity of labor.

Lenin once characterized socialism as "the Soviet power plus electrification". That epigram, whose one-sidedness was due to the propaganda aims of the moment, assumed at least as a minimum starting point the capitalist level of electrification. At present in the Soviet Union there is 1/3rd as much electrical energy per head of the population as in the advanced countries. If you take into consideration that the soviets have given place in the meantime to a political machine that is independent of the masses, the Communist International has nothing left but to declare that socialism is bureaucratic power plus 1/3rd of the capitalist electrification. Such a definition would be photographically accurate, but for socialism it is not quite enough! In a speech to the Stakhanovists in November 1935, Stalin, obedient to the empirical aims of the conference, unexpectedly announced:

> "Why can and should and necessarily will socialism conquer the capitalist system of economy? Because it can give... a higher productivity of labor."

Incidentally rejecting the resolution of the Communist International adopted three months before upon the same question, and also his own oft-repeated announcements, Stalin here speaks of the "triumph" of socialism in the future tense. Socialism will conquer the capitalist system, he says, when it surpasses it in the productivity of labour. Not only the tenses of the verbs but the social criteria change, as we see, from moment to moment. It is certainly not easy for the Soviet citizen to keep up with the "general line".

Finally, on 1 March, 1936, in a conversation with Roy Howard, Stalin offered a new definition of the Soviet regime:

> "That social organization which we have created may be called a Soviet socialist organization, still not wholly completed, but at root a socialist organization of society."

In this purposely vague definition there are almost as many contradictions as there are words. The social organization is called "Soviet socialist", but the Soviets are a form of state, and socialism is a social regime. These designations are not only not identical but, from the point of view of our interest, antagonistic. Insofar as the social organization has become socialistic, the Soviets ought to drop away like the scaffolding after a building is finished. Stalin introduces a correction: Socialism is "still not wholly completed". What does "not wholly" mean? By 5 per cent, or by 75 per cent? This they do not tell us, just as they do not tell us what they mean by an organization of society that is "socialistic at root". Do they mean forms of property or technique? The very mistiness of the definition, however, implies a retreat from the immeasurably more categorical formula of 1931–35. A further step along the same road would be to acknowledge that the "root" of every social organization is the productive forces, and that the Soviet root is just what is not mighty enough for the socialist trunk and for its leafage: human welfare.

## Chapter 4

# THE STRUGGLE FOR PRODUCTIVITY OF LABOUR

### 1. Money and Plan

We have attempted to examine the Soviet regime in the cross-section of currency. These two problems, state and money, have a number of traits in common, for they both reduce themselves in the last analysis to the problem of problems: productivity of labour. State compulsion like money compulsion is an inheritance from the class society, which is incapable of defining the relations of man by man except in the form of fetishes, churchly or secular, after appointing to defend them the most alarming of all fetishes, the state, with a great knife between its teeth. In a communist society, the state and money will disappear. Their gradual dying away ought consequently to begin under socialism. We shall be able to speak of the actual triumph of socialism only at that historical moment when the state turns into a semi-state, and money begins to lose its magic power. This will mean that socialism, having freed itself from capitalist fetishes, is beginning to create a more lucid, free and worthy relation among men. Such characteristically anarchist demands as the "abolition" of money, "abolition" of wages, or "liquidation" of the state and family, possess interest merely as models of mechanical thinking. Money cannot be arbitrarily "abolished", nor the state and the old family "liquidated". They have to exhaust their historic mission, evaporate, and fall away. The deathblow to money fetishism will be struck only upon that stage when the steady growth of social wealth has made us bipeds forget our miserly attitude toward every excess minute of labour, and our humiliating fear about the size of our ration. Having lost its ability to bring happiness or trample men in the dust, money will turn into mere bookkeeping receipts for the convenience of statisticians and for planning purposes. In the still more distant future, probably these receipts will not be needed. But we can leave this question entirely to posterity, who will be more intelligent than we are.

The nationalization of the means of production and credit, the co-operative or state-izing of internal trade, the monopoly of foreign trade, the collectivization of agriculture, the law on inheritance—set strict limits upon the personal accumulation of money and hinder its conversion into private capital (usurious, commercial and industrial). These functions of money, however, bound as they are with exploitation, are not liquidated at the beginning of a proletarian revolution, but in a modified form are transferred to the state, the universal merchant, creditor and industrialist. At the same time the more elementary functions of money, as measures of value, means of exchange and medium of payment, are not only preserved, but acquire a broader field of action than they had under capitalism.

Administrative planning has sufficiently revealed its power— but therewith also the limits of its power. An a priori economic plan— above all in a backward country with 170 million population, and a profound contradiction between city and country—is not a fixed gospel, but a rough working hypothesis, which must be verified and reconstructed in the process of its fulfillment. We might indeed lay down a rule: the more "accurately" an administrative task is fulfilled, the worse is the economic leadership. For the regulation and application of plans two levers are needed: the political lever, in the form of a real participation in leadership of the interested masses themselves, a thing which is unthinkable without Soviet democracy; and a financial lever, in the form of a real testing out of a priori calculations with the help of a universal equivalent, a thing that is unthinkable without a stable money system.

The role of money in the Soviet economy is not only

unfinished but, as we have said, still has a long growth ahead. The transitional epoch between capitalism and socialism taken as a whole does not mean a cutting down of trade, but, on the contrary, its extraordinary extension. All branches of industry transform themselves and grow. New ones continually arise, and all are compelled to define their relations to one another both quantitatively and qualitatively. The liquidation of the consummatory peasant economy, and at the same time of the shut-in family life, means a transfer to the sphere of social interchange, and ipso facto money circulation, of all the labour energy which was formerly expended within the limits of the peasant's yard, or within the walls of his private dwelling. All products and services begin for the first time in history to be exchanged for one another.

On the other hand, a successful socialist construction is unthinkable without including in the planned system the direct personal interests of the producer and consumer, their egoism,—which in its turn may reveal itself fruitfully only if it has in its service the customary reliable and flexible instrument, money. The raising of the productivity of labour and bettering of the quality of its products is quite unattainable without an accurate measure freely penetrating into all the cells of industry— that is, without a stable unit of currency. Hence it is clear that in the transitional economy, as also under capitalism, the sole authentic money is that based upon gold. All other money is only a substitute. To be sure, the Soviet state has in its hand at the same time the mass of commodities and the machinery for printing money. However, this does not change the situation. Administrative manipulations in the sphere of commodity prices do not in the slightest degree create, or replace, a stable money unit either for domestic or foreign trade. Deprived of an independent basis —that is, a gold basis—the money system of the Soviet Union, like that of a number of capitalist countries, has necessarily a shut-in character. For the world market the ruble does not exist. If the Soviet Union can endure the adverse aspects of this money system more easily than Germany and Italy, it is only in part due to the natural wealth of the country. Only this makes it possible not to struggle in the clutches of autarchy. The historic task, however, is not merely not avoid strangling, but to create face to face with the highest achievements of the world market a powerful economy, rational through and through, which will guarantee the greatest saving of time and consequently the highest flowering of culture.

The dynamic Soviet economy, passing as it does through continual technical revolutions and large-scale experiments, needs more than any other continual testing by means of a stable measure of value. Theoretically there cannot be the slightest doubt that if the Soviet economy had possessed a gold ruble, the result of the five-year plans would be incomparably more favourable than they are now. Of course you cannot "poss the impossible" [Ha nyet cuda nyet]. But you must not make a virtue of necessity, for that leads in turn to additional economic mistakes and losses.

## 2. "Socialist" Inflation

The history of the Soviet currency is not only a history of economic difficulties, successes and failures, but also a history of the zigzags of bureaucratic thought.

The restoration of the ruble in 1922–24, in connection with the transfer to the NEP, was directly bound up with the restoration of the "norms of bourgeois right" in the distribution of objects of consumption. So long as the course toward the well-to-do farmer continued, the chervonetz was an object of governmental concern. During the first period of the five-year plan, on the contrary, all the sluices of inflation were opened. From 0.7 billion rubles at the beginning of 1925, the total issue of currency had arisen by the beginning of 1928 to the comparatively modest sum of 1.7 billion, which is approximately comparable to the paper money circulation of tzarist Russia on the eve of the war—but this, of course, without its former metallic basis. The subsequent curve of inflation from year to year is depicted in the following feverish series: 2.0—2.8—4.3 —5.5—8.4! The final figure 8.4 billion rubles were reached at the beginning of 1933. After that came the years of reconsideration and retreat: 6.9 —7.7—7.9 billion

(1935). The ruble of 1924, equal in the official exchange to 13 francs, had been reduced in November 1935 to 3 francs— that is, to less than a fourth of its value, or almost as much as the French franc was reduced as a result of the war. Both parties, the old and the new, are very conditional in character; the purchasing power of the ruble in world prices now hardly equals 1.5 francs. Nevertheless the scale of devaluation shows with what dizzy speed the Soviet valuta was sliding downhill until 1934.

In the full flight of his economic adventurism, Stalin promised to send the NEP—that is, market relations—"to the devil". The entire press wrote, as in 1918, about the final replacement of merchant sale by "direct socialist distribution", the external sigh of which was the food card. At the same time, inflation was categorically rejected as a phenomenon inconsistent with the Soviet system.

"The stability of the Soviet valuta," said Stalin in 1933, "is guaranteed primarily by the immense quantity of commodities in the hands of the state put in circulation at stable prices."

Notwithstanding the fact that this enigmatical aphorism received neither development nor elucidation (partly indeed because of this), it became a fundamental law of the Soviet theory of money—or, more accurately, of that very inflation which it rejected. The chervonetz proved thereafter to be not a universal equivalent, but only the universal shadow of an "immense" quantity of commodities. And like all shadows, it possessed the right to shorten and lengthen itself. If this consoling doctrine made any sense at all, it was only this: the Soviet money has ceased to be money; it serves no longer as a measure of value; "stable prices" are designated by the state power; the chervonetz is only a conventional label of the planned economy—that is, a universal distribution card. In a word, socialism has triumphed "finally and irrevocably".

The most utopian views of the period of military communism were thus restored on a new economic basis—a little higher, to be sure, but alas still inadequate for the liquidation of money circulation. The ruling circles were completely possessed by the opinion that with a planned economy inflation is not to be feared. This means approximately that if you possess a compass there is no danger in a leaking ship. In reality, currency inflation, inevitably producing a credit inflation, entails a substitution of fictitious for real magnitudes, and corrodes the planned economy from within.

It is needless to say that inflation meant a dreadful tax upon the toiling masses. As for the advantages to socialism achieved with its help, they are more than dubious. Industry, to be sure, continued its rapid growth, but the economic efficiency of the grandiose construction was estimated statistically and not economically. Taking command of the ruble—giving it, that is, various arbitrary purchasing powers in different strata of the population and sectors of the economy—the bureaucracy deprived itself of the necessary instrument for objectively measuring its own successes and failures. The absence of correct accounting, disguised on paper by means of combinations with the "conventional ruble", led in reality to a decline of personal interest, to a low productivity, and to a still lower quality of goods.

In the course of the first five-year plan, this evil assumed threatening proportions. In July 1931, Stalin came out with his famous "six conditions", whose chief aim was to lower the production cost of industrial goods. These "conditions" (payment according to individual productivity of labour, production-cost accounting, etc.) contained nothing new. The "norms of bourgeois right" had been advanced at the dawn of the NEP, and developed at the 12th Congress of the party at the beginning of 1923. Stalin happened upon them only in 1931, under the influence of the declining efficiency of capital investments. During the following two years hardly an article appeared in the Soviet press without references to the salvation power of these "conditions". Meanwhile, with inflation continuing, the diseases caused by it were naturally not getting cured. Severe measures of repression against wreckers and sabotagers did as little to help things forward.

The fact seems almost unbelievable now that in opening a struggle against "impersonality" and "equalization"—which means anonymous "average" labour and similar "average" pay for all—the bureaucracy was at the same time sending "to the devil" the NEP, which means the money evaluation of all goods, including labour power. Restoring "bourgeois norms" with one hand, they were destroying with the other the sole implement of any use under them. With the substitution of "closed distributors" for commerce, and with complete chaos in prices, all correspondence between individual labour and individual wages necessarily disappeared, and therewith disappeared the personal interestedness of the worker.

The strictest instructions in regard to economic accounting, quality, cost of production and productivity, were left hanging in the air. This did not prevent the leaders from declaring the cause of all economic difficulties to be the malicious unfulfillment of the six prescriptions of Stalin. The most cautious references to inflation they likened to a state crime. With similar conscientiousness the authorities on occasion have accused teachers of breaking the rules of school hygiene while at the same time forbidding them to mention the absence of soap.

The question of the fate of the chervonetz has occupied a prominent place in the struggle of factions in the Communist party. The platform of factions in the Communist party. The platform of the Opposition (1927) demanded "a guarantee of the unconditional stability of the money unit". This demand became a leit motif during the subsequent years. "Stop the process of inflation with an iron hand," wrote the émigré organ of the Opposition in 1932, "and restore a stable unit of currency," even at the price of "a bold cutting down of capital investments." The defenders of the "tortoise tempo" and the superindustrializers had, it seemed, temporarily changed places. In answer to the boast that they would send the market "to the devil", the Opposition recommended that the State Planning Commission hang up the motto: "Inflation is the syphilis of a planned economy".

* * *

In the sphere of agriculture, inflation brought no less heavy consequences.

During the period when the peasant policy was still oriented upon the well-to-do farmer, it was assumed that the socialist transformation in agriculture, setting out upon the basis of the NEP, would be accomplished in the course of decades by means of the co-operatives. Assuming one after another purchasing, selling, and credit functions, the co-operatives should in the long run also socialize production itself. All this taken together was called "the co-operative plan of Lenin". The actual development, as we know, followed a completely different and almost an opposite course — dekulakization by violence and integral collectivization. Of the gradual socialization of separate economic functions, in step with the preparation of the material and cultural conditions for it, nothing more was said. Collectivization was introduced as though it were the instantaneous realization of the communist regime in agriculture.

The immediate consequence was not only an extermination of more than half of the livestock, but, more important, a complete indifference of the members of the collective farms to the socialized property and the results of their own labour. The government was compelled to make a disorderly retreat. They again supplied the peasants with chickens, pigs, sheep, and cows as personal property. They gave them private lots adjoining the farmsteads. The film of collectivization began to be run off backwards.

In thus restoring small personal farm holdings, the state adopted a compromise, trying to buy off, as it were, the individualistic tendencies of the peasant. The collective farms were retained, and at first glance, therefore, the retreat might seem of secondary importance. In reality, its significance could hardly be overestimated. If you leave aside the collective farm aristocracy, the daily needs of the average peasant are still met to a greater degree by his work "on his own", than by his participation in the collective. A peasant's income from individual enterprises, especially when he takes up technical culture, fruit, or stock farming, amounts frequently to three times as much as the earnings of the same peasant in the collective economy. This fact, testified to in the Soviet press itself, very clearly reveals on the one hand a completely barbarous squandering of tens of million of human forces, especially those of women, in midget enterprises, and, on the other, the still extremely low productivity of labour in the collective farms.

In order to raise the standard of large-scale collective agriculture, it was necessary again to talk to the peasant in the language he understands —that is, to resurrect the markets and return from taxes in kind to trade —in a word, to ask back from Satan the NEP which had been prematurely sent to him. The transition to a more or less stable money accounting thus became a necessary condition for the further development of agriculture.

### 3. The Rehabilitation of the Ruble

The owl of wisdom flies, as is well known, after sunset. Thus the theory of a "socialist" system of money and prices was developed only after the twilight of inflationist illusions. In developing the above enigmatical words of Stalin, the obedient professors managed to create an entire theory according to which the Soviet price, in contrast to the market price, has an exclusively planning or directive character. That is, it is not an economic, but an administrative category, and thus serves the better for the redistribution of the people's income in the interests of socialism. The professors forgot to explain how you can estimate real costs if all prices express the will of a bureaucracy and not the amount of socially necessary labour expended. In reality, for the redistribution of the people's income the government has in its hands such mighty levers as taxes, the state budget of expenditures for 1936, over 37.6 billion rubles are allotted directly, and many billions indirectly, to financing the various branches of economy. The budget and credit mechanism is wholly adequate for a planned distribution of the national income. And as to prices, they will serve the cause of socialism better, the more honestly they being to express the real economic relations of the present day.

Experience has managed to say its decisive word on this subject. "Directive" prices were less impressive in real life than in the books of scholars. On one and the same commodity, prices of different categories were established. In the broad cracks between these categories, all kinds of speculation, favouritism, parasitism, and other vices found room, and this rather as the rule than the exception. At the same time, the chervonetz, which ought to have been the steady shadow of stable prices, became in reality nothing but its own shadow.

It was again necessary to make a sharp change of course—this time as a result of difficulties, which grew out of the economic successes. Nineteen-thirty-five opened with the abolition of bread cards. By October, cards for other food products were liquidated. By January 1936, cards for industrial products of general consumption were abolished. The economic relations of the city and the country to the state, and to each other, were translated into the language of money. The ruble is an instrument for the influence of the population upon economic plans, beginning with the quantity and quality of the objects of consumption. In no other manner is it possible to rationalize the Soviet economy.

The president of the State Planning Commission announced in December 1935:

> "The present system of mutual relations between the banks and industry must be revised, and the banks must seriously realize control by the ruble."

Thus the superstition of administrative plan and the illusion of administrative prices were shipwrecked. If the approach to socialism means in the fiscal sphere the approach of the ruble to a distribution card, then the reforms of 1935 would have to be regarded as a departure from socialism. In reality, however, such an appraisal would be a crude mistake. The replacement of the card by the ruble is merely a rejection of fictions, and an open acknowledgment of the necessity of creating the premises for socialism by means of a return to bourgeois methods of distribution.

At a session of the Central Executive Committee in January

1936, the People's Commissar of Finance announced: "The Soviet ruble is stable as is not other valuta in the world." It would be wrong to read this announcement as sheer boasting. The state budget of the Soviet Union is balanced with a yearly increase of income over expenses. Foreign trade, to be sure, although insignificant in itself, gives an active balance. The gold reserve of the State Bank, which amounted in 1926 to 164 million rubles, in now more than a billion. The output of gold in the country is rising rapidly. In 1936, this branch of industry is calculated to take first place in the world. The growth of commodity circulation under the restored market has become very rapid. Paper-money inflation was actually stopped in 1934. The elements of a certain stabilization of the ruble exist. Nevertheless, the announcement of the People's Commissar of Finance must be explained to a considerable extent by an inflation of optimism. If the Soviet ruble possesses a mighty support in the general rise of industry, still its Achilles heel is the intolerably high cost of production. The ruble will become the most stable valuta only from that moment when the Soviet productivity of labour exceeds that of the rest of the world, and when, consequently, the ruble itself will be mediating on its final hour.

From a technically fiscal point of view, the ruble can still less lay claim to superiority. With a gold reserve of over a billion, about 8 billions of bank notes are in circulation in the country. The coverage, therefore, amounts to only 12.5 per cent. The gold in the State Bank is still considerably more in the nature of an inviolate reserve for the purposes of war, than the basis of a currency. Theoretically, to be sure, it is not impossible that at a higher stage of development the Soviets will resort to a gold currency, in order to make domestic economic plans precise and simplify economic relations with foreign countries. Thus, before giving up the ghost, the currency might once more flare up with the gleam of pure gold. But this in any case is not a problem of the immediate future.

In the period to come, there can be no talk of going over to the gold standard. Insofar, however, as the government, by increasing the gold reserve, is trying to raise the percentage even of a purely theoretical coverage; insofar as the limits of banknote emission are objectively determined and not dependent upon the will of the bureaucracy, to that extent the Soviet ruble may achieve at least a relative stability. That alone would be of enormous benefit. With a firm rejection of inflation in the future, the currency, although deprived of the advantage of the gold standard, could indubitably help to cure the many deep wounds inflicted upon the economy by the bureaucratic subjectivism of the preceding years.

### 4. The Stakhanov Movement

"All economy," said Marx,—and that means all human struggle with nature at all stages of civilization—"comes down in the last analysis to an economy of time." Reduced to its primary basis, history is nothing but a struggle for an economy of working time. Socialism could not be justified by the abolition of exploitation alone; it must guarantee to society a higher economy of time than is guaranteed by capitalism. Without the realization of this condition, the mere removal of exploitation would be but a dramatic episode without a future. The first historical experiment in the application of socialist methods has revealed the great possibilities contained in them. But the Soviet economy is still far from learning to make use of time, that most precious raw material of culture. The imported technique, the chief implement for the economy of time, still fails to produce on the Soviet soil those results, which are normal in its capitalist fatherlands. In that sense, decisive for all civilization, socialism has not yet triumphed. It has shown that it can and should triumph. But it has not yet triumphed. All assertions to the contrary are the fruit of ignorance and charlatanism.

Molotov, who sometimes—to do him justice—reveals a little more freedom from the ritual phrase than other Soviet leaders, declared in January 1936 at a session of the Central Executive Committee:

> "Our average level of productivity of labor... is still considerably below that of America and Europe."

It would be well to make these words precise approximately thus: three, five, and sometimes even 10 times as low as that of Europe and America, and our cost of production is correspondingly considerably higher. In the same speech, Molotov made a more general confession:

> "The average level of culture of our workers still stands below the corresponding level of the workers of a number of capitalist countries."

To this should be added: also the average standard of living. There is no need of explaining how mercilessly these sober words, spoken in passing, refute the boastful announcements of the innumerable official authorities, and the honeyed outpourings of the foreign "friends"!

The struggle to raise the productivity of labour, together with concern about defence, is the fundamental content of the activity of the Soviet government. At various stages in the evolution of the Union this struggle has assumed various characters. The methods applied during the years of the first five-year plan and the beginning of the second, the methods of "shock brigade-ism" were based upon agricultural, personal example, administrative pressure and all kinds of group encouragements and privileges. The attempt to introduce a kind of piecework payment, on the basis of the "six conditions" of 1931, came to grief against the spectral character of the valuta and the heterogeneity of prices. The system of state distribution of products had replaced the flexible differential valuation of labour with a so-called "premium system" which meant, in essence, bureaucratic caprice. In the strife for copious privileges, there appeared in the ranks of shock brigades an increasing number of chiselers with special pull. In the long run, the whole system came into complete opposition with its own aims.

Only the abolition of the card system, the beginning of stabilization and the unification of prices, created the condition for the application of piecework payment. Upon this basis, shock brigade-ism was replaced with the so-called Stakhanov movement. In the chase after the ruble, which had now acquired a very real meaning, the workers began to concern themselves more about their machines, and make a more careful use of their working time. The Stakhanov movement to a degree comes down to an intensification of labour, and even to a lengthening of the working day. During the so-called "nonworking" time, the Stakhanovists put their benches and tools in order and sort their raw material, the brigadiers instruct their brigades, etc. Of the seven-hour working day there thus remains nothing but the name.

It was not the Soviet administrators who invented the secret of piecework payment. That system, which strains the nerves without visible external compulsion, Marx considered "the most suitable to capitalistic methods of production". The workers greeted this innovation not only without sympathy, but with hostility. It would have been unnatural to expect anything else of them. The participation in the Stakhanov movement of the genuine enthusiasts of socialism is indubitable. To what extent they exceed the number of mere careerists and cheats, especially in the sphere of administration, it would be hard to say. But the main mass of the workers approaches the new mode of payment from the point of view of the ruble, and is often compelled to perceive that it is getting shorter.

Although at first glance the return of the Soviet government, after "the final and irrevocable triumph of socialism", to piecework payment might seem a retreat to capitalist relations, in reality it is necessary to repeat here what was said about the rehabilitation of the ruble: It is not a question of renouncing socialism, but merely of abandoning crude illusions. The form of wage payment is simply brought into better correspondence with the real resources of the country. "Law can never be higher than the economic structure."

However, the ruling stratum of the Soviet Union cannot yet get along without a social disguise. In a report to the Central Executive Committee in January 1936, the president of the State Planning Commission, Mezhlauk, said:

"The ruble is becoming the sole real means for the realization of a socialist (!) principle of payment for labor."

Although in the old monarchy everything, even down to

the public pissoirs, was called royal, this does not mean that in a workers' state everything automatically becomes socialist. The ruble is the "sole real means" for the realization of a *capitalist* principle of payment for labor, even though on a basis of socialist forms of property. This contradiction is already familiar to us. In instituting the new myth of a "socialist" piecework payment, Mezhlauk added:

"The fundamental principle of socialism is that each one works according to his abilities and receives payment according to the labor performed by him."

Those gentlemen are certainly not diffident in manipulating theories! When the rhythm of labour is determined by the chase after the ruble, then people do not expend themselves "according to ability"—that is, according to the condition of their nerves and muscles—but in violation of themselves. This method can only be justified conditionally and by reference to stern necessity. To declare it "the fundamental principle of socialism" means cynically to trample the idea of a new and higher culture in the familiar filth of capitalism.

Stalin has taken one more step upon this road, presenting the Stakhanov movement as a "preparation of the conditions for the transition from socialism to communism". The reader will see now how important it may be to give a scientific definition to those notions, which are employed in the Soviet Union according to administrative convenience. Socialism, or the lowest stage of communism, demands, to be sure, a strict control of the amount of labour and the amount of consumption, but it assumes in any case more humane forms of control than those invented by the exploitive genius of capital. In the Soviet Union, however, there is now taking place a ruthlessly severe fitting in of backward human material to the technique borrowed from capitalism. In the struggle to achieve European and American standards, the classic methods of exploitation, such as piecework payment, are applied in such naked and crude forms as would not be permitted even by reformist trade unions in bourgeois countries. The consideration that in the Soviet Union the workers work "for themselves" is true only in historical perspective, and only on condition—we will anticipate ourselves to say —that the workers do not submit to the saddle of an autocratic bureaucracy. In any case, state ownership of the means of production does not turn manure into gold, and does not surround with a halo of sanctity the sweatshop system, which wears out the greatest of all productive forces: man. As to the preparation of a "transition from socialism to communism" that will begin at the exactly opposite end—not with the introduction of piecework payment, but with its abolition as a relic of barbarism.

* * *

It is still early to cast the balance of the Stakhanov movement, but it is already possible to distinguish certain traits characteristic not only of the movement, but of the regime as a whole. Certain achievements of individual workers are undoubtedly extremely interesting as evidence of the possibilities open only to socialism. However, from these possibilities to their realization on the scale of the whole economy, is a long road. With the close dependence of one productive process upon another, a continual high output cannot be the result of mere personal efforts. The elevation of the average productivity cannot be achieved without a reorganization of production both in the separate factory and in the relations between enterprises. Moreover, to raise millions to a small degree of technical skill is immeasurably harder than to spur on a few thousand champions.

The leaders themselves, as we have heard, complain at times that the Soviet workers lack skill. However, that is only half of the truth, and the smaller half. The Russian worker is enterprising, ingenious, and gifted. Any hundred Soviet workers transferred into the conditions, let us say, of American industry, after a few months, and even weeks, would probably not fall behind the American workers of a corresponding category. The difficulty lies in the general organization of labour. The Soviet administrative personnel are, as a general rule, far less equal to the new productive tasks than the worker.

With a new technique, piecework payment should inevitably lead to a systematic raising of the now very low productivity of labour. But the creation of the necessary elementary conditions for this demands a raising of the level of administration itself, from the shop foreman to the leaders in the Kremlin. The Stakhanov movement only in a very small degree meets this demand. The bureaucracy tries fatally to leap over difficulties, which it cannot surmount. Since piecework payment of itself does not give the immediate miracles expected of it, a furious administrative pressure rushes to its help, with premiums and ballyhoos on the one side, and penalties on the other.

The first steps of the movement were signalized with mass repressions against the technical engineering personnel and the workers accused of resistance, sabotage and, in some cases, even of the murder of Stakhanovists. The severity of repressions testifies to the strength of the resistance. The bosses explained this so-called "sabotage" as a political opposition. In reality, it was most often rooted in technical, economic, and cultural difficulties, a considerable portion of which found their source in the bureaucracy itself. The "sabotage" was soon apparently broken. The discontented were frightened; the perspicuous were silenced. Telegrams flew around about unheard-of achievements. And in reality so long as it was a question of individual pioneers, the local administrations, obedient to orders, arranged their work with extraordinary forethought, although at the expense of the other workers in the mine or guild. But when hundreds and thousands of workers are suddenly numbered among "Stakhanovists", the administration gets into utter confusion. Not knowing how, and not being objectively able, to put the regime of production in order in a short space of time, it tries to violate both labor power and technique. When the clockworks slow down, it pokes the little wheels with a nail. As a result of the "Stakhanovist" days and ten-day periods, complete chaos was introduced into many enterprises. This explains the fact, at first glance astonishing, that a growth in the number of Stakhanovists is frequently accompanied, not with an increase, but a decrease of the general productivity of the enterprise.

At present, the "heroic" period of the movement is apparently past. The everyday grind begins. It is necessary to learn. Those especially have much to learn who teach others. But they are just the ones who least of all wish to learn. The name of that social guild which holds back and paralyzes all the guilds of the Soviet economy is—the bureaucracy.

## *Chapter 5*

# THE SOVIET THERMIDOR

### 1. Why Stalin Triumphed

The historians of the Soviet Union cannot fail to conclude that the policy of the ruling bureaucracy upon great questions has been a series of contradictory zigzags. The attempt to explain or justify them "by changing circumstances" obviously won't hold water. To guide means at least in some degree to exercise foresight. The Stalin faction has not in the slightest degree foreseen the inevitable results of the development; they have been caught napping every time. They have reacted with mere administrative reflexes. The theory of each successive turn has been created after the fact, and with small regard for what they were teaching yesterday. On the basis of the same irrefutable facts and documents, the historian will be compelled to conclude that the so-called "Left Opposition" offered an immeasurably more correct analysis of the processes taking place in the country, and far more truly foresaw their further development.

This assertion is contradicted at first glance by the simple fact that the fiction, which could not see ahead, was steadily victorious, while the more penetrating group suffered defeat after defeat. That kind of objection, which comes automatically to mind, is convincing, however, only for those who think rationalistically, and see in politics a logical argument or a chess match. A political struggle is in its essence a struggle of interests and forces, not of arguments. The quality of the leadership is, of course, far from a matter of indifference for the outcome of the conflict, but it is not the only factor, and in the last analysis is not decisive. Each of the struggling camps moreover demands leaders in its own image.

The February revolution raised Kerensky and Tsereteli to power, not because they were "cleverer" or "more astute" than the ruling tzarist clique, but because they represented, at least temporarily, the revolutionary masses of the people in their revolt against the old regime. Kerensky was able to drive Lenin underground and imprison other Bolshevik leaders, not because he excelled them in personal qualifications, but because the majority of the workers and soldiers in those days were still following the patriotic petty bourgeoisie. The personal "superiority" of Kerensky, if it is suitable to employ such a word in this connection, consisted in the fact that he did not see farther than the overwhelming majority. The Bolsheviks in their turn conquered the petty bourgeois democrats, not through the personal superiority of their leaders, but through a new correlation of social forces. The proletariat had succeeded at last in leading the discontented peasantry against the bourgeoisie.

The consecutive stages of the great French Revolution, during its rise and fall alike, demonstrate no less convincingly that the strength of the "leaders" and "heroes" that replaced each other consisted primarily in their correspondence to the character of those classes and strata which supported them. Only this correspondence, and not any irrelevant superiorities whatever, permitted each of them to place the impress of his personality upon a certain historic period. In the successive supremacy of Mirabeau, Brissot, Robespierre, Barras and Bonaparte, there is an obedience to objective law incomparably more effective than the special traits of the historic protagonists themselves.

It is sufficiently well known that every revolution up to this time has been followed by a reaction, or even a counter-revolution. This, to be sure, has never thrown the nation all the way back to its starting point, but it has always taken from the people the lion's share of their conquests. The victims of the first revolutionary wave have been, as a general rule, those pioneers, initiators, and instigators who stood at the head of the masses in the period of the revolutionary offensive. In their stead people of the second line, in league with the former enemies of the revolution, have been advanced to the front. Beneath this dramatic duel of "coryphées" on the open political scene, shifts have taken place in the relations between classes, and, no less important, profound changes in the psychology of the recently revolutionary masses.

Answering the bewildered questions of many comrades as to what has become of the activity of the Bolshevik party and the working class— where is its revolutionary initiative, its spirit of self-sacrifice and plebian pride—why, in place of all this, has appeared so much vileness, cowardice, pusillanimity and careerism—Rakovsky referred to the life story of the French revolution of the 18th century, and offered the example of Babuef, who on emerging from the Abbaye prison likewise wondered what had become of the heroic people of the Parisian suburbs. A revolution of the heroic people of the Parisian suburbs. A revolution is a mighty devourer of human energy, both individual and collective. The nerves give way. Consciousness is shaken and characters are worn out. Events unfold too swiftly for the flow of fresh forces to replace the loss. Hunger, unemployment, the death of the revolutionary cadres, the removal of the masses from administration, all this led to such a physical and moral impoverishment of the Parisian suburbs that they required three decades before they were ready for a new insurrection.

The axiomatic assertions of the Soviet literature, to the effect that the laws of bourgeois revolutions are "inapplicable" to a proletarian revolution, have no scientific content whatever. The proletarian character of the October Revolution was determined by the world situation and by a special correlation of internal forces. But the classes themselves were formed in the barbarous circumstances of tzarism and backward capitalism, and were anything but made to order for the demands of a socialist revolution. The exact opposite is true. It is for the very reason that a proletariat still backward in many respects achieved in the space of a few months the unprecedented leap from a semi-feudal monarchy to a socialist dictatorship, that the reaction in its ranks was inevitable. This reaction has developed in a series of consecutive waves. External conditions and events have vied with each other in nourishing it. Intervention followed intervention. The revolution got no direct help from the West. Instead of the expected prosperity of the country an ominous destitution reigned for long. Moreover, the outstanding representatives of the working class either died in the civil war, or rose a few steps higher and broke away from the masses. And thus after an unexampled tension of forces, hopes and illusions, there came a long period of weariness, decline and sheer disappointment in the results of the revolution. The ebb of the "plebian pride" made room for a flood of pusillanimity and careerism. The new commanding caste rose to its place upon this wave.

The demobilization of the Red Army of five million played no small role in the formation of the bureaucracy. The victorious commanders assumed leading posts in the local Soviets, in economy, in education, and they persistently introduced everywhere that regime which had ensured success in the civil war. Thus on all sides the masses were pushed away gradually from actual participation in the leadership of the country.

The reaction within the proletariat caused an extraordinary flush of hope and confidence in the petty bourgeois strata of town and country, aroused as they were to new life by the NEP, and growing bolder and bolder. The young bureaucracy, which had arisen at first as an agent of the proletariat, began now to feel itself a court of arbitration between classes. Its independence increased from mouth to mouth.

The international situation was pushing with mighty forces in the same direction. The Soviet bureaucracy became more self-confident, the heavier blows dealt to the working class. Between these two facts there was not only a chronological, but a causal connection, and one, which worked in two directions. The leaders of the bureaucracy promoted the proletarian defeats; the defeats promoted the rise of the bureaucracy. The crushing of the Bulgarian insurrection in 1924, the treacherous liquidation of the General Strike in England

and the unworthy conduct of the Polish workers' party at the installation of Pilsudski in 1926, the terrible massacre of the Chinese revolution in 1927, and, finally, the still more ominous recent defeats in Germany and Austria—these are the historic catastrophes which killed the faith of the Soviet masses in world revolution, and permitted the bureaucracy to rise higher and higher as the sole light of salvation.

As to the causes of the defeat of the world proletariat during the last thirteen years, the author must refer to his other works, where he has tried to expose the ruinous part played by the leadership in the Kremlin, isolated from the masses and profoundly conservative as it is, in the revolutionary movement of all countries. Here we are concerned primarily with the irrefutable and instructive fact that the continual defeats of the revolution in Europe and Asia, while weakening the international position of the Soviet Union, have vastly strengthened the Soviet bureaucracy. Two dates are especially significant in this historic series. In the second half of 1923, the attention of the Soviet workers was passionately fixed upon Germany, where the proletariat, it seemed, had stretched out its hand to power. The panicky retreat of the German Communist Party was the heaviest possible disappointment to the working masses of the Soviet Union. The Soviet bureaucracy straightway opened a campaign against the theory of "permanent revolution", and dealt the Left Opposition its first cruel blow. During the years 1926 and 1927 the population of the Soviet Union experienced a new tide of hope. All eyes were now directed to the East where the drama of the Chinese revolution was unfolding. The Left Opposition had recovered from the previous blows and was recruiting a phalanx of new adherents. At the end of 1927 the Chinese revolution was massacred by the hangman, Chiang-kai-shek, into whose hands the Communist International had literally betrayed the Chinese workers and peasants. A cold wave of disappointment swept over the masses of the Soviet Union. After an unbridled baiting in the press and at meetings, the bureaucracy finally, in 1928, ventured upon mass arrests among the Left Opposition.

To be sure, tens of thousands of revolutionary fighters gathered around the banner of the Bolshevik-Leninists. The advanced workers were indubitably sympathetic to the Opposition, but that sympathy remained passive. The masses lacked faith that the situation could be seriously changed by a new struggle. Meantime the bureaucracy asserted:

"For the sake of an international revolution, the Opposition proposes to drag us into a revolutionary war. Enough of shake-ups! We have earned the right to rest. We will build the socialist society at home. Rely upon us, your leaders!"

This gospel of repose firmly consolidated the apparatchiki and the military and state officials and indubitably found an echo among the weary workers, and still more the peasant masses. Can it be, they asked themselves, that the Opposition is actually ready to sacrifice the interests of the Soviet Union for the idea of "permanent revolution"? In reality, the struggle had been about the life interests of the Soviet state. The false policy of the International in Germany resulted ten years later in the victory of Hitler—that is, in a threatening war danger from the West. And the no less false policy in China reinforced Japanese imperialism and brought very much nearer the danger in the East. But periods of reaction are characterized above all by a lack of courageous thinking.

The Opposition was isolated. The bureaucracy struck while the iron was hot, exploiting the bewilderment and passivity of the workers, setting their more backward strata against the advanced, and relying more and more boldly upon the kulak and the petty bourgeois ally in general. In the course of a few years, the bureaucracy thus shattered the revolutionary vanguard of the proletariat.

It would be naive to imagine that Stalin, previously unknown to the masses, suddenly issued from the wings full armed with a complete strategical plan. No indeed. Before he felt out his own course, the bureaucracy felt out Stalin himself. He brought it all the necessary guarantees: the prestige of an old Bolshevik, a strong character, narrow vision, and close bonds with the political machine as the sole source of his influence. The success, which fell upon him, was a surprise at first to Stalin himself. It was the friendly welcome of the new ruling group, trying to free itself from the old principles and from the control of the masses, and having need of a reliable arbiter in its inner affairs. A secondary figure before the masses and in the events of the revolution, Stalin revealed himself as the indubitable leader of the Thermidorian bureaucracy, as first in its midst.

The new ruling caste soon revealed soon revealed its own ideas, feelings and, more important, its interests. The overwhelming majority of the older generation of the present bureaucracy had stood on the other side of the barricades during the October Revolution. (Take, for example, the Soviet ambassadors only: Troyanovsky, Maisky, Potemkin, Suritz, Khinchuk, etc.) Or at best they had stood aside from the struggle. Those of the present bureaucrats who were in the Bolshevik camp in the October days played in the majority of cases no considerable role. As for the young bureaucrats, they have been chosen and educated by the elders, frequently from among their own offspring. These people could not have achieved the October Revolution, but they were perfectly suited to exploit it.

Personal incidents in the interval between these two historic chapters were not, of course, without influence. Thus the sickness and death of Lenin undoubtedly hastened the denouement. Had Lenin lived longer, the pressure of the bureaucratic power would have developed, at least during the first years, more slowly. But as early as 1926 Krupskaya said, of Left Oppositionists: "If Ilych were alive, he would probably already be in prison." The fears and alarming prophecies of Lenin himself were then still fresh in her memory, and she cherished no illusions as to his personal omnipotence against opposing historic winds and currents.

The bureaucracy conquered something more than the Left Opposition. It conquered the Bolshevik party. It defeated the program of Lenin, who had seen the chief danger in the conversion of the organs of the state "from servants of society to lords over society". It defeated all these enemies, the Opposition, the party and Lenin, not with ideas and arguments, but with its own social weight. The leaden rump of bureaucracy outweighed the head of the revolution. That is the secret of the Soviet's Thermidor.

## 2. The Degeneration of the Bolshevik Party

The Bolshevik party prepared and insured the October victory. It also created the Soviet state, supplying it with a sturdy skeleton. The degeneration of the party became both cause and consequence of the bureaucratization of the state. It is necessary to show at least briefly how this happened.

The inner regime of the Bolshevik party was characterized by the method of democratic centralism. The combination of these two concepts, democracy and centralism, is not in the least contradictory. The party took watchful care not only that its boundaries should always be strictly defined, but also that all those who entered these boundaries should enjoy the actual right to define the direction of the party policy. Freedom of criticism and intellectual struggle was an irrevocable content of the party democracy. The present doctrine that Bolshevism does not tolerate factions is a myth of epoch decline. In reality the history of Bolshevism is a history of the struggle of factions. And, indeed, how could a genuinely revolutionary organization, setting itself the task of overthrowing the world and uniting under its banner the most audacious iconoclasts, fighters and insurgents, live and develop without intellectual conflicts, without groupings and temporary factional formations? The farsightedness of the Bolshevik leadership often made it possible to soften conflicts and shorten the duration of factional struggle, but no more than that. The Central Committee relied upon this seething democratic support. From this it derived the audacity to make decisions and give orders. The obvious correctness of the leadership at all critical stages gave it that high authority which is the priceless moral capital of centralism.

The regime of the Bolshevik party, especially before it came to power, stood thus in complete contradiction to the regime of the present sections of the Communist International, with their "leaders" appointed from above, making complete changes of policy at a word of command, with their uncontrolled apparatus, haughty in its attitude to the rank and file, servile in its attitude to the Kremlin. But in the first years after the conquest of power also, even when the administrative rust was already visible on the party, every Bolshevik, not excluding Stalin, would have denounced as a malicious slanderer anyone who should have shown him on a screen the image of the party ten or fifteen years later.

The very centre of Lenin's attention and that of his colleagues was occupied by a continual concern to protect the Bolshevik ranks from the vices of those in power. However, the extraordinary closeness and at times actual merging of the party with the state apparatus had already in those first years done indubitable harm to the freedom and elasticity of the party regime. Democracy had been narrowed in proportion as difficulties increased. In the beginning, the party had wished and hoped to preserve freedom of political struggle within the framework of the Soviets. The civil war introduced stern amendments into this calculation. The Opposition parties were forbidden one after the other. This measure, obviously in conflict with the spirit of Soviet democracy, the leaders of Bolshevism regarded not as a principle, but as an episodic act of self-defence.

The swift growth of the ruling party, with the novelty and immensity of its tasks, inevitably gave rise to inner disagreements. The underground oppositional currents in the country exerted a pressure through various channels upon the sole legal political organization, increasing the acuteness of the factional struggle. At the moment of completion of the civil war, this struggle took such sharp forms as to threaten to unsettle the state power. In March 1921, in the days of the Kronstadt revolt, which attracted into its ranks no small number of Bolsheviks, the 10th Congress of the party thought it necessary to resort to a prohibition of factions—that is, to transfer the political regime prevailing in the state to the inner life of the ruling party. This forbidding of factions was again regarded as an exceptional measure to be abandoned at the first serious improvement in the situation. At the same time, the Central Committee was extremely cautious in applying the new law, concerning itself most of all lest it lead to a strangling of the inner life of the party.

However, what was in its original design merely a necessary concession to a difficult situation, proved perfectly suited to the taste of the bureaucracy, which had then begun to approach the inner life of the party exclusively from the viewpoint of convenience in administration. Already in 1922, during a brief improvement in his health, Lenin, horrified at the threatening growth of bureaucratism, was preparing a struggle against the faction of Stalin, which had made itself the axis of the party machine as a first step toward capturing the machinery of state. A second stroke and then death prevented him from measuring forces with this internal reaction.

The entire effort of Stalin, with whom at that time Zinoviev and Kamenev were working hand in hand, was thenceforth directed to freeing the party machine from the control of the rank-and-file members of the party. In this struggle for "stability" of the Central Committee, Stalin proved the most consistent and reliable among his colleagues. He had no need to tear himself away from international problems; he had never been concerned with them. The petty bourgeois outlook of the new ruling stratum was his own outlook. He profoundly believed that the task of creating socialism was national and administrative in its nature. He looked upon the Communist International as a necessary evil, which should be used so far as possible for the purposes of foreign policy. His own party kept a value in his eyes merely as a submissive support for the machine.

Together with the theory of socialism in one country, there was put into circulation by the bureaucracy a theory that in Bolshevism the Central Committee is everything and the party nothing. This second theory was in any case realized with more success than the first. Availing itself of the death of Lenin, the ruling group announced a "Leninist levy". The gates of the party, always carefully guarded, were now thrown wide open. Workers, clerks, petty officials, flocked through in crowds. The political aim of this manoeuver was to dissolve the revolutionary vanguard in raw human material, without experience, without independence, and yet with the old habit of submitting to the authorities. The scheme was successful. By freeing the bureaucracy from the control of the proletarian vanguard, the "Leninist levy" dealt a death blow to the party of Lenin. The machine had won the necessary independence. Democratic centralism gave place to bureaucratic centralism. In the party apparatus itself there now took place a radical reshuffling of personnel from top to bottom. The chief merit of a Bolshevik was declared to be obedience. Under the guise of a struggle with the opposition, there occurred a sweeping replacement of revolutionists with chinovniks [professional governmental functionaries]. The history of the Bolshevik party became a history of its rapid degeneration.

The political meaning of the developing struggle was darkened for many by the circumstances that the leaders of all three groupings, Left, Centre and Right, belonged to one and the same staff in the Kremlin, the Politburo. To superficial minds it seemed to be a mere matter of personal rivalry, a struggle for the "heritage" of Lenin. But in the conditions of iron dictatorship social antagonisms could not show themselves at first except through the institutions of the ruling party. Many Thermidorians emerged in their day from the circle of the Jacobins. Bonaparte himself belonged to that circle in his early years, and subsequently it was from among former Jacobins that the First Consul and Emperor of France selected his most faithful servants. Times changed and the Jacobins with them, not excluding the Jacobins of the twentieth century.

Of the Politburo of Lenin's epoch there now remains only Stalin. Two of its members, Zinoviev and Kamenev, collaborators of Lenin throughout many years as émigrés, are enduring then-year prison terms for a crime, which they did not commit. Three other members, Rykov, Bukharin and Tomsky, are completely removed from the leadership, but as a reward for submission occupy secondary posts.

[TRANSLATOR'S NOTE: Zinoviev and Kamenev were executed in August 1936 for alleged complicity in a "terrible plot" against Stalin; Tomsky committed suicide or was shot in connection with the same case; Rykov was removed from his post in connection with the plot; Bukharin, although suspected, is still at liberty.]

And, finally, the author of these lines is in exile. The widow of Lenin, Krupskaya, is also under the ban, having proved unable with all her efforts to adjust herself completely to the Thermidor.

The members of the present Politburo occupied secondary posts throughout the history of the Bolshevik party. If anybody in the first years of the revolution had predicted their future elevation, they would have been the first in surprise, and there would have been no false modesty in their surprise. For this very reason, the rule is more stern at present that the Politburo is always right, and in any case that no man can be right against Stalin, who is unable to make mistakes and consequently cannot be right against himself.

Demands for party democracy were through all this time the slogans of all the oppositional groups, as insistent as they were hopeless. The above-mentioned platform of the Left Opposition demanded in 1927 that a special law be written into the Criminal Code "punishing as a serious state crime every direct or indirect persecution of a worker for criticism". Instead of this, there was introduced into the Criminal Code an article against the Left Opposition itself.

Of party democracy there remained only recollections in the memory of the older generation. And together with it had disappeared the democracy of the Soviets, the trade unions, the co-operatives, the cultural and athletic organizations. Above each and every one of them there reigns an unlimited hierarchy of party secretaries. The regime had become "totalitarian" in character several years before this word arrived from Germany.

"By means of demoralizing methods, which convert thinking communists into machines, destroying will, character and human dignity," wrote Rakovsky in 1928, "the ruling circles have succeeded in converting themselves into an unremovable and inviolate oligarchy, which replaces the class and the party."

Since these indignant lines were written, the degeneration of the regime has gone immeasurably farther. The GPU has become the decisive factor in the inner life of the party. If Molotov in March 1936 was able to boast to a French journalist that the ruling party no longer contains any factional struggle, it is only because disagreements are now settled by the automatic intervention of the political police. The old Bolshevik party is dead and no force will resurrect it.

* * *

Parallel with the political degeneration of the party, there occurred a moral decay of the uncontrolled apparatus. The word "sovbour"—Soviet bourgeois—as applied to a privileged dignitary appeared very early in the workers' vocabulary. With the transfer to the NEP bourgeois tendencies received a more copious field of action. At the 11th Congress of the party, in March 1922, Lenin gave warning of the danger of a degeneration of the ruling stratum. It has occurred more than once in history, he said, that the conqueror took over the culture of the conquered, when the latter stood on a higher level. The culture of the Russian bourgeoisie and the old bureaucracy was, to be sure, miserable, but alas the new ruling stratum must often take off its hat to that culture. "Four thousand seven hundred responsible communists" in Moscow administer the state machine. "Who is leading whom? I doubt very much whether you can say that the communists are in the lead..." In subsequent congresses, Lenin could not speak. But all his thoughts in the last months of his active life were of warning and arming the workers against the oppression, caprice and decay of the bureaucracy. He, however, saw only the first symptoms of the disease.

Christian Rakovsky, former president of the soviet of People's Commissars of the Ukraine, and later Soviet Ambassador in London and Paris, sent to his friends in 1928, when already in exile, a brief inquiry into the Soviet bureaucracy, which we have quoted above several times, for it still remains the best that has been written on this subject.

"In the mind of Lenin, and in all our minds," says Rakovsky, "the task of the party leadership was to protect both the party and the working class from the corrupting action of privilege, place and patronage on the part of those in power, from rapprochement with the relics of the old nobility and burgherdom, from the corrupting influence of the NEP, from the temptation of bourgeois morals and ideologies.... We must say frankly, definitely and loudly that the party apparatus has not fulfilled this task, that it has revealed a complete incapacity for its double role of protector and educator. It has failed. It is bankrupt."

It is true that Rakovsky himself, broken by the bureaucratic repressions, subsequently repudiated his own critical judgments. But the 70-year-old Galileo too, caught in the vice of the Holy Inquisition, found himself compelled to repudiate the system of Copernicus—which did not prevent the earth from continuing to revolve around the sun. We do not believe in the recantation of the 60-year-old Rakovsky, for he himself has more than once made a withering analysis of such recantations. As to his political criticisms, they have found in the facts of the objective development a far more reliable support than in the subjective stout-heartedness of their author.

The conquest of power changes not only the relations of the proletariat to other classes, but also its own inner structure. The wielding of power becomes the speciality of a definite social group, which is the more impatient to solve its own "social problem", the higher its opinion of the own mission.

> "In a proletarian state, where capitalist accumulation is forbidden to the members of the ruling party, the differentiation is at first functional, but afterward becomes social. I do not say it becomes a class differentiation, but a social one..."

Rakovsky further explains:

> "The social situation of the communist who has at his disposition an automobile, a good apartment, regular vacations, and receives the party maximum of salary, differs from the situation of the communist who works in the coal mines, where he receives from 50 to 60 rubles a month."

Counting over the causes of the degeneration of the Jacobins when in power—the chase after wealth, participation in government contracts, supplies, etc., Rakovsky cites a curious remark of Babeuf to the effect that the degeneration of the new ruling stratum was helped along not a little by the former young ladies of the aristocracy toward whom the Jacobins were very friendly. "What are you doing, small-hearted plebians?" cries Babeuf. "Today they are embracing you and tomorrow they will strangle you." A census of the wives of the ruling stratum in the Soviet Union would show a similar picture. The well-known Soviet journalist, Sosnovsky, pointed out the special role played by the "automobile-harem factor" in forming the morals of the Soviet bureaucracy. It is true that Sosnovsky, too, following Rakovsky, recanted and was returned from Siberia. But that did not improve the morals of the bureaucracy. On the contrary, that very recantation is proof of a progressing demoralization.

The old articles of Sosnovsky, passed about in manuscript from hand to hand, were sprinkled with unforgettable episodes from the life of the new ruling stratum, plainly showing to what vast degree the conquerors have assimilated the morals of the conquered. Not to return, however, to past years—for Sosnovsky finally exchanged his whip for a lyre in 1934—we will confine ourselves to wholly fresh examples from the Soviet press. And we will not select the abuses and co-called "excesses", either, but everyday phenomena realized by official social opinion.

The director of a Moscow factory, a prominent communist, boasts in *Pravda* of the cultural growth of the enterprise directed by him. "A mechanic telephones: 'What is your order, sir, check the furnace immediately or wait?' I answer: 'Wait.'" *[TRANSLATOR's NOTE: It is impossible to convey the flavour of this dialogue in English. The second person singular is used either with intimates in token of affection, or with children, servants and animals in token of superiority.]* The mechanic addresses the director with extreme respect, using the second person plural, while the director answers him in the second person singular. And this disgraceful dialogue, impossible in any culture's capitalist country, is related by the director himself on the pages of *Pravda* as something entirely normal! The editor does not object because he does not notice it. The readers do not object because they are accustomed to it. We are also not surprised, for at solemn sessions in the Kremlin, the "leaders" and People's Commissars address in the second person singular directors of factories subordinate to them, presidents of collective farms, shop foremen and working women, especially invited to receive decorations. How can they fail to remember that one of the most popular revolutionary slogans in tzarist Russia was the demand for the abolition of the use of the second person singular by bosses in addressing their subordinates!

These Kremlin dialogues of the authorities with "the people", astonishing in their lordly ungraciousness, unmistakably testify that, in spite of the October Revolution, the nationalization of the means of production, collectivization, and "the liquidation of the kulaks as a class", the relations among men, and that at the very heights of the Soviet pyramid, have not only not yet risen to socialism, but in many respects are still lagging behind a cultured capitalism. In recent years enormous backward steps have been taken in this very important sphere. And the source of this revival of genuine Russian barbarism is indubitably the Soviet Thermidor, which has given complete independence and freedom from control to a bureaucracy possessing little culture, and has given to the masses the well-known gospel of obedience and silence.

We are far from intending to contrast the abstraction of dictatorship with the abstraction of democracy, and weight their merits on the scales of pure reason. Everything is relative in this world, where change alone endures. The dictatorship of the Bolshevik party proved one of the most powerful instruments of progress in history. But here too, in the words of the poet, "Reason becomes unreason, kindness a pest". The prohibition of oppositional parties brought after it the prohibition of factions. The prohibition of factions ended in a prohibition to think otherwise than the infallible leaders. The police-manufactured monolithism of the party resulted in a bureaucratic impunity, which has become the sources of all kinds of wantonness and corruption.

### 3. The Social Roots of Thermidor

We have defined the Soviet Thermidor as a triumph of the bureaucracy over the masses. We have tried to disclose the historic conditions of this triumph. The revolutionary vanguard of the proletariat was in part devoured by the administrative apparatus and gradually demoralized, in part annihilated in the civil war, and in part thrown out and crushed. The tired and disappointed masses were indifferent to what was happening on the summits. These conditions, however, are inadequate to explain why the bureaucracy succeeded in raising itself above society and getting its fate firmly into its own hands. Its own will to this would in any case be inadequate; the arising of a new ruling stratum must have deep social causes.

The victory of the Thermidorians over the Jacobins in the 18th century was also aided by the weariness of the masses and the demoralization of the leading cadres, but beneath these essentially incidental phenomena a deep organic process was taking place. The Jacobins rested upon the lower petty bourgeoisie lifted by the great wave. The revolution of the 18th century, however, corresponding to the course of development of the productive forces, could not but bring the great bourgeoisie to political ascendancy in the long run. The Thermidor was only one of the stages in this inevitable process. What similar social necessity found expression in the Soviet Thermidor? We have tried already in one of the preceding chapters to make a preliminary answer to the question why the gendarme triumphed. We must now prolong out analysis of the conditions of the transition from capitalism to socialism, and the role of the state in this process. Let us again compare theoretic prophecy with reality.

"It is still necessary to suppress the bourgeoisie and its resistance," wrote Lenin in 1917, speaking of the period which should begin immediately after the conquest of power, "but the organ of suppression here is now the majority of the population, and not the minority as had heretofore always been the case.... In that sense the state is beginning to die away."

In what does this dying away express itself? Primarily in the fact that "in place of special institutions of a privileged minority (privileged officials, commanders of a standing army), the majority itself can directly carry out" the functions of suppression. Lenin follows this with a statement axiomatic and unanswerable:

> "The more universal becomes the very fulfillment of the functions of the state power, the less need is there of this power."

The annulment of private property in the means of production removes the principal task of the historic state—defence of the proprietary privileges of the minority against the overwhelming majority.

The dying away of the state begins, then, according to Lenin, on the very day after the expropriation of the expropriators—that is, before the new regime has had time to take up its economic and cultural problems. Every success in the solution of these problems means a further step in the liquidation of the state, its dissolution in the socialist society. The degree of this dissolution is the best index of the depth and efficacy of the socialist structure. We may lay down approximately this sociological theorem: The strength of the compulsion exercised by the masses in a workers' state is directly proportional to the strength of the exploitive tendencies, or the danger of a restoration of capitalism, and inversely proportional to the strength of the social solidarity and the general loyalty to the new regime. Thus the bureaucracy—that is, the "privileged officials and commanders of the standing army"—represents a special kind of compulsion which the masses cannot or do not wish to exercise, and which, one way or another, is directed against the masses themselves.

If the diplomatic Soviets had preserved to this day their original strength and independence, and yet were compelled to resort to repressions and compulsions on the scale of the first years, this circumstance might of itself give rise to serious anxiety. How much greater must be the alarm in view of the fact that the mass Soviet have entirely disappeared from the scene, having turned over the function of compulsion to Stalin, Yagoda and company. And what forms of compulsion! First of all we must ask ourselves: What social cause stands behind its policification? The importance of this question is obvious. In dependence upon the answer, we must either radically revise out traditional views of the socialist society in general, or as radically reject the official estimates of the Soviet Union.

Let us now take from the latest number of a Moscow newspaper a stereotyped characterization of the present Soviet regime, one of those which are repeated throughout the country from day to day and which school children learn by heart:

> "In the Soviet Union the parasitical classes of capitalists, landlords and kulaks are completely liquidated, and thus is forever ended the exploitation of man by man. The whole national economy has become socialistic, and the growing Stakhanov movement is preparing the conditions for a transition from socialism to communism." **(*Pravda,* April 4, 1936)**

The world press of the Communist International, it goes without saying, has no other thing to say on this subject. But if exploitation is "ended forever", if the country is really now on the road from socialism, that is, the lowest stage of communism, to its higher stage, then there remains nothing for society to do but throw off at last the straightjacket of the state. In place of this—it is hard even to grasp this contrast with the mind!—the Soviet state has acquired a totalitarian-bureaucratic character.

The same fatal contradiction finds illustration in the fate of the party. Here the problem may be formulated approximately thus: Why, from 1917 to 1921, when the old ruling classes were still fighting with weapons in the hands, when they were actively supported by the imperialists of the whole world, when the kulaks in arms were sabotaging the army and food supplies of the country—why was it possible to dispute openly and fearlessly in the party about the most critical questions of policy? Why now, after the cessation of intervention, after the shattering of the exploiting classes, after the indubitable successes of industrialization, after the collectivization of the overwhelming majority of the peasants, is it impossible to permit the slightest word of criticism of the unremovable leaders? Why is it that any Bolshevik who should demand a calling of the congress of the party in accordance with its constitution would be immediately expelled, any citizen who expressed out loud a doubt of the infallibility of Stalin would be tried and convicted almost as though a participant in a terrorist plot? Whence this terrible, monstrous and unbearable intensity of repression and of the police apparatus?

Theory is not a note, which you can present at any moment to reality for payment. If a theory proves mistaken we must revise it or fill out its gaps. We must find out those real social forces that have given rise to the contrast between Soviet reality and the traditional Marxian conception. In any case we must not wander in the dark, repeating ritual phrases, useful for the prestige of the leaders, but which nevertheless slap the living reality in the face. We shall now see a convincing example of this.

In a speech at a session of the Central Executive Committee in January 1936, Molotov, the president of the Council of People's Commissars, declared:

> "The national economy of the country has become socialistic. (applause) In that sense [?] we have solved the problem of the liquidation of classes." (applause) However, there still remain from the past "elements in their nature hostile to us," fragments of the former ruling classes. Moreover, among the collectivized farmers, state employees and sometimes also the workers, spekulantiki ["petty speculators"] are discovered, "grafters in relation to the collective and state wealth, anti-Soviets gossip, etc." And hence results the necessity of a further reinforcement of the dictatorship. In opposition to Engels, the workers' state must not "fall asleep", but on the contrary become more and more vigilant.

The picture drawn by the head of the Soviet government would be reassuring in the highest degree, were it not murderously self-contradictory. Socialism completely reigns in the country: "In that sense" classes are abolished. (If they are abolished in that sense, then they are in every other.) To be sure, the social harmony is broken here and there by fragments and remnants of the past, but it is impossible to think that scattered dreamers of a restoration of capitalism, deprived of power and property, together with "petty speculators" (not even speculators!) and "gossips" are capable of overthrowing the classless society. Everything is getting along, it seems, the very best you can imagine. But what is the use then of the iron dictatorship of the bureaucracy.

Those reactionary dreamers, we must believe, will gradually die out. The "petty speculators" and "gossips" might be disposed of with a laugh by the super-democratic Soviets.

"We are not utopians," responded Lenin in 1917 to the bourgeois and reformist theoreticians of the bureaucratic state, and "by no means deny the possibility and inevitability of excesses on the part of individual persons, and likewise the necessity for suppressing such excesses. But... for this there is no need of a special machine, a special apparatus of repression. This will be done by the armed people themselves, with the same simplicity and ease with which any crowd of civilized people even in contemporary society separate a couple of fighters or stop an act of violence against a woman."

Those words sound as though the author has especially foreseen the remarks of one of his successors at the head of the government. Lenin is taught in the public schools of the Soviet Union, but apparently not in the Council of People's Commissars. Otherwise it would be impossible to explain Molotov's daring to resort without reflection to the very construction against which Lenin directed his well-sharpened weapons. The flagrant contradictions between the founder and his epigones are before us! Whereas Lenin judged that even the liquidation of the exploiting classes might be accomplished without a bureaucratic apparatus, Molotov, in explaining why after the liquidation of classes the bureaucratic machine has strangled the independence of the people, finds no better pretext than a reference to the "remnants" of the liquidated classes.

To live on these "remnants" becomes, however, rather difficult since, according to the confession of authoritative representatives of the bureaucracy itself, yesterday's class enemies are being successfully assimilated by the Soviet society. Thus Postyshev, one of the secretaries of the Central Committee of the party, said in April 1936, at a congress of the League of Communist Youth:

"Many of the sabotagers... have sincerely repented and joined the ranks of the Soviet people." In view of the successful carrying out of collectivization, "the children of kulaks are not to be held responsible for their parents." And yet more: "The kulak himself now hardly believes in the possibility of a return to his former position of exploiter in the village."

Not without reason did the government annul the limitations connected with social origins! But if Postyshev's assertion, wholly agreed to by Molotov, makes any sense it is only this: Not only has the bureaucracy become a monstrous anachronism, but state compulsion in general has nothing whatever to do in the land of the Soviets. However, neither Molotov nor Postyshev agrees with that immutable inference. They prefer to hold the power even at the price of self-contradiction.

In reality, too, they cannot reject the power. Or, to translate this into objective language: The present Soviet society cannot get along without a state, nor even—within limits—without a bureaucracy. But the case of this is by no means the pitiful remnants of the past, but the mighty forces and tendencies of the present. The justification for the existence of a Soviet state as an apparatus of compulsion lies in the fact that the present transitional structure is still full of social contradictions, which in the sphere of consumption—most closely and sensitively felt by all—are extremely tense, and forever threaten to break over into the sphere of production. The triumph of socialism cannot be called either final or irrevocable.

The basis of bureaucratic rule is the poverty of society in

objects of consumption, with the resulting struggle of each against all. When there are enough goods in a store, the purchasers can come whenever they want to. When there are little goods, the purchasers are compelled to stand in line. When the lines are very long, it is necessary to appoint a policeman to keep order. Such is the starting point of the power of the Soviet bureaucracy. It "knows" who is to get something and who has to wait.

A raising of the material and cultural level ought, at first glance, to lessen the necessity of privileges, narrow the sphere of application of "bourgeois law", and thereby undermine the standing ground of its defenders, the bureaucracy. In reality the opposite thing has happened: the growth of the productive forces has been so far accompanied by an extreme development of all forms of inequality, privilege and advantage, and therewith of bureaucratism. That too is not accidental.

In its first period, the Soviet regime was undoubtedly far more equalitarian and less bureaucratic than now. But that was an equality of general poverty. The resources of the country were so scant that there was no opportunity to separate from the masses of the population any broad privileged strata. At the same time the "equalizing" character of wages, destroying personal interestedness, became a brake upon the development of the productive forces. Soviet economy had to lift itself from its poverty to a somewhat higher level before fat deposits of privilege became possible. The present state of production is still far from guaranteeing all necessities to everybody. But it is already adequate to give significant privileges to a minority, and convert inequality into a whip for the spurring on of the majority. That is the first reason why the growth of production has so far strengthened not the socialist, but the bourgeois features of the state.

But that is not the sole reason. Alongside the economic factor dictating capitalist methods of payment at the present stage, there operates a parallel political factor in the person of the bureaucracy itself. In its very essence it is the planter and protector of inequality. It arose in the beginning as the bourgeois organ of a workers' state. In establishing and defending the advantages of a minority, it of course draws off the cream for its own use. Nobody who has wealth to distribute ever omits himself. Thus out of a social necessity there has developed an organ which has far outgrown its socially necessary function, and become an independent factor and therewith the source of great danger for the whole social organism.

The social meaning of the Soviet Thermidor now begins to take form before us. The poverty and cultural backwardness of the masses has again become incarnate in the malignant figure of the ruler with a great club in his hand. The deposed and abused bureaucracy, from being a servant of society, has again become its lord. On this road it has attained such a degree of social and moral alienation from the popular masses, that it cannot now permit any control over its activities or its income.

The bureaucracy's seemingly mystic fear of "petty speculators, grafters, and gossips" thus finds a wholly natural explanation. Not yet able to satisfy the elementary needs of the population, the Soviet economy creates and resurrects at every step tendencies to graft and speculation. On the other side, the privileges of the new aristocracy awaken in the masses of the population a tendency to listen to anti-Soviet "gossips"—that is, to anyone who, albeit in a whisper, criticizes the greedy and capricious bosses. It is a question, therefore, not of spectres of the past, not of the remnants of what no longer exists, not, in short, of the snows of yesteryear, but of new, mighty, and continually reborn tendencies to personal accumulation. The first still very meagre wave of prosperity in the country, just because of its meagreness, has not weakened, but strengthened, these centrifugal tendencies. On the other hand, there has developed simultaneously a desire of the unprivileged to slap the grasping hands of the new gentry. The social struggle again grows sharp. Such are the sources of the power of the bureaucracy. But from those same sources comes also a threat to its power.

# Chapter 6

# THE GROWTH OF INEQUALITY AND SOCIAL ANTAGONISMS

## 1. Want, luxury and speculation

After starting out with "socialist distribution", the Soviet power found itself obliged in 1921 to return to the market. The extreme stretching of material means in the epoch of the five-year-plan again led to state distribution—that is, a repetition of the experiment of "military Communism" on a higher basis. This basis too, however, proved inadequate. In the year 1935, the system of planned distribution again gave way to trade. Thus, a second time it is made evident that practicable methods of distribution depend more upon the level of technique and the existing material resources, than even upon forms of property.

The raising of the productivity of labour, in particular through piecework payment, promises in the future an increase of the mass of commodities, a lowering of prices, and a consequent rise in the standard of living of the population. But that is only one aspect of the matter—an aspect which has also been observed under capitalism in its flourishing epoch. Social phenomena and processes must, however, be taken in their connections and interactions. A raising of the productivity of labour on the basis of commodity circulation, means at the same time a growth of inequality. The rise in the prosperity of the commanding strata is beginning to exceed by far the rise in the standard of living of the masses. Along with an increase of state wealth goes a process of new social differentiation.

According to the conditions of its daily life, Soviet society is already divided into a secure and privileged minority, and a majority getting along in want. At its extremes, moreover, this inequality assumes the character of flagrant contrast. Products designed for broad circulation are as a rule, in spite of their high prices, of low quality, and the farther from the centres the more difficult to obtain. Not only speculation but the downright theft of objects of consumption assumes in these circumstances a mass character. And while up to yesterday these acts supplemented the planned distribution, they now serve as a corrective to Soviet trade.

The "friends" of the Soviet Union have a professional habit of collecting impressions with closed eyes and cotton in their ears. We cannot rely upon them. The enemies frequently propagate malicious slanders. Let us turn, therefore, to the bureaucracy itself. Since it is at least not hostile to itself, its official self-accusations, evoked always by some sort of urgent practical demand, deserve a great deal more confidence than its more frequent and noisy self-praise.

The industrial plan of 1935, as is well known, was more than carried out. But in the matter of housing, it was carried out only 55.7 per cent. Moreover the construction of houses for the workers proceeded most slowly, badly and sloppily of all. As for the members of collective farms, they live as formerly in the old huts with their calves and cockroaches. On the other hand, the Soviet dignitaries complain in the press that not all the houses newly constructed for them possess "rooms for houseworkers" —that is, for domestic servants.

Every regime has its monumental reflection in buildings and architecture. Characteristic of the present Soviet epoch are the numerous palaces and houses of the Soviets, genuine temples of the bureaucracy sometimes costing as much as ten million rubles, expensive theatres, houses of the Red Army — that is, military clubs chiefly for officers—luxurious subways for those who can pay, and therewith an extreme and unchanging backwardness in the construction of workers' dwellings even of the barrack type.

In the matter of transporting state freight on the railroads, genuine progress has been attained. But the simple Soviet human being has gained very little from that. Innumerable orders from the heads of the Department of Roads and Communications complain of the unsanitary condition of the cars and passenger stations, of "the intolerable fact of inaction in the service of passengers on the road", "the great number of abuses, thieveries and cheatings with railroad tickets ... concealment of vacant seats and speculation on them, bribe-taking ... robbing of luggage at the stations and on the road". Such facts are "a disgrace to socialist transport"! As a matter of fact they are criminal offences in capitalist transport. These repeated complaints of the eloquent administrator bear certain witness to the extreme inadequacy of the means of transport for the use of the population, the bitter want of those products, which are transported, and, finally, the cynical neglect of simple mortals on the part of railroad officials as of all other persons in authority. The bureaucracy is admirably able to provide service for itself on land and water and in the air, as we learn from the great number of Soviet parlour cars, special trains and special steamers—and these more and more giving place to the best of automobiles and aeroplanes.

In characterizing the successes of Soviet industry, the president of the Leningrad Central Committee, Zhdanov, to the applause of his immediately interested audience, promised that in a year "our active workers will arrive for the conference not in the present modest Fords, but in limousines". The Soviet technique, insofar as its face is turned toward mankind, directs its efforts primarily to satisfying the high-class demands of a chosen minority. The streetcars, where they exist at all, are as before filled to suffocation.

When the People's Commissar of Food Industries, Mikoyan, boasts that the lowest kind of confections are rapidly being crowded out of production by the highest, and that "our women" are demanding fine perfumes, this only means that industry, with the transfer to money circulation, is accommodating itself to the better qualified consumer. Such are the laws of the market, in which by no means the last place is occupied by the highly placed "wives". Together with this it becomes known that sixty-eight co-operative shops out of ninety-five investigated in the Ukraine in 1935, had no confections at all, and that the demand for pastries was only 15 to 20 per cent satisfied, and this with a very low quality of goods. "The factories are working," complains *Isvestia*, "without regard to the demands of the consumer." Naturally, if the consumer is not one who is able to stand up for himself.

Professor Bakh, who approaches the question from the standpoint of organic chemistry, finds that "our bread is sometimes intolerably bad". The working man and woman, although not initiated into the mysteries of yeast and its fermentation, think the very same thought. In distinction from the esteemed professor, however, they have not the opportunity to express their appraisal in the pages of the press.

In Moscow, the garment trust advertises variegated fashions of silk dresses designed by the special "house of fashions". In the provinces, even in the great industrial cities, the workers as formerly cannot, without standing in lines and submitting to other vexations, obtain a cotton print shirt: There aren't enough! It is much harder to supply the needs of the many than to supply luxuries to the few. All history vouches for that.

In listing his achievements, Mikoyan informs us: "The oleomargarine industry is new." It is true that this industry did not exist under the old regime. We need not rush to the conclusion, however, that the situation has become worse than under the tzar. The people saw no butter in those days, either. But the appearance of a substitute means at least that in the Soviet Union there are two classes of consumers: one prefers butter, the other gets along with margarine. "We supply plenty of *makhorka* to all who need it," boasts the same Mikoyan. He forgets to add that neither Europe nor America ever heard of such low-grade tobacco as *makhorka*.

One of the very clear, not to say defiant, manifestations of inequality is the opening in Moscow and other big cities of special stores with high-quality articles under the very expressive, although not very Russian, designation of "Luxe". At the same time ceaseless complaints of mass robbery in the food shops of Moscow and the provinces, mean that foodstuffs are adequate only for the minority, although everybody would like to have something to eat.

The worker-mother has her view of the social regime, and her "consumer's" criterion, as the functionary—very attentive, by the way, to his own consumption—scornfully expresses it, is in the last analysis decisive. In the conflict between the working woman and the bureaucracy, Marx and Lenin, and we with them, stand on the side of the working woman. We stand against the bureaucrat, who is exaggerating his achievements, blurring contradictions, and holding the working woman by the throat in order that she may not criticize.

Granted that margarine and *makhorka* are today unhappy necessities. Still it is useless to boast and ornament reality. Limousines for the "activists", fine perfumes for "our women", margarine for the workers, stores "de luxe" for the gentry, a look at delicacies through the store windows for the plebs—such socialism cannot but seem to the masses a new re-facing of capitalism, and they are not far wrong. On a basis of "generalized want", the struggle for the means of subsistence threatens to resurrect "all the old crap", and is partially resurrecting it at every step.

Present market relations differ from relations under the NEP (1921–28) in that they are supposed to develop directly without the middleman and the private trader between the state co-operative and collective farm organizations and the individual citizen. However, this is true only in principle. The swiftly growing turnover of retail trade, both state and co-operative, should in 19156, according to specifications, amount to one hundred billion rubles. The turnover of collective farm trade, which amounted to sixteen billion in 1965, is to grow considerably during the current year. It is hard to determine what place—at least not an insignificant one!—will be occupied by illegal and semi-legal middlemen both within this turnover and alongside it. Not only the individual peasants, but the collectives, and especially individual members of the collectives, are much inclined to resort to the middleman. The same road is followed by the home-industry workers, co-operators, and the local industries dealing with the peasants. From time to time, it unexpectedly transpires that the trade in meat, butter or eggs throughout a large district, has been cornered by "speculators". Even the most necessary articles of daily use, like salt, matches, flour, kerosene, although existing in the state storehouses in sufficient quantity, are lacking for weeks and months at a time in the bureaucratized rural co-operatives. It is clear that the peasants will get the goods they need by other roads. The Soviet press often speaks of the jobber as of something to be taken for granted.

As for the other forms of private enterprise and accumulation, they play, it seems, a smaller role. Independent cabmen, innkeepers, solitary artisans, are, like the independent peasants, semi-tolerated professions. In Moscow itself there is a considerable number of private small business and repair shops. Eyes are closed to them because they fill up important gaps in the economy. An incomparably greater number of private entrepreneurs work, however, under the false label of all kinds of artels and co-operatives, or hide under the roofs of the collective farms—as though for the special purpose of emphasizing the rifts in the planned economy. The G-men in Moscow arrest from time to time, in the character of malicious speculators, hungry women who are selling homemade berets or cotton shirts on the street.

"The basis of speculation in our land is destroyed," announced Stalin in the autumn of 1935, "and if we have speculators none the less, it can be explained by only one fact: lack of class vigilance and a liberal attitude toward the speculators in various links of the Soviet apparatus." An ideally pure culture of bureaucratic thinking! The economic basis of speculation is destroyed. But then there is no need of any vigilance whatever. If the state could, for example, guarantee the population a sufficient quantity of modest headdresses, there would be no necessity of arresting those unfortunate street traders. It is doubtful, indeed, if such a necessity exists now.

In itself the number of the private traders above

mentioned, like the quantity of their business, is not alarming. You cannot really fear an attack of truck drivers, traders in berets, watchmakers and buyers of eggs, upon the fortresses of the state property! But still the question is not decided by bare arithmetical correlations. An abundance and variety of speculators coming to the surface at the least sign of administrative weakness like a rash in a fever, testifies to the continual pressure of petty bourgeois tendencies. How much danger to the socialist future is represented by the speculation bacillus is determined wholly by the general power of resistance of the economic and political organism of the country.

The mood and conduct of the rank-and-file workers and collective farmers that is, about 90 per cent of the population—is determined primarily by changes in their own real wages. But no less significance must be given to the relation between their income and the income of the better-placed strata. The law of relativity proclaims itself most directly in the sphere of human consumption! The translation of all social relations into the language of money accounting will reveal to the bottom the actual share enjoyed by the different strata of society in the national income. Even when we understand the historic necessity of inequality for a prolonged period, questions remain open about its admissible limits and its social expediency in each concrete case. The inevitable struggle for a share of the national income necessarily becomes a political struggle. The question whether the present structure is socialist or not will be decided, not by the sophisms of the bureaucracy, but by the attitude toward it of the masses themselves—that is, the industrial workers and collectivized peasants.

## 2. The differentiation of the proletariat

One would think that in a workers' state data about real wages would be studied with especial care—indeed that all statistics of income according to categories of the population would be distinguished by complete lucidity and general accessibility. As a matter of fact this whole question, which touches the most vital interests of the toilers, is surrounded with an impenetrable veil. The budget of the worker's family in the Soviet Union, unbelievable as this may be, is a magnitude incomparably more enigmatical for the investigator than in any capitalist country. We have tried in vain to plot the curve of real wages of the different categories of the working class even for the period of the second five-year plan. The stubborn silence of the sources and authorities on this subject is as eloquent as their boasting about meaningless totals.

According to the report of the Commissar of Heavy Industry, Ordjonikidze, the monthly output of the worker rose, during the decade 1925 to 1935, 3.2 times, and money wages 4.5 times. What part of the latter so impressive-looking figure is swallowed by specialists in the upper layers of the working class and not less important, what is the expression of this nominal sum in real values—of this we can find out nothing either from his report or from the commentaries of the press. At a congress of the Soviet Youth in April 1936, the secretary of the Komsomol, Kossarov, declared: "From January 1931 to December 1935 the wages of the youth rose 340 per cent!" But even from the carefully selected young decoration wearers, generous in ovations, whom he addressed, this boast did not evoke one handclap. The listeners, like the orator, knew too well that the abrupt change to market prices had lowered the material situation of the basic mass of the workers.

The "average" wage per person, if you join together the director of the trust and the charwoman, was about 2800 rubles in 1935, and was to be in 1936 about 2500 rubles—that is, nominally 7500 French francs, although hardly more than 8500 to 4000 in real purchasing power. This figure, very modest in itself, goes still lower if you take into consideration that the rise of wages in 1936 is only a partial compensation for the abolition of special prices on objects of consumption, and the abolition of a series of free services. But the principal thing is that 2500 rubles a year, or 208 rubles a month, is, as we said, the *average* payment—that is, an arithmetical fiction whose function is to mask the real and cruel inequality in the payment of labor.

It is indubitable that the situation of the upper layer of the workers, especially the so-called Stakhanovists, has risen considerably during the last year. The press is not without foundation in eagerly listing the number of suits, shoes, gramophones, bicycles, or jars of conserves this or that decorated worker has bought himself. Incidentally it becomes clear how little these benefits are accessible to the rank-and-file worker. Speaking of the impelling motives of the Stakhanov movement, Stalin declared: "Life has become easier, life has become happier, and when life is happy then work goes fast." In that optimistic illumination of the piecework system, extremely characteristic of the ruling stratum, there is this amount of prosaic truth, that the formation of a workers' aristocracy has proven possible only thanks to the preceding economic successes of the country. The motive force of the Stakhanovists, however, is not a "happy" mood, but a desire to earn more money. Molotov introduced this correction of Stalin: "The immediate impulse to high productivity on the part of the Stakhanovists is a simple interest in increasing their earnings." That is true. In the course of a few months an entire stratum of workers has arisen whom they call "thousand men", since their earnings exceed a thousand rubles a month. There are others who earn even more than two thousand rubles a month, while the workers of the lower categories often receive less than a hundred.

It would seem as though this divergence of wages alone establishes a sufficient distinction between the "rich" and "unrich" workers. But that is not enough for the bureaucracy. They literally shower privileges upon the Stakhanovists. They give them new apartments or repair their old ones. They send them out of turn to resthouses and sanatoriums. They send free teachers and physicians to their houses. They give them free tickets to the moving pictures. In some places they even cut their hair and shave them free and out of turn. Many of these privileges seem to be deliberately calculated to injure and insult the average worker. The cause of this importunate good will on the part of the authorities is, in addition to careerism, a troubled conscience. The local ruling groups eagerly seize the chance to escape from their isolation by allowing the upper stratum of the workers to participate in their privileges. As a result, the real earnings of the Stakhanovists often exceed by twenty or thirty times the earnings of the lower categories of workers. And as for especially fortunate specialists, their salaries would in many cases pay for the work of eighty to a hundred unskilled laborers. In scope of inequality in the payment of labour, the Soviet Union has not only caught up to, but far surpassed the capitalist countries!

The best of the Stakhanovists, those who are really impelled by socialist motives, are not happy in their privileges, but irked by them. And no wonder. Their individual enjoyment of all kinds of material goods on a background of general scarcity surrounds them with a ring of envy and ill will, and poisons their existence. Relations of this kind are farther from socialist morals than the relations of the workers of a capitalist factory, joined together as they are in a struggle against exploitation.

In spite of all this, everyday life is not easy even for the skilled worker especially in the provinces. Aside from the fact that the seven-hour working day is being more and more sacrificed to higher productivity, no small number of hours is expended in a supplementary struggle for existence. As a symptom of the special prosperity of the better workers of the Soviet farms, for example, they point to the fact that the tractor men, combine operators, etc.—an already notorious aristocracy—own their own cows and pigs. The theory that socialism without milk is better than milk without socialism has been abandoned. It is now recognized that the workers in the state agricultural undertakings, where it would seem there is no lack either of cows or pigs, are compelled in order to guarantee their subsistence to create their own pocket economies. No less striking is the triumphal announcement that in Kharkov 96,000 workers have their own gardens—other towns are challenged to vie with Kharkov. What a terrible robbery of human power is implied by those words "his own cow" and "his own garden", and what a burden of medieval digging in manure and in the earth they lay upon the worker, and yet more upon his wife and children!

As concerns the fundamental masses, they, of course, have neither cows nor gardens, nor even in large part their own homes. The wages of unskilled workers are 1200 to 1500 rubles a year and even less—which under Soviet prices means a regime of destitution. Living conditions, the most reliable indicator of the material and cultural level, are extremely bad, often unbearable. The overwhelming majority of the workers huddle in common dwellings, which in equipment and upkeep are considerably worse than barracks. When it is necessary to justify industrial unsuccesses, malingerings and trashy products, the administration itself through its journalists gives such a picture as this of living conditions: "The workers sleep on the floor, since bedbugs eat them up in the beds. The chairs are broken; there are no mugs to drink water from, etc." "Two families live in one room. The roof leaks. When it rains they carry the water out of the room by pailfuls." "The privies are in a disgusting condition." Such descriptions, relating to different parts of the country, could be multiplied at will. As a result of these unbearable conditions, "the fluidity of labor" —writes, for example, the head of the oil industry—"has reached a very high point.... Owing to lack of workers, a great number of the drills are altogether abandoned." There are certain especially unfavorable regions, where only those will consent to work who have been fined or discharged from other places for various violations of discipline. Thus at the bottom of the proletariat there is accumulating a layer of rejected Soviet pariahs, possessing no rights, and of whom nevertheless such an important branch of industry as oil production is compelled to make use.

As a result of these flagrant differences in wages, doubled by arbitrary privileges, the bureaucracy has managed to introduce sharp antagonisms in the proletariat. Accounts of the Stakhanov campaign presented at times the picture of a small civil war. "The wrecking and breaking of mechanisms is the favorite [!] method of struggle against the Stakhanov movement," wrote, for example, the organ of the trade unions. "The class struggle," we read farther, "makes itself felt at every step." In this "class" struggle, the workers are on one side, the trade unions on the other. Stalin publicly recommended that those who resist should get it "in the teeth". Other members of the Central Committee have more than once threatened to sweep the "insolent enemy" from the face of the earth. The experience of the Stakhanov movement has made especially clear the deep alienation between the authorities and the proletariat, and the furious insistence with which the bureaucracy is applying the maxim—not, it is true, invented by itself: "Divide and rule!" Moreover, to console the workers, this forced piecework labour is called "socialist competition." The name sounds like a mockery!

Competition, whose roots lie in our biological inheritance, having purged itself of greed, envy and privilege, will indubitably remain the most important motive force of culture under communism too. But in the closer-by preparatory epoch the actual establishment of a socialist society can and will be achieved, not by these humiliating measures of a backward capitalism to which the Soviet government is resorting, but by methods more worthy of a liberated humanity—and above all not under the whip of a bureaucracy. For this very whip is the most disgusting inheritance from the old world. It will have to be broken in pieces and burned at a public bonfire before you can speak of socialism without a blush of shame.

### 3. Social contradictions in the collective village

If the industrial trusts are "in principle" socialist enterprises, this cannot be said of the collective farms.

They rest not upon state, but upon group property. This is a great step forward by comparison with individual scatteredness, but whether the collective enterprises will lead to socialism depends upon a whole series of circumstances, a part lying within the collectives, a part outside them in the general conditions of the Soviet system, and a part, finally, no less a part, on the world arena.

The struggle between the peasants and the state is far from ended. The present still very unstable organization of agriculture is nothing but a temporary compromise between the struggling camps, following the dreadful outbreak of civil war between them. To be sure, 90 per cent of the peasant farms are collectivized, and 94 per cent of the entire agricultural product is taken from the fields of the collective farms. Even if you take into consideration a certain percentage of fictitious collectives, behind which essentially individual farmers are hiding, you still have to concede, it would seem, that the victory over individual economy is at least nine tenths won. However, the real struggle of forces and tendencies in the rural districts is far from contained within the framework of a bare contrast between individual and collective farmers.

With the purpose of pacifying the peasants, the state has found itself compelled to make very great concessions to the proprietary and individualist tendencies of the village, beginning with the solemn transfer to the collectives of their land allotments for "eternal" use that is, in essence, the annulment of the socialization of the land. Is this a legal fiction? In dependence upon the correlation of forces, it might prove a reality and offer in the very near future immense difficulties for planned economy on a statewide scale. It is far more important, however, that the state was compelled to restore individual peasant farming on special midget farms with their own cows, pigs, sheep, domestic fowls, etc. In exchange for this transgressing of socialization and limiting of collectivization, the peasant agrees peaceably, although as yet without great zest, to work in the collective farms, which offer him the opportunity to fulfill his obligation to the state and get something into his own hands. The new relations still assume such immature forms that it would: be difficult to measure them in figures, even if the Soviet statistics were more honest. Many things, however, permit the conclusion that in the personal existence of the peasant his own midget holdings have no less significance than the collectives. This means that the struggle between individualistic and collective tendencies is still in progress throughout the whole mass of the villages, and that its outcome is not yet decided. Which way are the peasants inclined? They themselves do not as yet exactly know.

The People's Commissar of Agriculture said, at the end of

1935: "Up to the present moment, we have met great resistance from the side of the kulak elements to the fulfillment of the state plan of grain provisioning." This means, in other words, that the majority of collectivized peasants "up to recent times" (and today?) considered the surrender of grain to the state as an operation disadvantageous to themselves, and was tending toward private trade. The same thing is testified to in another manner by the draconic laws for the protection of collective property against plunder by the collectivized peasants themselves. It is very instructive that the property of the collectives is insured with the state for twenty billion rubles, and the private property of the collectivized peasants for twenty-one billion. If this correlation does not necessarily mean that the peasants taken separately are richer than the collectives, it does at any rate mean that the peasants insure their personal more carefully than their common property.

No less indicative from our point of view is the course of development in stockbreeding. While the number of horses continued to decline up to 1935, and only as a result of a series of governmental measures has begun during the last year to rise slightly, the increase of horned cattle during the preceding year had already amounted to four million head. The plan for horses was fulfilled in the favourable year 1935 only up to 94 per cent, while in the matter of horned cattle it was considerably exceeded. The meaning of these data becomes clear in the fact that horses exist only as collective property, while cows are already among the personal possessions of the majority of collectivized peasants. It remains only to add that in the steppe regions, where the collectivized peasants are permitted as an exception to possess a horse, the increase of horses is considerably more rapid than in the collective farms, which in their turn are ahead of the Soviet farms. From all this it is not to be inferred that private small economy is superior to large-scale socialized economy, but that the transition from the one to the other, from barbarism to civilization, conceals many difficulties which cannot be removed by mere administrative pressure.

"Law can never stand higher than the economic structure

and the cultural development conditioned by it." The renting of land, although forbidden by law, is really very widely practised, and moreover in its most pernicious form of share-cropping. Land is rented by one collective farm to another, and sometimes to an outsider, and finally, sometimes to its own more enterprising members. Unbelievable as it is, the Soviet farms —that is, the "socialist" enterprises resort to the rental of land. And, what is especially instructive, this is practised by the Soviet farms of the G.P.U.! Under the protection of this high institution, which stands guard over the laws, the director of the Soviet farm imposes upon the peasant renter conditions almost copied from the old landlord-peon contracts. We thus have cases of the exploitation of peasants by the bureaucrats, no longer in the character of agents of the state, but in the character of semi-legal landlords.

Without in the least exaggerating the scope of such ugly phenomena, which are of course not capable of statistical calculation, we still cannot fail to see their enormous symptomatic significance. They unmistakably testify to the strength of bourgeois tendencies in this still extremely backward branch of economy, which comprises the overwhelming majority of the population. Meanwhile, market relations are inevitably strengthening the individualistic tendencies, and deepening the social differentiation of the village, in spite of the new structure of property relations.

On the average, the income of each collective farm is about 4,000 rubles. But in relation to the peasants, "average" figures are even more deceptive than in relation to the workers. It was reported in the Kremlin, for example, that the collective fishermen earned in 1935 twice as much as in 1934, or 1,919 rubles each, and the applause offered to this last figure showed how considerably it rises above the earnings of the principal mass of the collectives. On the other hand, there are collectives in which the income amounts to 80,000 rubles for each household, not counting either income in money and kind from individual holdings, or the income in kind of the whole enterprise. In general, the income of every one of these big collective farmers is ten to fifteen times more than the wage of the "average" worker and the lower-grade collectivized peasant.

The gradations of income are only in part determined by skill and assiduousness in labour. Both the collectives and the personal allotments of the peasants are of necessity placed in extraordinarily unequal conditions, depending upon climate, soil, kind of crop, and also upon position in relation to the towns and industrial centers. The contrast between the city and the village not only was not softened during the five-year plan, but on the contrary was greatly sharpened as a result of the feverish growth of cities and new industrial regions. This fundamental social contrast in Soviet society inevitably creates derivative contradictions among the collectives and within the collectives, chiefly thanks to differential rent.

The unlimited power of the bureaucracy is a no less forceful instrument of social differentiation. It has in its hand such levers as wages, prices, taxes, budget and credit. The completely disproportionate income of a series of central Asiatic cotton collectives depends much more upon the correlation of prices established by the government than upon the work of the members of the collectives. The exploitation of certain strata of the population by other strata has not disappeared, but has been disguised. The first tens of thousands of "well-off" collectives have prospered at the expense of the remaining mass of the collectives and the industrial workers. To raise all the collectives to a level of well-being is an incomparably more difficult and prolonged task than to give privileges to the minority at the expense of a majority. In 1927 the Left Opposition declared that "the income of the kulak has increased immeasurably more than that of the workers," and this proposition retains its force now too, although in a changed form. The income of the upper class of collectives has grown immeasurably more than the income of the fundamental peasant and worker mass. The differentiation of material levels of existence is now, perhaps, even more considerable than on the eve of dekulakization.

The differentiation taking place *within* the collectives finds its expression partly in the sphere of personal consumption; partly it precipitates itself in the personal enterprises adjoining the collectives, since the fundamental property of the collective itself is socialized. The differentiation *between* collectives is already having deeper consequences, since the rich collective has the opportunity to apply more fertilizer and more machines, and consequently to get rich quicker. The successful collectives often hire labour power from the poor ones, and the authorities shut their eyes to this. The deeding over of land allotments of unequal value to the collectives greatly promotes a further differentiation between them, and consequently the crystallizing of a species of bourgeois collectives, or "millionaire collectives" as they are even now called.

Of course the state power is able to interfere as a regulator in the process of social differentiation among the peasantry. But in what direction and within what limits? To attack the kulak collectives and members of collectives would be to open up a new conflict with the more "progressive" layers of the peasantry, who are only now, after a painful interruption, beginning to feel an exceptionally greedy thirst for a "happy life". Moreover —and this is the chief thing—the state power itself becomes less and less capable of socialist control. In agriculture as in industry, it seeks the support and friendship of strong, successful "Stakhanovists of the fields," of millionaire collectives. Starting with a concern for the development of the productive forces, it invariably ends with a concern about itself. It is exactly in agriculture, where consumption is so closely bound with production, that collectivization has opened up grandiose opportunities for the parasitism of the bureaucracy, and therewith for its intergrowth with the upper circles of the collectives. Those complimentary "gifts", which the collective farmers present to the leaders at solemn sessions in the Kremlin, are only the symbolic expression of an unsymbolic tribute, which they place at the disposal of the local representatives of power.

Thus in agriculture immeasurably more than in industry, the low level of production comes into continual conflict with the socialist and even co-operative (collective farm) forms of property. The bureaucracy, which in the last analysis grew out of this contradiction, deepens it in turn.

**4. The social physiognomy of the ruling stratum**

In Soviet political literature you often meet with accusations of "bureaucratism" as a bad custom of thought or method of work. (The accusation is always directed from above downward and is a method of self-defence on the part of the upper circles.) But what you cannot meet anywhere is an investigation of the bureaucracy as a ruling stratum —its numbers and structure, its flesh and blood, its privileges and appetites, and the share of the national income which it swallows up. Nevertheless it exists. And the fact that it so carefully conceals its social physiognomy proves that it possesses the specific consciousness of a ruling "class" which, however, is still far from confident of its right to rule.

It is absolutely impossible to describe the Soviet bureaucracy in accurate figures, and that for reasons of two kinds. In the first place, in a country where the state is almost the sole employer it is hard to say where the administrative apparatus ends. In the second place, upon this question the Soviet statisticians, economists and publicists preserve, as we have said, an especially concentrated silence. And they are imitated by their "friends". We remark in passing that in all the twelve hundred pages of their labour of compilation, the Webbs never once mention the Soviet bureaucracy as a social category. And no wonder, for they wrote, in the essence of the matter, under its dictation!

The central state apparatus numbered on 1 November, 1933, according to official figures about 55,000 people in the directing personnel. But in this figure, which has increased extraordinarily in recent years, there are not included, on the one hand, the military and naval departments and the G.P.U., and, on the other, the co-operative centers and the series of so-called social organizations such as the Ossoaviokhim. [Society for the Defense of the Soviet Union and Development of Its deviation and Chemical Industries.] Each of the republics, moreover, has its own governmental apparatus.

Parallel with the state, trade union, co-operative and other general staffs, and partly interwoven with them, there stands the powerful staff of the party. We will hardly be exaggerating if we number the commanding upper circles of the Soviet Union and the individual republics at 400,000 people. It is possible that at the present time this number has already risen to the half-million mark. This does not include functionaries, but, so to speak, "dignitaries", "leaders", a ruling caste in the proper sense of the word, although, to be sure, hierarchically divided in its turn by very important horizontal boundaries.

This half-million upper caste is supported by a heavy administrative pyramid with a broad and many-faceted foundation. The executive committees of the provincial town and district soviets, together with the parallel organs of the party, the trade unions, the Communist Youth, the local organs of transport, the commanding staffs of the army and fleet, and the agentry of the G.P.U., should give a number in the vicinity of two million. And we must not forget also the presidents of the soviets of six hundred thousand towns and villages.

The immediate administration of the industrial enterprises was concentrated in 1933 (there are no more recent data) in the hands of 17,000 directors and vice-directors. The whole administrative and technical personnel of the shops, factories and mines, counting lower links down to and including the foremen, amounted to about 250,000 people (although, of these, 54,000 were specialists without administrative functions in the proper sense of the word). To this we must add the party and trade-union apparatus in the factories, where administration is carried on, as is well known, in the manner of the "triangle." A figure of half a million for the administration of the industrial enterprises of all-union significance will not be at the present time exaggerated. And to this we must add the administrative personnel of the undertakings of the separate republics and the local soviets.

In another cross-section the official statistics indicate for 1933 more than 860,000 administrators and specialists in the whole Soviet economy—in industry over 480,000, in transport over 100,000, in agriculture 93,000, in commerce 25,000. In this number are included, to be sure, specialists without administrative power, but on the other hand neither collective farms nor co-operatives are included. These data, too, have been left far behind during the last two and a half years.

For 250,000 collective farms, if you count only the presidents and party organizers, there are a half-million administrators. In actual reality, the number is immeasurably higher. If you add the Soviet farms and the tractor and machinery stations, the general number of commanders of the socialized agriculture far exceeds a million.

The state possessed, in 1935, 115,000 trade departments, the co-operatives 200,000. The leaders of both are in essence not commercial employees, but functionaries of the state, and moreover monopolists. Even the Soviet press from time to time complains that "the co-operators have ceased to regard the members of the collective as their electors"—as though the mechanism of the co-operatives could be qualitatively distinguished from that of the trade unions, soviets and the party itself! This whole stratum, which does not engage directly in productive labour, but administers, orders, commands, pardons and punishes—teachers and students we are leaving aside must be numbered at five or six million. This total figure, like the items composing it, by no means pretends to accuracy, but it will do well enough for a first approach. It is sufficient to convince us that "the general line" of the leadership is not a disembodied spirit.

In the various stages or stories of this ruling structure, passing from below upward, the communist filling amounts to from 20 to 90 per cent. In the whole mass of the bureaucracy, the communists together with the Communist Youth constitute a block of 1½ to 2 million—at present, owing to continued purgations, rather less than more. This is the backbone of the state power. These same communist administrators are the backbone of the party, and of the Communist Youth. The former Bolshevik party is now no longer the vanguard of the proletariat, but the political organization of the bureaucracy. The remaining mass of the members of the party and the

Communist Youth serve only as a source for the formation of this "active" —that is, a reserve for the replenishment of the bureaucracy. The nonparty "active" serves the same purpose. Hypothetically, we may assume that the labour and collectivized peasant aristocracy, the Stakhanovists, the nonparty "active", trusted personages, their relatives and relatives-in-law, approximate the same figure that we adopted for the bureaucracy, that is, five to six million. With their families, these two interpenetrating strata constitute as many as twenty to twenty-five million. We make a comparatively low estimate of the numbers in a family for the reason that often husband and wife, and sometimes also son and daughter, occupy a place in the apparatus. Moreover, the wives of the ruling group find it much easier to limit the size of their family than working women, and above all peasant women. The present campaign against abortion was set in motion by the bureaucracy, but does not apply to it. Twelve per cent, or perhaps 15 per cent, of the population —that is the authentic social basis of the autocratic ruling circles.

Where a separate room and sufficient food and neat clothing are still accessible only to a small minority, millions of bureaucrats, great and small, try to use the power primarily in order to guarantee their own well-being. Hence the enormous egoism of this stratum, its firm inner solidarity, its fear of the discontent of the masses, its rabid insistence upon strangling all criticism, and finally its hypocritically religious kowtowing to "the Leader", who embodies and defends the power and privileges of these new lords.

The bureaucracy itself is still far less homogeneous than the proletariat or the peasantry. There is a gulf between the president of the rural soviet and the dignitary of the Kremlin. The life of the lower functionaries of various categories proceeds essentially upon a very primitive level—lower than the standard of living of the skilled worker of the West. But everything is relative, and the level of the surrounding population is considerably lower. The fate of the president of the collective farm, of the party organizer, of the lower order of co-operator, like that of the highest bosses, does not in the least depend upon so-called "electors". Any one of these functionaries can be sacrificed at any moment by the bosses next above, in order to quiet some discontent. Moreover each of them can on occasion raise himself a step higher. They are all, at least up to the first serious shock, bound together by mutual guarantees of security with the Kremlin.

In its conditions of life, the ruling stratum comprises all gradations, from the petty bourgeoisie of the backwoods to the big bourgeoisie of the capitals. To these material conditions correspond habits, interests and circles of ideas. The present leaders of the Soviet trade unions are not much different in their psychological type from the Citrines, Jonhaux's and Greens. Other phraseology, but the same scornfully patronizing relation to the masses, the same conscienceless astuteness in second-rate maneuvers, the same conservativism, the same narrowness of horizon, the same hard concern for their own peace, and finally the same worship for the most trivial forms of bourgeois culture. The Soviet colonels and generals are in the majority little different from the colonels and generals of the rest of the earth, and in any case are trying their best to be like them. The Soviet diplomats have appropriated from the Western diplomats not only their tailcoats, but their modes of thought. The Soviet journalists fool the readers no less than their foreign colleagues, although they do it in a special manner.

If it is difficult to estimate the numbers of the bureaucracy, it is still harder to determine their income. As early as 1927, the Left Opposition protested that the "swollen and privileged administrative apparatus is devouring a very considerable part of the surplus value". On the Opposition platform it was estimated that the trade apparatus alone "devours an enormous share of the national income more than one tenth of the total production." After that the authorities took the necessary measures to make such estimates impossible. But for that very reason overhead expenses have not been cut down, but have grown.

It is no better in other spheres than in the sphere of trade. It required, as Rakovsky wrote in 1930, a fleeting quarrel between the party and the trade-union bureaucrats in order that the population should find out from the press that out of the budget of the trade unions, amounting to 400,000,000 rubles, 80,000,000 go for the support of the personnel. And here, we remark, it was a question only of the legal budget. Over and above this, the bureaucracy of the trade unions receives from the industrial bureaucracy in token of friendship immense gifts of money, apartments, means of transport, etc. "How much goes for the support of party, co-operative, collective farm, Soviet farm, industrial and administrative apparatus with all their ramifications?" asked Rakovsky. And he answered: "We possess not even hypothetical information."

Freedom from control inevitably entails abuse of office, including pecuniary malfeasance. On 29 September, 1931; the government, compelled again to raise the question of the bad work of the co-operatives, established over the signatures of Molotov and Stalin, and not for the first time, "the presence of immense plunderings and squanderings and losses in the work of many of the rural consumers' societies". At a session of the Central Executive Committee in January 1936, the People's Commissar of Finance complained that local executive committees permit completely arbitrary expenditures of state funds. If the Commissar was silent about the central institutions, it was only because he himself belongs to their circle. There is no possibility of estimating what share of the national income is appropriated by the bureaucracy. This is not only because it carefully conceals even its legalized incomes. It is not only because standing on the very boundary of malfeasance, and often stepping over the boundary, it makes a wide use of unforeseen incomes. It is chiefly because the whole advance in social well being, municipal utilities, comfort, culture, art, still serves chiefly, if not exclusively, this upper privileged stratum. In regard to the bureaucracy as a consumer, we may, with the necessary changes, repeat what was said about the bourgeoisie. There is no reason or sense in exaggerating its appetite for articles of personal consumption. But the situation changes sharply as soon as we take into consideration its almost monopolistic enjoyment of the old and new conquests of civilization. Formally, these good things are, of course, available to the whole population, or at least to the population of the cities. But in reality they are accessible only in exceptional cases. The bureaucracy, on the contrary, avails itself of them as a rule when and to what extent it wishes as of its personal property. If you count not only salaries and all forms of service in kind, and every type of semi-legal supplementary source of income, but also add the share of the bureaucracy and the Soviet aristocracy in the theatres, rest palaces, hospitals, sanatoriums, summer resorts, museums, clubs, athletic institutions, etc., it would probably be necessary to conclude that 15 per cent, or, say, 20 per cent, of the population enjoys not much less of the wealth than is enjoyed by the remaining 80 to 85 per cent.

The "friends" will want to dispute our figures? Let them give us others more accurate. Let them persuade the bureaucracy to publish the income and expense book of Soviet society. Until they do, we shall hold to our opinion. The distribution of this earth's goods in the Soviet Union, we do not doubt, is incomparably more democratic than it was in tzarist Russia, and even than it is in the most democratic countries of the West. But it has as yet little in common with socialism.

## *Chapter 7*

# FAMILY, YOUTH AND CULTURE

### 1. Thermidor in the family

The October Revolution honestly fulfilled its obligations in relation to woman. The young government not only gave her all political and legal rights in equality with man, but, what is more important, did all that it could, and in any case incomparably more than any other government ever did, actually to secure her access to all forms of economic and cultural work. However, the boldest revolution, like the "all-powerful" British parliament, cannot convert a woman into a man—or rather, cannot divide equally between them the burden of pregnancy, birth, nursing and the rearing of children. The revolution made a heroic effort to destroy the so-called "family hearth"—that archaic, stuffy and stagnant institution in which the woman of the toiling classes performs galley labour from childhood to death. The place of the family as a shut-in petty enterprise was to be occupied, according to the plans, by a finished system of social care and accommodation: maternity houses, crèches, kindergartens, schools, social dining rooms, social laundries, first-aid stations, hospitals, sanatoria, athletic organizations, moving-picture theaters, etc. The complete absorption of the housekeeping functions of the family by institutions of the socialist society, uniting all generations in solidarity and mutual aid, was to bring to woman, and thereby to the loving couple, a real liberation from the thousand-year-old fetters. Up to now this problem of problems has not been solved. The forty million Soviet families remain in their overwhelming majority nests of medievalism, female slavery and hysteria, daily humiliation of children, feminine and childish superstition. We must permit ourselves no illusions on this account. For that very reason, the consecutive changes in the approach to the problem of the family in the Soviet Union best of all characterize the actual nature of Soviet society and the evolution of its ruling stratum.

It proved impossible to take the old family by storm—not because the will was lacking, and not because the family was so firmly rooted in men's hearts. On the contrary, after a short period of distrust of the government and its crèches, kindergartens and like institutions, the working women, and after them the more advanced peasants, appreciated the immeasurable advantages of the collective care of children as well as the socialization of the whole family economy. Unfortunately society proved too poor and little cultured. The real resources of the state did not correspond to the plans and intentions of the Communist Party. You cannot "abolish" the family; you have to replace it. The actual liberation of women is unrealizable on a basis of "generalized want". Experience soon proved this austere truth, which Marx had formulated eighty years before.

During the lean years, the workers wherever possible, and in part their families, ate in the factory and other social dining rooms, and this fact was officially regarded as a transition to a socialist form of life. There is no need of pausing again upon the peculiarities of the different periods: military communism, the NEP and the first five-year plan. The fact is that from the moment of the abolition of the food-card system in 1935, all the better-placed workers began to return to the home dining table. It would be incorrect to regard this retreat as a condemnation of the socialist system, which in general was never tried out. But so much the more withering was the judgment of the workers and their wives upon the "social feeding" organized by the bureaucracy. The same conclusion must be extended to the social laundries, where they tear and steal linen more than they wash it. Back to the family hearth! But home cooking and the home washtub, which are now half shamefacedly celebrated by orators and journalists, mean the return of the workers' wives to their pots and pans that is, to the old slavery. It is doubtful if the resolution of the Communist International on the "complete and irrevocable triumph of socialism in the Soviet Union" sounds very convincing to the women of the factory districts!

The rural family, bound not only with home industry but with agriculture, is infinitely more stable and conservative than that of the town. Only a few, and as a general rule, anaemic agricultural communes introduced social dining rooms and crèches in the first period. Collectivization, according to the first announcements, was to initiate a decisive change in the sphere of the family. Not for nothing did they expropriate the peasant's chickens as well as his cows. There was no lack, at any rate, of announcements about the triumphal march of social dining rooms throughout the country. But when the retreat began, reality suddenly emerged from the shadow of this bragging. The peasant gets from the collective farm, as a general rule, only bread for himself and fodder for his stock. Meat, dairy products and vegetables, he gets almost entirely from the adjoining private lots. And once the most important necessities of life are acquired by the isolated efforts of the family, there can no longer be any talk of social dining rooms. Thus the midget farms, creating a new basis for the domestic hearthstone, lay a double burden upon woman.

The total number of steady accommodations in the crèches amounted, in 1932, to 600,000, and of seasonal accommodations solely during work in the fields to only about 4,000,000. In 1935 the cots numbered 5,600,000, but the steady ones were still only an insignificant part of the total. Moreover, the existing crèches, even in Moscow, Leningrad and other centres, are not satisfactory as a general rule to the least fastidious demands. "A crèche in which the child feels worse than he does at home is not a crèche but a bad orphan asylum," complains a leading Soviet newspaper. It is no wonder that the better-placed workers' families avoid crèches. But for the fundamental mass of the toilers, the number even of these "bad orphan asylums" is insignificant. Just recently the Central Executive Committee introduced a resolution that foundlings and orphans should be placed in private hands for bringing up. Through its highest organ, the bureaucratic government thus acknowledged its bankruptcy in relation to the most important socialist function. The number of children in kindergartens rose during the five years 1930–1935 from 370,000 to 1,181,000. The lowness of the figure for 1930 is striking, but the figure for 1935 also seems only a drop in the ocean of Soviet families. A further investigation would undoubtedly show that the principal, and in any case the better part of these kindergartens, appertain to the families of the administration, the technical personnel, the Stakhanovists, etc.

The same Central Executive Committee was not long ago compelled to testify openly that the "resolution on the liquidation of homeless and uncared-for children is being weakly carried out". What is concealed behind this dispassionate confession? Only by accident, from newspaper remarks printed in small type, do we know that in Moscow more than a thousand children are living in "extraordinarily difficult family conditions"; that in the so-called children's homes of the capital there are about 1,500 children who have nowhere to go and are turned out into the streets; that during the two autumn months of 1935 in Moscow and Leningrad "7,500 parents were brought to court for leaving their children without supervision". What good did it do to bring them to court? How many thousand parents have avoided going to court? How many children in "extraordinarily difficult conditions" remained unrecorded? In what do *extraordinarily* difficult conditions differ from *simply* difficult ones? Those are the questions, which remain unanswered. A vast amount of the homelessness of children, obvious and open as well as disguised, is a direct result of the great social crisis in the course of which the old family continues to dissolve far faster than the new institutions are capable of replacing it.

From these same accidental newspaper remarks and from episodes in the criminal records, the reader may find out about the existence in the Soviet Union of prostitution —that is, the extreme degradation of woman in the interests of men who can pay for it. In the autumn of the past year *Izvestia* suddenly informed its readers, for example, of the arrest in Moscow of "as many as a thousand women who were secretly selling themselves on the streets of the proletarian capital". Among those arrested were 177 working women, 92 clerks, 5 university students. What drove them to the sidewalks? Inadequate wages, want, the necessity to "get a little something for a dress, for shoes". We should vainly seek the approximate dimensions of this social evil. The modest bureaucracy orders the statistician to remain silent. But that enforced silence itself testifies unmistakably to the numerousness of the "class" of Soviet prostitutes. Here there can be essentially no question of "relics of the past"; prostitutes are recruited from the younger generation. No reasonable person, of course, would think of placing special blame for this sore, as old as civilization, upon the Soviet regime. But it is unforgivable in the presence of prostitution to talk about the triumph of socialism. The newspapers assert, to be sure insofar as they are permitted to touch upon this ticklish theme—that "prostitution is decreasing". It is possible that this is really true by comparison with the years of hunger and decline (1931–1933). But the restoration of money relations which has taken place since then, abolishing all direct rationing, will inevitably lead to a new growth of prostitution as well as of homeless children. Wherever there are privileged there are pariahs!

The mass homelessness of children is undoubtedly the most unmistakable and most tragic symptom of the difficult situation of the mother. On this subject even the optimistic *Pravda is* sometimes compelled to make a bitter confession: "The birth of a child is for many women a serious menace to their position." It is just for this reason that the revolutionary power gave women the right to abortion, which in conditions of want and family distress, whatever may be said upon this subject by the eunuchs and old maids of both sexes, is one of her most important civil, political and cultural rights. However, this right of women too, gloomy enough in itself, is under the existing social inequality being converted into a privilege. Bits of information trickling into the press about the practice of abortion are literally shocking. Thus through only one village hospital in one district of the Urals, there passed in 1935 "195 women mutilated by midwives"—among them 33 working women, 28 clerical workers, 65 collective farm women, 58 housewives. This Ural district differs from the majority of other districts only in that information about it happened to get into the press. How many women are mutilated every day throughout the extent of the Soviet Union?

Having revealed its inability to serve women who are compelled to resort to abortion with the necessary medical aid and sanitation, the state makes a sharp change of course, and takes the road of prohibition. And just as in other situations, the bureaucracy makes a virtue of necessity. One of the members of the highest Soviet court, Soltz, a specialist on matrimonial questions, bases the forthcoming prohibition of abortion on the fact that in n socialist society where there are no unemployed, etc., no woman has no right to decline "the joys of motherhood." The philosophy of a priest endowed also with the powers of a gendarme. We just heard from the central organ of the ruling party that the birth of a child is for many women, and it would be truer to say for the overwhelming majority, "a menace to their position". We just heard from the highest Soviet institution that "the liquidation of homeless and uncared for children is being weakly carried out," which undoubtedly means a new increase of homelessness. But here the highest Soviet judge informs U8 that in a country where "life is happy" abortion should be punished with imprisonment—just exactly as in capitalist countries where life is grievous. It is clear in advance that in the Soviet Union as in the West those who will fall into the claws of the jailer will be chiefly working women, servants, peasant wives, who find it hard to conceal their troubles. As far as concerns "our women", who furnish the demand for fine perfumes and other pleasant things, they will, as formerly, do what they find necessary under the very nose of an indulgent justiciary. "We have need of people," concludes Soltz, closing his eyes to the homeless. "Then have the kindness to bear them yourselves," might be the answer to the high judge of millions of toiling women, if the bureaucracy had not sealed their lips with the seal of silence.

These gentlemen have, it seems, completely forgotten that socialism was to remove the cause, which impels woman to abortion, and not force, her into the "joys of motherhood" with the help of foul police interference in what is to every woman the most intimate sphere of life.

The draft of the law forbidding abortion was submitted to so-called universal popular discussion, and even through the fine sieve of the Soviet press many bitter complaints and stifled protests broke out. The discussion was cut off as suddenly as it had been announced, and on June 27th the Central Executive Committee converted the shameful draft into a thrice shameful law. Even some of the official apologists of the bureaucracy were embarrassed. Louis Fischer declared this piece of legislation something in the nature of a deplorable misunderstanding. In reality the new law against women—with an exception in favour of ladies—is the natural and logical fruit of a Thermidorian reaction.

The triumphal rehabilitation of the family, taking place simultaneously—what a providential coincidence!—with the rehabilitation of the ruble, is caused by the material and cultural bankruptcy of the state. Instead of openly saying, "We have proven still too poor and ignorant for the creation of socialist relations among men, our children and grandchildren will realize this aim", the leaders are forcing people to glue together again the shell of the broken family, and not only that, but to consider it, under threat of extreme penalties, the sacred nucleus of triumphant socialism. It is hard to measure with the eye the scope of this retreat.

Everybody and everything is dragged into the new course: lawgiver and litterateur, court and militia, newspaper and schoolroom. When a naive and honest communist youth makes bold to write in his paper: "You would do better to occupy yourself with solving the problem how woman can get out of the clutches of the family," he receives in answer a couple of good smacks and—is silent. The ABCs of communism are declared a "leftist excess". The stupid and stale prejudices of uncultured philistines are resurrected in the name of a new morale. And what is happening in daily life in all the nooks and corners of this measureless country? The press reflects only in a faint degree the depth of the Thermidorian reaction in the sphere of the family.

Since the noble passion of evangelism grows with the growth of sin, the seventh commandment is acquiring great popularity in the ruling stratum. The Soviet moralists have only to change the phraseology slightly. A campaign is opened against too frequent and easy divorces. The creative thought of the lawgivers had already invented such a "socialistic" measure as the taking of money payment upon registration of divorces, and increasing it when divorces were repeated. Not for nothing we remarked above that the resurrection of the family goes hand in hand with the increase of the educative role of the ruble. A tax indubitably makes registration difficult for those for whom it is difficult to pay. For the upper circles, the payment, we may hope, will not offer any difficulty. Moreover, people possessing nice apartments, automobiles and other good things arrange their personal affairs without unnecessary publicity and consequently without registration. It is only on the bottom of society that prostitution has a heavy and humiliating character. On the heights of the Soviet society, where power is combined with comfort, prostitution takes the elegant form of small mutual services, and even assumes the aspect of the "socialist family". We have already heard from Sosnovsky about the importance of the "automobile-harem factor" in the degeneration of the ruling stratum.

The lyric, academical and other "friends of the Soviet Union" have eyes in order to see nothing. The marriage and family laws established by the October Revolution, once the object of its legitimate pride, are being made over and mutilated by vast borrowings from the law treasuries of the bourgeois countries. And as though on purpose to stamp treachery with ridicule, the same arguments which were earlier advanced in favour of unconditional freedom of divorce and abortion—"the liberation of women," "defense of the rights of personality," "protection of motherhood"—are repeated now in favor of their limitation and complete prohibition.

The retreat not only assumes forms of disgusting hypocrisy,

but also is going infinitely farther than the iron economic necessity demands. To the objective causes producing this return to such bourgeois forms as the payment of alimony, there is added the social interest of the ruling stratum in the deepening of bourgeois law. The most compelling motive of the present cult of the family is undoubtedly the need of the bureaucracy for a stable hierarchy of relations, and for the disciplining of youth by means of 40,000,000 points of support for authority and power.

While the hope still lived of concentrating the education of the new generations in the hands of the state, the government was not only unconcerned about supporting the authority of the "elders", and, in particular of the mother and father, but on the contrary tried its best to separate the children from the family, in order thus to protect them from the traditions of a stagnant mode of life. Only a little while ago, in the course of the first five-year plan, the schools and the Communist Youth were using children for the exposure, shaming and in general "re-educating" of their drunken fathers or religious mothers with what success is another question. At any rate, this method meant a shaking of parental authority to its very foundations. In this not unimportant sphere too, a sharp turn has now been made. Along with the seventh, the fifth commandment is also fully restored to its rights as yet, to be sure, without any references to God. But the French schools also get along without this supplement, and that does not prevent them from successfully inculcating conservatism and routine.

Concern for the authority of the older generation, by the way, has already led to a change of policy in the matter of religion. The denial of God, his assistance and his miracles, was the sharpest wedge of all those which the revolutionary power drove between children and parents. Outstripping the development of culture, serious propaganda and scientific education, the struggle with the churches, under the leadership of people of the type of Yaroslavsky, often degenerated into buffoonery and mischief. The storming of heaven, like the storming of the family, is now brought to a stop. The bureaucracy, concerned about their reputation for respectability, have ordered the young "godless" to surrender their fighting armour and sit down to their books. In relation to religion, there is gradually being established a regime of ironical neutrality. But that is only the first stage. It would not be difficult to predict the second and third, if the course of events depended only upon those in authority.

The hypocrisy of prevailing opinion develops everywhere and always as the square, or cube, of the social contradictions. Such approximately is the historic law of ideology translated into the language of mathematics. Socialism, if it is worthy of the name, means human relations without greed, friendship without envy and intrigue, love without base calculation. The official doctrine declares these ideal norms already realized—and with more insistence the louder the reality protests against such declarations. "On a basis of real equality between men and women," says, for example, the new programme of the Communist Youth, adopted in April 1986, "a new family is coming into being, the flourishing of which will be a concern of the Soviet state." An official commentary supplements the program: "Our youth in the choice of a life-friend—wife or husband—know only one motive, one impulse: love. The bourgeois marriage of pecuniary convenience does not exist for our growing generation." (*Pravda*, April 4, 19136.) So far as concerns the rank-and-file workingman and woman, this is more or less true. But "marriage for money" is comparatively little known also to the workers of capitalist countries. Things are quite different in the middle and upper strata. New social groupings automatically place their stamp upon personal relations. The vices which power and money create in sex relations are flourishing as luxuriously in the ranks of the Soviet bureaucracy as though it had set itself the goal of outdoing in this respect the Western bourgeoisie.

In complete contradiction to the just quoted assertion of *Pravda*, "marriage for convenience", as the Soviet press itself in moments of accidental or unavoidable frankness confesses, is now fully resurrected. Qualifications, wages, employment, number of chevrons on the military uniform, are acquiring more and more significance, for with them are bound questions of shoes, and fur coats, and apartments, and bathrooms, and—the ultimate dream—automobiles. The mere struggle for a room unites and divorces no small number of couples every year in Moscow. The question of relatives has acquired exceptional significance. It is useful to have as a father-in-law a military commander or an influential communist, as a mother-in-law the sister of a high dignitary. Can we wonder at this? Could it be otherwise?

One of the very dramatic chapters in the great book of the Soviets will be the tale of the disintegration and breaking up of those Soviet families where the husband as a party member, trade unionist, military commander or administrator, grew and developed and acquired new tastes in life, and the wife, crushed by the family, remained on the old level. The road of the two generations of the Soviet bureaucracy is sown thick with the tragedies of wives rejected and left behind. The same phenomenon is now to be observed in the new generation. The greatest of all crudities and cruelties are to be met perhaps in the very heights of the bureaucracy, where a very large percentage are parvenus of little culture, who consider that everything is permitted to them. Archives and memoirs will some day expose downright crimes in relation to wives, and to women in genera], on the part of those evangelists of family morals and the compulsory "joys of motherhood", who are, owing to their position, immune from prosecution.

No, the Soviet woman is not yet free. Complete equality before the law has so far given infinitely more to the women of the upper strata, representatives of bureaucratic, technical, pedagogical and, in general, intellectual work, than to the working women and yet more the peasant women. So long as society is incapable of taking upon itself the material concern for the family, the mother can successfully fulfill a social function only on condition that she has in her service a white slave: nurse, servant, cook, etc. Out of the 40,000,000 families, which constitute the population of the Soviet Union, 5 per cent, or maybe 10, build their "hearthstone" directly or indirectly upon the labor of domestic slaves. An accurate census of Soviet servants would have as much significance for the socialistic appraisal of the position of women in the Soviet Union as the whole Soviet law code, no matter how progressive it might be. But for this very reason the Soviet statistics hide servants under the name of "working woman" or "and others"! The situation of the mother of the family who is an esteemed communist, has a cook, a telephone for giving orders to the stores, an automobile for errands, etc., has little in common with the situation of the working woman who is compelled to run to the shops, prepare dinner herself, and carry her children on foot from the kindergarten —if, indeed, a kindergarten is available. No socialist labels can conceal this social contrast, which is no less striking than the contrast between the bourgeois lady and the proletarian woman in any country of the West.

The genuinely socialist family, from which society will remove the daily vexation of unbearable and humiliating cares, will have no need of any regimentation, and the very idea of laws about abortion and divorce will sound no better within its walls than the recollection of houses of prostitution or human sacrifices. The October legislation took a bold step in the direction of such a family. Economic and cultural backwardness has produced a cruel reaction. The Thermidorian legislation is beating a retreat to the bourgeois models, covering its retreat with false speeches about the sacredness of the "new" family. On this question, too, socialist bankruptcy covers itself with hypocritical respectability.

There are sincere observers who are, especially upon the question of children, shaken by the contrast here between high principles and ugly reality. The mere fact of the furious criminal measures that have been adopted against homeless children is enough to suggest that the socialist legislation in defense of women and children is nothing but crass hypocrisy. There are observers of an opposite kind who are deceived by the broadness and magnanimity of those ideas that have been dressed up in the form of laws and administrative institutions. When they see destitute mothers, prostitutes and homeless children, these optimists tell themselves that a further growth of material wealth will gradually fill the socialist laws with flesh and blood. It is not easy to decide which of these two modes of approach is more mistaken and more harmful. Only people stricken with historical blindness can fail to see the broadness and boldness of the social plan, the significance of the first stages of its development, and the immense possibilities opened by it. But on the other hand, it is impossible not to be indignant at the passive and essentially indifferent optimism of those who shut their eyes to the growth of social contradictions, and comfort themselves with gazing into a future, the key to which they respectfully propose to leave in the hands of the bureaucracy. As though the equality of rights of women and men were not already converted into an equality of deprivation of rights by that same bureaucracy! And as though in some book of wisdom it were firmly promised that the Soviet bureaucracy will not introduce a new oppression in place of liberty.

How man enslaved woman, how the exploiter subjected them both, how the toilers have attempted at the price of blood to free themselves from slavery and have only exchanged one chain for another—history tells us much about all this. In essence, it tells us nothing else. But how in reality to free the child, the woman and the human being? For that we have as yet no reliable models. All past historical experience, wholly negative, demands of the toilers at least and first of all an implacable distrust of all privileged and uncontrolled guardians.

## 2. The struggle against the youth

Every revolutionary party finds its chief support in the younger generation of the rising class. Political decay expresses itself in a loss of ability to attract the youth under one's banner. The parties of bourgeois democracy, in withdrawing one after another from the scene, are compelled to turn over the young either to revolution or fascism. Bolshevism when underground was always a party of young workers. The Mensheviks relied upon the more respectable skilled upper stratum of the working class, always prided themselves on it, and looked down upon the Bolsheviks. Subsequent events harshly showed them their mistake. At the decisive moment the youth carried with them the more mature stratum and even the old folks.

The revolution gave a mighty historical impulse to the new Soviet generation. It cut them free at one blow from conservative forms of life, and exposed to them the great secret—the first secret of the dialectic—that there is nothing unchanging on this earth, and that society is made out of plastic materials. How stupid is the theory of unchanging racial types in the light of the events of our epoch! The Soviet Union is an immense melting pot in which the characters of dozens of nationalities are being mixed. The mysticism of the "Slavic soul" is coming off like scum.

But the impulse given to the younger generation has not yet found expression in a corresponding historic enterprise. To be sure, the youth are very active in the sphere of economics. In the Soviet Union there are 7,000,000 workers under twenty-three—3,140,000 in industry, 700,000 in the railroads, 700,000 in the building trades. In the new giant factories, about half the workers are young. There are now 1,200,000 Communist Youth in the collective farms. Hundreds of thousands of members of the Communist Youth have been mobilized during recent years for construction work, timber work, coal mining, gold production, for work in the Arctic, Sakhalin, or in Amur where the new town of Komsomolsk is in process of construction. The new generation is putting out shock brigades, champion workers, Stakhanovists, foremen, under-administrators. The youth are studying, and a considerable part of them are studying assiduously. They are as active, if not more so, in the sphere of athletics in its most daring or warlike forms, such as parachute jumping and marksmanship. The enterprising and audacious are going on all kinds of dangerous expeditions.

"The better part of our youth," said recently the well-known polar explorer, Schmidt, "are eager to work where difficulties await them." This is undoubtedly true. But in all spheres the post-revolutionary generation is still under guardianship. They are told from above what to do, and how to do it. Politics, as the highest form of command, remains wholly in the hands of the so-called "Old Guard", and in all the ardent and frequently flattering speeches they address to the youth the old boys are vigilantly defending their own monopoly.

Not conceiving of the development of a socialist society without the dying away of the state that is, without the replacement of all kinds of police oppression by the self-administration of educated producers and consumers— Engels laid tile accomplishment of this task upon the younger generation, "who will grow up in new, free social conditions, and will be in a position to cast away all this rubbish of state-ism". Lenin adds on his part: "... every kind of state-ism, the democratic-republican included." The prospect of the construction of a socialist society stood, then, in the mind of Engels and Lenin approximately thus: The generation which conquered the power, the "Old Guard", will begin the work of liquidating the state; the next generation will complete it.

How do things stand in reality? Forty-three per cent of the population of the Soviet Union was born after the October Revolution. If you take the age of twenty-three as the boundary between the two generations, then over 50 per cent of Soviet humanity has not yet reached this boundary. A big half of the population of the country, consequently, knows nothing by personal recollection of any regime except that of the Soviets. But it is just this new generation, which is forming itself, not in "free social conditions", as Engels conceived it, but under intolerable and constantly increasing oppression from the ruling stratum composed of those same ones who—according to the official fiction—achieved the great revolution. In the factory, the collective farm, the barracks, the university, the schoolroom, even in the kindergarten, if not in the crèche, the chief glory of man is declared to be: personal loyalty to the leader and unconditional obedience. Many pedagogical aphorisms and maxims of recent times might seem to have been copied from Goebbels, if he himself had not copied them in good part from the collaborators of Stalin.

The school and the social life of the student are saturated

with formalism and hypocrisy. The children have learned to sit through innumerable deadly dull meetings, with their inevitable honorary presidium, their chants in honour of the dear leaders, their predigested righteous debates in which, quite in the manner of their elders, they say one thing and think another. The most innocent groups of school children who try to create oases in this desert of officiousness are met with fierce measures of repression. Through its agentry the G.P.U. introduces the sickening corruption of treachery and tale bearing into the so-called "socialist schools". The more thoughtful teachers and children's writers, in spite of the enforced optimism, cannot always conceal their horror in the presence of this spirit of repression, falsity and boredom, which is killing school life. Having no experience of class struggle and revolution, the new generations could have ripened for independent participation in the social life of the country only in conditions of soviet democracy, only by consciously working over the experience of the past and the lessons of the present. Independent character like independent thought cannot develop without criticism. The Soviet youth, however, are simply denied the elementary opportunity to exchange thoughts, make mistakes and try out and correct mistakes, their own as well as others'. All questions, including their very own, are decided for them. Theirs only to carry out the decision and sing the glory of those who made it. To every word of criticism, the bureaucracy answers with a twist of the neck. All who are outstanding and unsubmissive in the ranks of the young are systematically destroyed, suppressed or physically exterminated. This explains the fact that out of the millions upon millions of communist youth there has not emerged a single big figure.

In throwing themselves into engineering, science, literature, sport or chess playing, the youth are, so to speak, winning their spurs for future great action. In all these spheres they compete with the badly prepared older generation, and often equal and best them. But at every contact with politics they burn their fingers. They have, thus, but three possibilities open to them: participate in the bureaucracy and make a career;

submit silently to oppression, retire into economic work, science or their own petty personal affairs; or, finally, go underground and learn to struggle and temper their character for the future. The road of the bureaucratic career is accessible only to a small minority. At the other pole a small minority enter the ranks of the Opposition. The middle group, the overwhelming mass, is in turn very heterogeneous. But in it, under the iron press, extremely significant although hidden processes are at work, which will to a great extent determine the future of the Soviet Union.

The ascetic tendencies of the epoch of the civil war gave way in the period of the NEP to a more epicurean, not to say avid, mood. The first five-year plan again became a time of involuntary asceticism—but now only for the masses and the youth. The ruling stratum had firmly dug themselves in positions of personal prosperity. The second five-year plan is undoubtedly accompanied by n sharp reaction against asceticism. A concern for personal advancement has seized upon broad circles of the population, especially the young. The fact is, however, that in the new Soviet generation well-being and prosperity are accessible only to that thin layer who manage to rise above the mass and one way or another accommodate themselves to the ruling stratum. The bureaucracy on its side is consciously developing and sorting out machine politicians and careerists.

Said the chief speaker at a Congress of the Communist Youth (April 1936): "Greed for profits, philistine pettiness and base egotism are not the attributes of Soviet youth." These words sound sharply discordant with the reigning slogans of a "prosperous and handsome life", with the methods of piecework, premiums and decorations. Socialism is not ascetic; on the contrary, it is deeply hostile to the asceticism of Christianity. It is deeply hostile, in its adherence to *this* world, and this only, to all religion. But socialism has its gradations of earthly values. Human personality begins for socialism not with the concern for a prosperous life, but on the contrary with the cessation of this concern. However, no generation can jump over its own head. The whole Stakhanov movement is for the present built upon "base egotism". The very measures of success—the number of trousers and neckties earned—testify to nothing but "philistine pettiness". Suppose that this historic stage is unavoidable. All right. It is still necessary to see it as it is. The restoration of market relations opens an indubitable opportunity for a considerable rise of personal prosperity. The broad trend of the Soviet youth toward the engineering profession is explained, not so much by the allurements of socialist construction, as by the fact that engineers earn incomparably more than physicians or teachers. When such tendencies arise in circumstances of intellectual oppression and ideological reaction, and with a conscious unleashing from above of careerist instincts, then the propagation of what is called "socialist culture" often turns out to be education in the spirit of the most extreme antisocial egotism.

Still it would be a crude slander against the youth to portray them as controlled exclusively, or even predominantly, by personal interests. No, in the general mass they are magnanimous, responsive, enterprising. Careerism colours them only from above. In their depths are various unformulated tendencies grounded in heroism and still only awaiting application. It is upon these moods in particular that the newest kind of Soviet patriotism is nourishing itself. It is undoubtedly very deep, sincere and dynamic. But in this patriotism, too, there is a rift, which separates the young from the old.

Healthy young lungs find it intolerable to breathe in the atmosphere of hypocrisy inseparable from a Thermidor— from a reaction, that is, which is still compelled to dress in the garments of revolution. The crying discord between the socialist posters and the reality of life undermines faith in the official canons. A considerable stratum of the youth takes pride in its contempt for politics, in rudeness and debauch. In many cases, and probably a majority, this indifferentism and cynicism is but the initial form of discontent and of a hidden desire to stand up on one's own feet. The expulsion from the Communist Youth and the party, the arrest and exile, of hundreds of thousands of young "white guards" and "opportunists", on the one hand, and "Bolshevik-Leninists" on the other, proves that the wellsprings of conscious political opposition, both right and left, are not exhausted. On the contrary, during the last couple of years they have been bubbling with renewed strength. Finally, the more impatient, hot-blooded, unbalanced, injured in their interests and feelings, are turning their thoughts in the direction of terrorist revenge. Such, approximately, is the spectrum of the political moods of the Soviet youth.

The history of individual terror in the Soviet Union clearly marks the stages in the general evolution of the country. At the dawn of the Soviet power, in the atmosphere of the still unfinished civil war, terrorist deeds were perpetrated by white guards or Social Revolutionaries. When the former ruling classes lost hope of a restoration, terrorism also disappeared. The kulak terror, echoes of which have been observed up to very recent times, had always a local character and supplemented the guerrilla warfare against the Soviet regime. As for the latest outburst of terrorism, it does not rest either upon the old ruling classes or upon the kulak. The terrorists of the latest draft are recruited exclusively from among the young, from the ranks of the Communist Youth and the party—not infrequently from the offspring of the ruling stratum. Although completely impotent to solve the problems, which it sets itself, this individual terror has nevertheless an extremely important symptomatic significance. It characterizes the sharp contradiction between the bureaucracy and the broad masses of the people, especially the young.

All taken together—economic hazards, parachute jumping, polar expeditions, demonstrative indifferentism, "romantic hooligans", terroristic mood, and individual acts of terror—are preparing an explosion of the younger generation against the intolerable tutelage of the old. A war would undoubtedly serve as a vent for the accumulating vapors of discontent—but not for long. In a war the youth would soon acquire the necessary fighting temper and the authority, which it now so sadly lacks. At the same time the reputation of the majority of "old men" would suffer irremediable damage. At best, a war would give the bureaucracy only a certain moratorium. The ensuing political conflict would be so much the more sharp.

It would be one-sided, of course, to reduce the basic political problem of the Soviet Union to the problem of the two generations. There are many open and hidden foes of the bureaucracy among the old, just as there are hundreds of thousands of perfected yes-men among the young. Nevertheless, from whatever side the attack came against the position of the ruling stratum, from left or right, the attackers would recruit their chief forces among the oppressed and discontented youth deprived of political rights. The bureaucracy admirably understands this. It is in general exquisitely sensitive to everything, which threatens its dominant position. Naturally, in trying to consolidate its position in advance, it erects the chief trenches and concrete fortifications against the younger generation.

In April 1936, as we have said, there assembled in the Kremlin the tenth congress of the Communist Youth. Nobody bothered to exclaim, of course, why in violation of its constitution, the congress had not been called for an entire five years. Moreover, it soon became clear that this carefully sifted and selected congress was called at this time exclusively for the purpose of a political expropriation of the youth. According to the new constitution the Communist Youth League is now even juridically deprived of the right to participate in the social life of the country. Its sole sphere henceforth is to be education and cultural training. The General Secretary of the Communist Youth, under orders from above, declared in his speech: "We must ... *end the chatter* about industrial and financial planning, about the lowering, of production costs, economic accounting, crop sowing, and other important state problems *as though we were going to decide them.*" The whole country might well repeat those last words: "as though we were going, to decide them!" That insolent rebuke: "End the chatter!" welcomed with anything but enthusiasm even by this supersubmissive congress—is the more striking when you remember that the Soviet law defines the age of political maturity as 18 years, giving all electoral rights to young men and women of that age, whereas the age limit for Communist Youth members, according to the old Constitution, was 23 years, and a good third of the members of the organization were in reality older than that. This last congress adopted two simultaneous reforms: It legalized membership in the Communist Youth for people of greater age, thus increasing the number of Communist Youth electors, and at the same time deprived the organization as a whole of the right to intrude into the sphere, not only of general politics—of that there can never be any question!—but of the current problems of economy. The abolition of the former age limit was dictated by the fact that transfer from the Communist Youth into the party, formerly an almost automatic process, has now been made extremely difficult. This annulment of the last remnant of political rights, and even of the appearance of them, was caused by a desire fully and finally to enslave the Communist Youth to the well-purged party. Both measures, obviously contradicting each other, derive nevertheless from the same source: the bureaucracy's fear of the younger generation.

The speakers at the congress, who according to their own statements were carrying out the express instructions of Stalin—they gave these warnings in order to forestall in advance the very possibility of a debate explained the aim of the reform with astonishing frankness: "We have no need of any second party". This argument reveals the fact that in the opinion of the ruling circles the Communist Youth League, if it is not decisively strangled, threatens to become a second party. As though on purpose to define these possible tendencies, another speaker warningly declared: "In his time, no other than Trotsky himself attempted to make a demagogic play for the youth, to inspire it with the anti-Leninist, anti-Bolshevik idea of creating a second party, etc." The speaker's historic allusion contains an anachronism. In reality, Trotsky "in his time" only gave warning that a further bureaucratization of the regime would inevitably lead to a break with the youth, and produce the danger of a second party. But never mind: the course of events, in confirming that warning, has converted it ipso facto into a programme. The degenerating party has kept its attractive power only for careerists. Honest and thinking young men and girls cannot but be nauseated by the Byzantine slavishness, the false rhetoric, concealing privilege and caprice, the braggadocio of mediocre bureaucrats singing praises to each other—at all these marshals who because they can't catch the stars in heaven have to stick them on their own bodies in various places. *[Translator's note: The phrase "he does not catch the stars in heaven" is a proverbial way of saying that a man is mediocre.]* Thus it is no longer a question of the "danger" as it was twelve or thirteen years ago of a second party, but of its historic necessity as the sole power capable of further advancing the cause of the October Revolution. The change in the constitution of the Communist Youth League, although reinforced with fresh police threats, will not, of course, halt the political maturing of the youth, and will not prevent their hostile clash with the bureaucracy.

Which way will the youth turn in case of a great political disturbance? Under what banner will they assemble their ranks? Nobody can give a sure answer to that question now, least of all the youth themselves. Contradictory tendencies are furrowing their minds. In the last analysis, the alignment of the principal mass will be determined by historic events of world significance, by a war, by new successes of fascism, or, on the contrary, by the victory of the proletarian revolution in the West. In any case the bureaucracy will find out that these youth deprived of rights represent a historic charge with mighty explosive power.

In 1894 the Russian autocracy, through the lips of the young tzar Nicholas II, answered the Zemstvos, which were timidly dreaming of participating in political life, with the famous words: "Meaningless fancies!" In 1936 the Soviet bureaucracy answered the as yet vague claims of the younger generation with the still ruder cry: "Stop your chatter!" Those words, too, will become historic. The regime of Stalin may pay no less dear for them than the regime headed by Nicholas II.

### 3. Nationality and culture

The policy of Bolshevism on the national question, having ensured the victory of the October Revolution, also helped the Soviet Union to hold out afterward notwithstanding inner centrifugal forces and a hostile environment. The bureaucratic degeneration of the state has rested like a millstone upon the national policy. It was upon the national question that Lenin intended to give his first battle to the bureaucracy, and especially to Stalin, at the 12th Congress of the party in the spring of 1923. But before the congress met Lenin had gone from the ranks. The documents, which he then prepared, remain even now suppressed by the censor.

The cultural demands of the nations aroused by the revolution require the widest possible autonomy. At the same time, industry can successfully develop only by subjecting all parts of the Union to a general centralized plan. But economy and culture are not separated by impermeable partitions. The tendencies of cultural autonomy and economic centralism come naturally from time to time into conflict. The contradiction between them is, however, far from irreconcilable. Although there can be no once-and-for-all prepared formula to resolve the problem, still there is the resilient will of the interested masses themselves. Only their actual participation in the administration of their own destinies can at each new stage draw the necessary lines between the legitimate demands of economic centralism and the living gravitations of national culture. The trouble is, however, that the will of the population of the Soviet Union in all its national divisions is now wholly replaced by the will of a bureaucracy, which approaches both economy and culture from the point of view of convenience of administration and the specific interests of the ruling stratum.

It is true that in the sphere of national policy, as in the sphere of economy, the Soviet bureaucracy still continues to carry out a certain part of the progressive work, although with immoderate overhead expenses. This is especially true of the backward nationalities of the Union, which must of necessity pass through a more or less prolonged period of borrowing, imitation and assimilation of what exists. The bureaucracy is laying down a bridge for them to the elementary benefits of bourgeois, and in part even pre-bourgeois, culture. In relation to many spheres and peoples, the Soviet power is to a considerable extent carrying out the historic work fulfilled by Peter I and his colleagues in relation to the old Muscovy, only on a larger scale and at a swifter tempo.

In the schools of the Union, lessons are taught at present in no less than eighty languages. For a majority of them, it was necessary to compose new alphabets, or to replace the extremely aristocratic Asiatic alphabets with the more democratic Latin. Newspapers are published in the same number of languages—papers that for the first time acquaint the peasants and nomad shepherds with the elementary ideas of human culture. Within the far-flung boundaries of the tzar's empire, a native industry is arising. The old semi-clan culture is being destroyed by the tractor. Together with literacy, scientific agriculture and medicine are coming into existence. It would be difficult to overestimate the significance of this work of raising up new human strata. Marx was right when he said that revolution is the locomotive of history.

But the most powerful locomotive cannot perform miracles. It cannot change the laws of space, and can only accelerate movement. The very necessity of acquainting tens of millions of grown-up people with the alphabet and the newspaper, or with the simple laws of hygiene, shows what a long road must be travelled before you can really pose the question of a new socialist culture. The press informs us, for example, that in western Siberia the Oirots who formerly did not know what a bath means, have now "in many villages baths to which they sometimes travel 30 kilometers to wash themselves". This extreme example, although taken at the lowest level of culture, nevertheless truthfully suggests the height of many other achievements, and that not only in the backward regions. When the head of a government, in order to illustrate the growth of culture, refers to the fact that in the collective farms a demand has arisen for "iron bedsteads, wall clocks, knit underwear, sweaters, bicycles, etc.," this only means that the well-off upper circles of the Soviet villages are beginning to use those articles of manufacture which were long ago in common use among the peasant masses of the West. From day to day, in speeches and in the press, lessons are pronounced on the theme of "cultured socialist trade". In the essence, it is a question of giving a clean attractive look to the government stores, supplying them with the necessary technical implements and a sufficient assortment of goods, not letting the apples rot, throwing in darning cotton with stockings, and teaching the selling clerk to be polite and attentive to the customer—in other words, acquiring the commonplace methods of capitalist trade. We are still far from solving this extremely important problem—in which, however, there is not a drop of socialism.

If we leave laws and institutions aside for a moment, and take the daily life of the basic mass of the population, and if we do not deliberately delude our minds or others', we are compelled to acknowledge that in life customs and culture the heritage of tzarist and bourgeois Russia in the Soviet country vastly prevails over the embryonic growth of socialism. Most convincing on this subject is the population itself, which at the least rise of the standard of living throws itself avidly upon the ready models of the West. The young Soviet clerks, and often the workers too, try both in dress and manner to imitate American engineers and technicians with whom they happen to come in contact in the factories. The industrial and clerical working girls devour with their eyes the foreign lady tourist in order to capture her modes and manners. The lucky girl who succeeds in this becomes an object of wholesale imitation. Instead of the old bangs, the better-paid working girl acquires a "permanent wave". The youth are eagerly joining "Western dancing circles". In a certain sense all this means progress, but what chiefly expresses itself here is not the superiority of socialism over capitalism, but the prevailing of petty bourgeois culture over patriarchal life, the city over the village, the centre over the backwoods, the West over the East.

The privileged Soviet stratum does its borrowing meanwhile in the higher capitalistic spheres. And in this field the pacemakers are the diplomats, directors of trusts, engineers, who have to make frequent trips to Europe and America. Soviet satire is silent on this question, for it is simply forbidden to touch the upper "ten thousand". However, we cannot but remark with sorrow that the loftiest emissaries of the Soviet Union have been unable to reveal in the face of capitalist civilization either a style of their own, or any independent traits whatever. They have not found sufficient inner stability to enable them to scorn external shine and observe the necessary aloofness. Their chief ambition ordinarily is to differ as little as possible from the most finished snobs of the bourgeoisie. In a word, they feel and conduct themselves in a majority of cases not as the representatives of a new world, but as ordinary parvenus!

To say that the Soviet Union is now performing that cultural work, which the advanced countries long ago performed on the basis of capitalism, would be, however, only half the truth. The new social forms are by no means irrelevant. They not only give to a backward country the possibility of gaining the level of the most advanced, but they permit it to achieve this task in a much shorter space of time than was needed formerly in the West. The explanation of this acceleration of tempo is simple. The bourgeois pioneers had to invent their technique and learn to apply it in the spheres both of economy and culture. The Soviet Union takes it ready made in its latest forms and, thanks to the socialized means of production, applies the borrowings not partially and by degrees but at once and on a gigantic scale.

Military authorities have more than once celebrated the role of the army as a carrier of culture, especially in relation to the peasantry. Without deceiving ourselves as to the specific kind of "culture", which bourgeois militarism inculcates, we cannot deny that many progressive customs have been instilled in the popular masses through the army. Not for nothing have former soldiers and under-officers in revolutionary and especially peasant movements usually stood at the head of the insurrectionists. The Soviet regime has an opportunity to influence the daily life of the people not only through the army, but also through the whole state apparatus, and interwoven with it the apparatus of have not found sufficient inner stability to enable them to scorn external shine and observe the necessary aloofness. Their chief ambition ordinarily is to differ as little as possible from the most finished snobs of the bourgeoisie. In a word, they feel and conduct themselves in a majority of cases not as the representatives of a new world, but as ordinary parvenus!

To say that the Soviet Union is now performing that cultural work, which the advanced countries long ago performed on the basis of capitalism, would, however, be only half the truth. The new social forms are by no means irrelevant. They not only give to a backward country the possibility of gaining the level of the most advanced, but they permit it to achieve this task in a much shorter space of time than was needed formerly in the West. The explanation of this acceleration of tempo is simple. The bourgeois pioneers had to invent their technique and learn to apply it in the spheres both of economy and culture. The Soviet Union takes it ready made in its latest forms and, thanks to the socialized means of production, applies the borrowings not partially and by degrees but at once and on a gigantic scale.

Military authorities have more than once celebrated the role of the army as a carrier of culture, especially in relation to the peasantry. Without deceiving ourselves as to the specific kind of "culture", which bourgeois militarism inculcates, we cannot deny that many progressive customs have been instilled in the popular masses through the army. Not for nothing have former soldiers and under-officers in revolutionary and especially peasant movements usually stood at the head of the insurrectionists. The Soviet regime has an opportunity to influence the daily life of the people not only through the army, but also through the whole state apparatus, and interwoven with it the apparatus of the Party, the Communist Youth and the trade unions. An appropriation of ready-made models of technique, hygiene, art, sport, in an infinitely shorter time than was demanded for their development in their homeland, is guaranteed by the state forms of property, the political dictatorship and the planned methods of administration.

If the October Revolution had given nothing but this accelerated forward movement, it would be historically justified, for the declining bourgeois regime has proved incapable during the last quarter century of seriously moving forward any one of the backward countries in any part of the earth. However, the Russian proletariat achieved the revolution in the name of much more far-reaching tasks. No matter how suppressed it is politically at present, in its better parts it has not renounced the communist programme nor the mighty hope bound with it. The bureaucracy is compelled to accommodate itself to the proletariat, partly in the very direction of its policy, but chiefly in the interpretation of it. Hence, every step forward in the sphere either of economy or culture, regardless of its actual historic content or its real significance in the life of the masses, is proclaimed as a hitherto unseen and unheard-of conquest of "socialist culture". There is not a doubt that to make toilet soap and a toothbrush the possession of millions who up to yesterday never heard of the simplest requirements of neatness is a very great cultural work. But neither soap nor a brush, nor even the perfumes, which "our women" are demanding, quite constitute a socialist culture, especially in conditions where these pitiable attributes of civilization are accessible only to some 15 per cent of the population.

The "making over of men" of which they talk so much in the Soviet press is truly in full swing. But to what degree is this socialist making over? The Russian people never knew in the past either a great religious reformation like the Germans, or a great bourgeois revolution like the French. Out of these two furnaces, if we leave aside the reformation-revolution of the British Islanders in the seventeenth century, came bourgeois individuality, a very important step in the development of human personality in general. The Russian revolutions of 1905 and 1917 necessarily meant the first awakening of individuality in the masses, its crystallization out of the primitive medium. That is to say, they fulfilled, in abridged form and accelerated tempo, the educational work of the bourgeois reformations and revolutions of the West. Long before this work was finished, however, even in the rough, the Russian revolution, which had broken out in the twilight of capitalism, was compelled by the course of the class struggle to leap over to the road of socialism. The contradictions in the sphere of Soviet culture only reflect and refract the economic and social contradictions, which grew out of this leap. The awakening of personality under these circumstances necessarily assumes a more or less petty bourgeois character, not only in economics, but also in family life and Iyric poetry. The bureaucracy itself has become the carrier of the most extreme, and sometimes unbridled, bourgeois individualism. Permitting and encouraging the development of economic individualism (piecework, private land allotments, premiums, decorations), it at the same time ruthlessly suppresses the progressive side of individualism in the realm of spiritual culture (critical views, the development of one's own opinion, the cultivation of personal dignity).

The more considerable the level of development of a given national group, or the higher the sphere of its cultural creation, or, again, the more closely it grapples with the problems of society and personality, the more heavy and intolerable becomes the pressure of the bureaucracy. There can be in reality no talk of uniqueness of national culture when one and the same conductor's baton, or rather one and the same police club, undertakes to regulate all the intellectual activities of all the peoples of the Soviet Union. The Ukrainian, White Russian, Georgian, or Turk newspapers and books are only translations of the bureaucratic imperative into the language of the corresponding nationality. Under the name of models of popular creativeness, the Moscow press daily publishes in Russian translation odes by the prize poets of the different nationalities in honour of the leaders, miserable verses in reality that differ only in the degree of their servility and u ant of talent.

The Great Russian culture, which has suffered from the regime of the guardhouse no less than the others, lives chiefly at the expense of the older generation formed before the revolution. The youth are suppressed as though with an iron plank. It is a question, therefore, not of the oppression of one nationality over another in the proper sense of the word, but of oppression by the centralized police apparatus over the cultural development of all the nations, starting with the Great Russian. We cannot, however, ignore the fact that 90 per cent of the publications of the Soviet Union are printed in the Russian language. If this percentage is, to be sure, in flagrant contradiction with the relative number of the Great Russian population, still it perhaps the better corresponds to the general influence of Russian culture, both in its independent weight and its role as mediator between the backward peoples of the country and the West. But with all that, does not the excessively high percentage of Great Russians in the publishing houses (and not only there, of course) mean an actual autocratic privilege of the Great Russians at the expense of the other nationalities of the Union? It is quite possible. To this vastly important question it is impossible to answer as categorically as one would wish, for in life it is decided not so much by collaboration, rivalry and mutual fertilizations of culture, as by the ultimate arbitrament of the bureaucracy. And since the Kremlin is the residence of the authorities, and the outlying territories are compelled to keep step with the centre, bureaucratism inevitably takes the colour of an autocratic Russification, leaving to the other nationalities the sole indubitable cultural right of celebrating the arbiter in their own language.

* * *

The official doctrine of culture changes in dependence upon economic zigzags and administrative expediencies. But with all its changes, it retains one trait—that of being absolutely categorical. Simultaneously with the theory of "socialism in one country", the previously frowned-on theory of "proletarian culture" received official recognition. The opponents of this theory pointed out that the regime of proletarian dictatorship has a strictly transitional character, that in distinction from the bourgeoisie the proletariat does not intend to dominate throughout a series of historical epochs, that the task of the present generation of the new ruling class reduces itself primarily to an assimilation of all that is valuable in bourgeois culture, that the longer the proletariat remains a proletariat —that is, bears the traces of its former oppression— the less is it capable of rising above the historic heritage of the past, and that the possibilities of new creation will really open themselves only to the extent that the proletariat dissolves itself in a socialist society. All this means, in other words, that the bourgeois culture should be replaced by a socialist, not a proletarian culture.

In a polemic against the theory of a "proletarian art" produced by laboratory methods, the author of these lines wrote: "Culture feeds upon the juices of industry, and a material excess is necessary in order that culture should grow, refine and complicate itself." Even the most successful solution of elementary economic problems "would far from signify as yet a complete victory of the new historic principle of socialism. Only a forward movement of scientific thought on an all-national basis and the development of a new art would mean that the historic kernel had produced a blossom as well as a stalk. In this sense the development of art is the highest test of the viability and significance of every epoch." This point of view, which had prevailed up to that moment, was in an official declaration suddenly proclaimed to be "capitulatory", and dictated by a "disbelief" in the creative powers of the proletariat. There opened the period of Stalin and Bukharin, the latter of whom had long before appeared as an evangel of "proletarian culture", and the former never given a thought to these questions. They both considered, in any case, that the movement toward socialism would develop with a "tortoise stride", and that the proletariat would have at its disposal decades for the creation of its own culture. As to the character of this culture, the ideas of these theoreticians were as vague as they were uninspiring.

The stormy years of the first five-year plan upset the tortoise perspective. In 1931, on the eve of a dreadful famine, the country had already "entered into socialism". Thus, before the officially patronized writers, artists and painters had managed to create a proletarian culture, or even the first significant models of it, the government announced that the proletariat had dissolved in the classless society. It remained for the artists to reconcile themselves with the fact that the proletariat did not possess the most necessary condition for the creation of a proletarian culture: time. Yesterday's conceptions were immediately abandoned to oblivion. "Socialist culture" was placed instantly upon the order of the day. We have already in part become acquainted with its content.

Spiritual creativeness demands freedom. The very purpose of communism is to subject nature to technique and technique to plan, and compel the raw material to give unstintingly everything to man that he needs. Far more than that, its highest goal is to free finally and once for all the creative forces of mankind from all pressure, limitation and humiliating dependence. Personal relations, science and art will not know any externally imposed "plan", nor even any shadow of compulsion. To what degree spiritual creativeness shall be individual or collective will depend entirely upon its creators.

A transitional regime is a different thing. The dictatorship reflects the past barbarism and not the future culture. It necessarily lays down severe limitations upon all forms of activity, including spiritual creation. The programme of the revolution from the very beginning regarded these limitations as a temporary evil, and assumed the obligation, in proportion as the new regime was consolidated, to remove one after the other all restrictions upon freedom. In any case, and in the hottest years of the civil war, it was clear to the leaders of the revolution that the government could, guided by political considerations, place limitations upon creative freedom, but in no case pretend to the role of commander in the sphere of science, literature and art. Although he had rather "conservative" personal tastes in art, Lenin remained politically extremely cautious in artistic questions, eagerly confessing his incompetence. The patronizing of all kinds of modernism by Lunacharsky, the People's Commissar of Art and Education, was often embarrassing to Lenin. But he confines himself to ironical remarks in private conversations, and remained remote from the idea of converting his literary tastes into law. In 1924, on the threshold of the new period, the author of this book thus formulated the relation of the state to the various artistic groups and tendencies: "while holding over them all the categorical criterion, *for* the revolution or *against* the revolution, to give them complete freedom in the sphere of artistic self-determination".

While the dictatorship had a seething mass-basis and a prospect of world revolution, it had no fear of experiments, searchings, the struggle of schools, for it understood that only in this way could a new cultural epoch be prepared. The popular masses were still quivering in every fibre, and were thinking aloud for the first time in a thousand years. All the best youthful forces of art were touched to the quick. During those first years, rich in hope and daring, there were created not only the most complete models of socialist legislation, but also the best productions of revolutionary literature. To the same times belongs, it is worth remarking, the creation of those excellent Soviet films which, in spite of a poverty of technical means, caught the imagination of the whole world with the freshness and vigour of their approach to reality.

In the process of struggle against the party Opposition, the literary schools were strangled one after the other. It was not only a question of literature, either. The process of extermination took place in all ideological spheres, and it took place more decisively since it was more than half unconscious. The present ruling stratum considers itself called not only to control spiritual creation politically, but also to prescribe its roads of development. The method of command-without-appeal extends in like measure to the concentration camps, to scientific agriculture and to music. The central organ of the party prints anonymous directive editorials, having the character of military orders, in architecture, literature, dramatic art, the ballet, to say nothing of philosophy, natural science and history.

The bureaucracy superstitiously fears whatever does not serve it directly, as well as whatever it does not understand. When it demands some connection between natural science and production, this is on a large scale right; but when it commands that scientific investigators set themselves goals only of immediate practical importance, this threatens to seal up the most precious sources of invention, including practical discoveries, for these most often arise on unforeseen roads. Taught by bitter experience, the natural scientists, mathematicians, philologists, military theoreticians, avoid all broad generalizations out of fear lest some "red professor", usually an ignorant careerist, threateningly pull up on them with some quotation dragged in by the hair from Lenin, or even from Stalin. To defend one's own thought in such circumstances, or one's scientific dignity, means in all probability to bring down repressions upon one's head.

But it is infinitely worse in the sphere of the social sciences. Economists, historians, even statisticians, to say nothing of journalists, are concerned above all things not to fall, even obliquely, into contradiction with the momentary zigzag of the official course. About Soviet economy, or domestic or foreign policy, one cannot write at all except after covering his rear and flanks with banalities from the speeches of the "leader", and having assumed in advance the task of demonstrating that everything is going exactly as it should go and even better. Although this 100 per cent conformism frees one from everyday unpleasantnesses, it entails the heaviest of punishments: sterility.

In spite of the fact that Marxism is formally a state doctrine in the Soviet Union, there has not appeared during the last twelve years one Marxian investigation--in economics, sociology, history or philosophy—which deserves attention and translation into foreign languages. The Marxian works do not transcend the limit of scholastic compilations, which say over the same old ideas, endorsed in advance, and shuffle over the same old quotations according to the demands of the current administrative conjuncture. Millions of copies are distributed through the state channels of books and brochures that are of no use to anybody, put together with the help of mucilage, flattery and other sticky substances. Marxists who might say something valuable and independent are sitting in prison, or forced into silence, and this in spite of the fact that the evolution of social forms is raising gigantic scientific problems at every step! Befouled and trampled underfoot is the one thing without which theoretical work is impossible: scrupulousness. Even the explanatory notes to the complete works of Lenin are radically worked over in every new edition from the point of view of the personal interests of the ruling staff: the names of "leaders" magnified, those of opponents vilified; tracks covered up. The same is true of the textbooks on the history of the party and the revolution. Facts are distorted, documents concealed or fabricated, reputations created or destroyed. A simple comparison of the successive variants of one and the same book during the last twelve years permits us to trace infallibly the process of degeneration of the thought and conscience of the ruling stratum.

No less ruinous is the effect of the "totalitarian" regime upon artistic literature. The struggle of tendencies and schools has been replaced by interpretation of the will of the leaders. There has been created for all groups a general compulsory organization, a kind of concentration camp of artistic literature. Mediocre but "right-thinking" storytellers like Serafimovich or Gladkov are inaugurated as classics. Gifted writers who cannot do sufficient violence to themselves are pursued by a pack of instructors armed with shamelessness and dozens of quotations. The most eminent artists either commit suicide, or find their material in the remote past, or become silent. Honest and talented books appear as though accidentally, bursting out from somewhere under the counter, and have the character of artistic contraband.

The life of Soviet art is a kind of martyrology. After the editorial orders in *Pravda* against "formalism", there began an epidemic of humiliating recantations by writers, artists, stage directors and even opera singers. One after another, they renounced their own past sins, refraining, however—in case of further emergencies—from any clear-cut definition of the nature of this "formalism". In the long run, the authorities were compelled by a new order to put an end to a too copious flow of recantations. Literary estimates are transformed within a few weeks, textbooks made over, streets renamed, statues brought forward, as a result of a few eulogistic remarks of Stalin about the poet Maiakovsky. The impressions made by the new opera upon high-up auditors are immediately converted into a musical directive for composers. The Secretary of the Communist Youth said at a conference of writers: "The suggestions of Comrade Stalin are a law for everybody," and the whole audience applauded, although some doubtless burned with shame. As though to complete the mockery of literature, Stalin, who does not know how to compose a Russian phrase correctly, is declared a classic in the matter of style. There is something deeply tragic in this Byzantinism and police rule, notwithstanding the involuntary comedy of certain of its manifestations.

The official formula reads: Culture should be socialist in content, national in form. As to the content of a socialist culture, however, only certain more or less happy guesses are possible. Nobody can grow that culture upon an inadequate economic foundation. Art is far less capable than science of anticipating the future. In any case, such prescriptions as, "portray the construction of the future", "indicate the road to socialism", "make over mankind", give little more to the creative imagination than does the price list of a hardware store, or a railroad timetable.

The national form of an art is identical with its universal accessibility. "What is not wanted by the people," *Pravda* dictates to the artists, "cannot have aesthetic significance." That old Narodnik formula, rejecting the task of artistically educating the masses, takes on a still more reactionary character when the right to decide what art the people want and what they don't want remains in the hands of the bureaucracy. It prints books according to its own choice. It sells them also by compulsion, offering no choice to the reader. In the last analysis the whole affair comes down in its eyes to taking care that art assimilates its interests, and finds such forms for them as will make the bureaucracy attractive to the popular masses.

In vain! No literature can fulfill that task. The leaders themselves are compelled tc acknowledge that "neither the first nor the second five-year plan has yet given us a new literary wave which can rise above the first wave born in October". That is very mildly said. In reality, in spite of individual exceptions, the epoch of the Thermidor will go into the history of artistic creation pre-eminently as an epoch of mediocrities, laureates and toadies.

# *Chapter 8*

# FOREIGN POLICY AND THE ARMY

## 1. From "World Revolution" to "Status Quo"

Foreign policy is everywhere and always a continuation of domestic policy, for it is conducted by the same ruling class and pursues the same historic goals. The degeneration of the governing stratum in the Soviet Union could not but be accompanied by a corresponding change of aims and methods in Soviet diplomacy. The "theory" of socialism in one country, first announced in the autumn of 1924, already signalized an effort to liberate Soviet foreign policy from the programme of international revolution. The bureaucracy, however, had no intention to liquidate therewith its connection with the Communist International. That would have converted the latter into a world oppositional organization, with resulting unfavourable consequences in the correlation of forces within the Soviet Union. On the contrary, the less the policy of the Kremlin preserved of its former internationalism, the more firmly the ruling clique clutched in its hands the rudder of the Communist International. Under the old name it was now to serve new ends. For the new ends, however, new people were needed. Beginning with the autumn of 1923, the history of the Communist International is a history of the complete renovation of its Moscow staff, and the staffs of all the national sections, by way of a series of palace revolutions, purgations from above, expulsions, etc. At the present time, the Communist International is a completely submissive apparatus in the service of Soviet foreign policy, ready at any time for any zigzag whatever.

The bureaucracy has not only broken with the past, but has deprived itself of the ability to understand the most important lessons of that past. The chief of these lessons was that the Soviet power could not have held out for 12 months without the direct help of the international— and especially the European—proletariat, and without a revolutionary movement of the colonial peoples. The only reason the Austro-German military powers did not carry their attack upon Soviet Russia through to the end was that they felt behind their back the hot breath of the revolution. In some three quarters of a year, insurrections in Germany and Austro-Hungary put an end to the Brest-Litovsk treaty. The revolt of the French sailors in the Black Sea in April 1919 compelled the government of the Third Republic to renounce its military operations in the Soviet South. The British government, in September 1919, withdrew its expeditionary forces from the Soviet North under direct pressure from its own workers. After the retreat of the Red Army from the vicinity of Warsaw in 1920, only a powerful wave of revolutionary protests prevented the Entente from coming to the aid of Poland and crushing the Soviets. The hands of Lord Curzon, when he delivered his threatening ultimatum to Moscow in 1923, were bound at the decisive moment by the resistance of the British workers' organizations. These clear episodes are not peculiar. They depict the whole character of the first and most difficult period of Soviet existence. Although the revolution triumphed nowhere outside the limits of Russia, the hopes of its triumph were far from being fruitless.

During those years, the Soviet government concluded a series of treaties with bourgeois governments: the Brest-Litovsk peace in 1918; a treaty with Estonia in 1920; the Riga peace with Poland in October 1920; the treaty of Rapallo with Germany in April 1922; and other less important diplomatic agreements. It could never have entered the mind of the Soviet government as a whole, however, nor any member of it, to represent its bourgeois counteragents as "friends of peace", and still less to invite the communist parties of Germany, Poland, or Estonia, to support with their votes the bourgeois governments which had signed these treaties. It is just this question, moreover, which is decisive for the revolutionary education of the masses. The Soviets could not help signing the Brest-Litovsk peace, just as exhausted strikers cannot help signing the most cruel conditions imposed by the capitalists. But the vote cast in favour of this peace by the German Social Democrats, in the hypothetical form of "abstention", was denounced by the Bolsheviks as a support of brigandage and brigands. Although the Rapallo agreement with democratic Germany was signed four years later on a formal basis of "equal rights" for both parties, nevertheless if the German communist party had made this a pretext to express confidence in the diplomacy of its country, it would have been forthwith expelled from the International. The fundamental line of the international policy of the Soviets rested on the fact that this or that commercial, diplomatic, or military bargain of the Soviet government with the imperialists, inevitable in the nature of the case, should in no case limit or weaken the struggle of the proletariat of the corresponding capitalist country, for in the last analysis the safety of the workers' state itself could be guaranteed only by the growth of the world revolution. When Chicherin, during the preparations for the Geneva Conference, proposed for the benefit of "public opinion" in America to introduce certain "democratic" changes in the Soviet Constitution, Lenin, in an official letter of 23 January, 1922, urgently recommended that Chicherin be sent immediately to a sanatorium. If anybody had dared in those days to propose that we purchase the good favour of "democratic" imperialism by adhering, let us say, to the false and hollow Kellog Pact, or by weakening the policy of the Communist International, Lenin would indubitably have proposed that the innovator be sent to an insane asylum —and he would hardly have met any opposition in the Politburo.

The leaders of those days were especially implacable in relation to all kinds of pacifist illusions—League of Nations, collective security, courts of arbitration, disarmament, etc.—seeing in them only a method of lulling the toiling masses in order to catch them unawares when a new war breaks out. In the programme of the party, drafted by Lenin and adopted at the Congress of 1919, we find the following unequivocal lines on this subject:

> "The developing pressure of the proletariat, and especially its victories in individual countries, are strengthening the resistance of the exploiters and impelling them to new forms of international consolidation of the capitalists (League of Nations, etc.) which, organizing on a world scale the systematic exploitation of all the peoples of the Earth, are directing their first efforts toward the immediate suppression of the revolutionary movements of the proletariat of all countries. All this inevitably leads to a combination of civil wars within the separate states with revolutionary wars, both of the proletarian countries defending themselves, and of the oppressed peoples against the yoke of the imperialist powers. In these conditions the slogans of pacifism, international disarmament under capitalism, courts of arbitration, etc., are not only reactionary utopias, but downright deceptions of the toilers designed to disarm the proletariat and distract it from the task of disarming the exploiters."

These lines, from the Bolshevik programme, constitute an advance estimate, and moreover a truly devastating one, of the present Soviet foreign policy and the policy of the Communist International, with all its pacifistic "friends" in every corner of the Earth.

After the period of intervention and blockade, the economic and military pressure of the capitalist world on the Soviet Union did, to be sure, prove considerably weaker than might have been feared. Europe was still thinking of the past and not the future war. Then came the unheard of economic world crisis, causing prostrations in the ruling classes of the whole world. It was only thanks to this that the Soviet Union could survive the trials of the first five-year plan, when the country again became an arena of civil war, famine, and epidemic. The first years of the second five-year plan, which have brought an obvious betterment of internal conditions, have coincided with the beginning of an economic revival in the capitalist world, and a new tide of hopes, appetites, yearnings and preparations for war. The danger of a combined attack on the Soviet Union takes palpable form in our eyes only because the country of the Soviets is still isolated, because to a considerable extent this "one-sixth of the Earth's surface" is a realm of primitive backwardness, because the productivity of labour in spite of the nationalization of the means of production is still far lower than in capitalist countries, and, finally—what is at present most important—because the chief detachments of the world proletariat are shattered, distrustful of themselves, and deprived of reliable leadership. Thus the October Revolution, in which its leaders saw only a prelude to world revolution, but which in the course of things has received a temporary independent significance, reveals in this new historic stage its deep dependence upon world development. Again it becomes obvious that the historic question, *Who shall prevail?* cannot be decided within national boundaries, that interior successes and failures only prepare more or less favourable conditions for its decision on the world arena.

The Soviet bureaucracy—we must do it this justice—has acquired a vast experience in directing popular masses, in lulling them to sleep, dividing and weakening them, or deceiving them outright for the purpose of unlimited domination over them. But for this very reason it has lost every trace of the faculty of revolutionary education of the masses. Having strangled independence and initiative in the lower ranks of the people at home, it naturally cannot provoke critical thought and revolutionary daring on the world arena. Moreover, as a ruling and privileged stratum, it values infinitely more the help and friendship of those who are kin to it in social type in the West—bourgeois radicals, reformist parliamentarians, trade-union bureaucrats—than of the rank-and-file workers who are separated from it by social chasms. This is not the place for a history of the decline and degeneration of the Third International, a subject to which the author has dedicated a series of independent investigations published in almost all the languages of the civilized world. The fact is that in its capacity as leader of the Communist International, the nationally limited and conservative, ignorant and irresponsible Soviet bureaucracy has brought nothing but misfortunes to the workers' movement of the world. As though in historic justice, the present international position of the Soviet Union is determined to a far higher degree by the consequences of the defeat of the world proletariat, than by the successes of an isolated Socialist construction. It is sufficient to recall that the defeat of the Chinese revolution in 1925–27, which untied the hands of Japanese militarism in the East, and the shattering of the German proletariat which led to the triumph of Hitler and the mad growth of German militarism, are alike the fruits of the policy of the Communist International.

Having betrayed the world revolution, but still feeling loyal to it, the Thermidorean bureaucracy has directed its chief efforts to "neutralizing" the bourgeoisie. For this it was necessary to seem a moderate, respectable, authentic bulwark of order. But in order to seem something successfully and for a long time, you have to be it. The organic evolution of the ruling stratum has taken care of that. Thus, retreating step-by-step before the consequences of its own mistakes, the bureaucracy has arrived at the idea of insuring the inviolability of the Soviet Union by including it in the system of the European-Asiastic status quo. What could be finer, when all is said and done, than an eternal pact of non-aggression between socialism and capitalism? The present official formula of foreign policy, widely advertised not only by the Soviet diplomacy, which is permitted to speak in the customary language of its profession, but by the Communist International, which is supposed to speak the language of revolution, reads: "We don't want an inch of foreign land, but we will not surrender an inch of our own". As though it were a question of mere quarrels about a bit of land, and not of the world struggle of two irreconcilable social systems!

When the Soviet Union considered it more sensible to surrender the Chinese-Eastern Railroad to Japan, this act of weakness, prepared by the collapse of the Chinese revolution, was celebrated as a manifestation of self-confident power in the service of peace. In reality, by surrendering to the enemy an extremely important strategic highway, the Soviet government promoted Japan's further seizures in North China and her present attempts upon Mongolia. That forced sacrifice did not mean a "neutralization" of the danger, but at the best a short breathing spell, and at the same time a mighty stimulus to the appetites of the ruling military clique in Tokyo.

The question of Mongolia is already a question of the strategic positions to be occupied by Japan in a future war against the Soviet Union. The Soviet government found itself this time compelled to announce openly that it would answer the intrusion of Japanese troops into Mongolia with war. Here, however, it is no question of the immediate defence of "our land": Mongolia is an independent state. A passive defence of the Soviet boundaries seemed sufficient only when nobody was seriously threatening them. The real method of defense of the Soviet Union is to weaken the positions of imperialism, and strengthen the position of the proletariat and the colonial peoples throughout the Earth. An unfavourable correlation of forces might compel us to surrender many "inches" of land, as it did at the moment of the Brest-Litovsk peace, the Riga peace, and in the matter of the handing over of the Chinese-Eastern Railroad. At the same time, the struggle for a favorable change in the correlation of world forces puts upon the workers' state a continual obligation to come to the help of the liberative movements in other countries. But it is just this fundamental task, which conflict absolutely with the conservative policy of the status quo.

## 2. The League of Nations and the Communist International

The *rapprochement* and subsequent outright military treaty with France, the chief defender of the status quo—a policy that resulted from the victory of German National Socialism—is infinitely more favourable to France than to the Soviets. The obligation to military from the side of the Soviets is, according to the treaty, unconditional; French help, on the contrary, is conditioned upon a preliminary agreement with England and Italy, which opens an unlimited field for hostile machinations against the Soviet Union. The events connected with the Rhineland demonstrated that, with a more realistic appraisal of the situation, and with more restraint, Moscow might have gotten better guarantees from France—if indeed treaties can be considered "guarantees" in an epoch of sharp changes of set-up, continued diplomatic crises, *rapprochements* and breaks. But this is not the first time it has become evident that the Soviet bureaucracy is far more firm in its struggles against the advanced workers of its own country, than in negotiation with the bourgeois diplomats.

The assertion that helps from the side of the Soviet Union is of little consequence in view of the fact that it has no common boundary with Germany, is not to be taken seriously. In case Germany attacks the Soviet Union, the common boundary will obviously be found by the attacking side. In the case of an attack by Germany on Austria, Czechoslovakia, and France, Poland cannot remain neutral for a day. If she recognizes her obligations as an ally of France, she will inevitably open the road to the Red Army; and if she breaks her treaty of alliance, she will immediately become a helpmate of Germany. In the latter case, the Soviet Union will have no difficulty in finding a "common boundary". Moreover, in a future war, the sea and air "boundaries" will play no less a role than those on land.

The entrance of the Soviet Union into the League of Nations— represented to the Russian population, with the help of a stage management worthy of Goebbels, as a triumph of socialism and a result of "pressure" from the world proletariat—was in reality acceptable to the bourgeoisie only as a result of the extreme weakening of the revolutionary danger. It was not a victory of the Soviet Union, but a capitulation of the Thermidorean bureaucracy to this hopelessly compromised Geneva institution, which, according to the above-quoted words of the Bolshevik programme, "will direct its future efforts to the suppression of revolutionary movements". What has changed so radically since the days of the Magna Carta of Bolshevism: the nature of the League of Nations, the function of pacifism in a capitalist society, or— the policy of the Soviets? To ask the question is to answer it.

Experience quickly proved that participation in the League

of Nations, while adding nothing to those practical advantages, which could be had by way of agreements with separate bourgeois states, imposes at the same time serious limitations and obligations. These the Soviet Union is performing with the most pedantic faithfulness in the interest of its still unaccustomed conservative prestige. The necessity of accommodation within the League not only to France, but also to her allies, compelled Soviet diplomacy to occupy an extremely equivocal position in the Italian-Abyssinian conflict. At the very time when Litvinov, who was nothing at Geneva but a shadow of Laval, expressed his gratitude to the diplomats of France and England for their efforts "in behalf of peace", efforts which so auspiciously resulted in the annihilation of Abyssinia, oil from the Caucausus continued to nourish the Italian fleet. Even if you can understand that the Moscow government hesitated openly to break a commercial treaty, still the trade unions were not obliged to take into consideration the undertakings of the Commissariat of Foreign Trade. An actual stoppage of exports to Italy by a decision of the Soviet trade unions would have evoked a world movement of boycott incomparably more real than the treacherous "sanctions", measured as they were in advance by diplomatists and jurists in agreement with Mussolini. And if the Soviet trade unions never lifted a finger this time, in contrast with 1926, when they openly collected millions of rubles for the British coal strike, it is only because such an initiative was forbidden by the ruling bureaucracy, chiefly to curry favour with France. In the coming world war, however, no military allies can recompense the Soviet Union for the lost confidence of the colonial peoples and of the toiling masses in general.

Can it be that this is not understood in the Kremlin?

> The fundamental aim of German fascism"—so answers the Soviet official newspaper—"is to isolate the Soviet Union.... Well, and what of it? The Soviet Union has today more friends in the world than ever before." **(*Izvestia* 17/9/35)**

The Italian proletariat is in the chains of fascism; the Chinese revolution is shattered, and Japan is playing the boss in China; the German proletariat is so crushed that Hitler's plebiscite encounters no resistance whatever; the proletariat of Austria is bound hand and foot; the revolutionary parties of the Balkans are trampled in the earth; in France, in Spain, the workers are marching at the tail of the radical bourgeoisie. In spite of all this, the Soviet government from the time of its entrance into the League of Nation has had "more friends in the world than ever before"! This boast, so fantastic at first glance, has a very real meaning when you apply it not to the workers' state, but to its ruling group. Was it not indeed the cruel defeats of the world proletariat which permitted the Soviet bureaucracy to usurp the power at home and earn a more or less favourable "public opinion" in the capitalist countries? The less the Communist International is capable of threatening the positions of capital, the more political credit is given to the Kremlin government in the eyes of French, Czechoslovak, and other bourgeoisies. Thus the strength of the bureaucracy, both domestic and international, is in inverse proportion to the strength of the Soviet Union as a socialist state and a fighting base of the proletarian revolution. However, that is only one side of the medal. There is another.

Lloyd George, in whose jumps and sensations there is often a glimmer of shrewd penetration, warned the House of Commons in November 1934 against condemning fascist Germany, which, according to his words, was destined to be the most reliable bulwark against communism in Europe. "We shall yet greet her as our friend." Most significant words! The half-patronizing, half-ironical praise addressed by the world bourgeoisie to the Kremlin is not of itself in the slightest degree a guarantee of peace, or even a simple mitigation of the war danger. The evolution of the Soviet bureaucracy is of interest to the world bourgeoisie in the last analysis from the point of view of possible changes in the forms of property. Napoleon I, after radically abandoning the traditions of Jacobinism, donning the crown, and restoring the Catholic cult, remained nevertheless an object of hatred to the whole of ruling semi-feudal Europe, because he continued to defend the new property system created by the revolution. Until the monopoly of foreign trade is broken and the rights of capital restored, the Soviet Union, in spite of all the services of its ruling stratum, remains in the eyes of the bourgeoisie of the whole world an irreconcilable enemy, and German National Socialism a friend, if not today, at least of tomorrow. Even during the negotiations of Barthou and Laval with Moscow, the big French bourgeoisie, in spite of the critical danger from the side of Hitler, and the sharp turn of the French Communist Party to patriotism, stubbornly refused to stake its game on the Soviet card. When he signed the treaty with the Soviet Union, Laval was accused from the Left of frightening Berlin with Moscow, while seeking in reality a *rapprochement* with Berlin and Rome against Moscow. This judgment was perhaps a little premature, but by no means in conflict with the natural development of events.

However one may judge the advantages of disadvantages of the Franco-Soviet pact, no serious revolutionary statesman would deny the right of the Soviet state to seek supplementary supports for its inviolability in temporary agreements with this or that imperialism. It is only necessary clearly and openly to show the masses the place of these partial and tactical agreements in the general system of historic forces. In order to make use particularly of the antagonism between France and Germany, there is not the slightest need of idealizing the bourgeois ally, or that combination of imperialists which temporarily hides behind the screen of the League of Nations. Not only Soviet diplomacy, however, but in its steps the Communist International systematically paints up the episodical allies of Moscow as "friends of peace", deceives the workers with slogans like "collective security" and "disarmament", and thus becomes in reality a political agent of the imperialists among the working classes.

The notorious interview given by Stalin to the president of the Scripps-Howard newspapers, Roy Howard, on 1 March, 1936, is a precious document for the characterization of bureaucratic blindness upon the great questions of world politics, and of that false relation which has been established between the leaders of the Soviet Union and the world workers' movement. To the question, Is war inevitable?, Stalin answers:

> **"I think that the position of the friends of peace is growing stronger; the friends of peace can work openly, they rely upon the strength of public opinion, they have at their disposal such instruments, for instance, as the League of Nations."**

In these words, there is not a glimmer of realism. The bourgeois states do not divide themselves into "friends" and "enemies" of peace—especially since "peace" as such does not exist. Each imperialist country is interested in preserving *its* peace, and the more sharply interested, the more unbearable this peace may be for its enemies. The formula common to Stalin, Baldwin, Leon Blum, and others, "peace would be really guaranteed if all states united in the League for its defense", means merely that peace would be guaranteed if there existed no causes for its violation. The thought is correct, if you please, but not exactly weighty. The great powers that are nonmembers of the League, like the United States, obviously value a free hand above the abstraction of "peace". For just what purpose they need these free hands they will show in due time. Those states, which withdraw from the League, like Japan and Germany, or temporarily take a "leave of absence" from it, like Italy, also have sufficiently material reasons for what they do. Their break with the League merely changes the diplomatic form of existent antagonisms, but not their nature and not the nature of the League. Those virtuous nations, which swear eternal loyalty to the League, compel themselves the more resolutely to employ it in support of *their* peace. But even so, there is no agreement. England is quite ready to extend the period of peace—at the expense of France's interests in Europe or in Africa. France, in her turn, is ready to sacrifice the safety of the British naval routes—for the support of Italy. But for the defence of their own interests, they are both ready to resort to war—to the most just, it goes without saying, of all wars. And, finally, the small states, which for the lack of anything better seek shelter in the shadow of the League, will show up in the long run not on the side of "peace", but on the side of the strongest combination in the war.

The League in its defence of the status quo is not an

organization of "peace", but an organization of the violence of the imperialist minority over the overwhelming majority of mankind. This "order" can be maintained only with the help of continual wars, little and big—today in the colonies, tomorrow between the great powers. Imperialist loyalty to the status quo has always a conditional, temporary, and limited character. Italy was yesterday defending the status quo of Europe, but not in Africa. What will be her policy in Europe tomorrow, nobody knows. But already the change of boundaries in Africa finds its reflection in Europe. Hitler made bold to lead his troops into the Rhineland only because Mussolini invaded Abyssinia. It would be hard to number Italy among the "friends" of peace. However, France values her friendship with Italy incomparably more than her friendship with the Soviet Union. England on her side seeks a friendship with Germany. The groupings change; the appetites remain. The task of the so-called partisans of the status quo is in essence to find in the League the most auspicious combination of forces, and the most advantageous cover for the preparation of a future war. Who will begin it and how, depends upon circumstances of secondary importance. Somebody will have to begin it, because the status quo is a cellarful of explosives.

A programme of "disarmament", while imperialist antagonisms survive, is the most pernicious of fictions. Even if it were realized by way of general agreement—an obviously fantastic assumption!—that would by no means prevent a new war. The imperialists do not make war because there are armaments; on the contrary, they forge arms when they need to fight. The possibilities of a new, and, moreover, very speedy, arming lie in contemporary technique. Under no matter what agreements, limitations and "disarmaments", the arsenals, the military factories, the laboratories, the capitalist industries as a whole, preserve their force. Thus Germany, disarmed by her conquerors under the most careful control (which, by the way, is the only real form of "disarmament"!) is again, thanks to her powerful industries, becoming the citadel of European militarism. She intends, in her turn, to "disarm" certain of her neighbours. The idea of a so-called "progressive disarmament" means only an attempt to cut down excessive military expenses in time of peace. But that task, too, remains unrealized. In consequence of differences of geographic position, economic power and colonial saturation, any standards of disarmament would inevitably change the correlation of forces to the advantage of some and to the disadvantage of others. Hence the fruitlessness of the attempts made in Geneva. Almost 20 years of negotiations and conversations about disarmament have led only to a new wave of armaments, which is leaving far behind everything that was ever seen before. To build the revolutionary policy of the proletariat on a programme of disarmament means to build it not on sand, but on the smoke screen of militarism.

The strangulation of the class struggle in the cause of an unhindered progress of imperialist slaughter can be ensured only with the mediation of the leaders of the mass workers' organizations. The slogans under which this task was fulfilled in 1914: "The last war", "War against Prussian militarism", "War for democracy", are too well discredited by the history of the last two decades. "Collective security" and "general disarmament" are their substitutes. Under the guise of supporting the League of Nations, the leaders of the workers' organizations of Europe are preparing a new edition of the "sacred union", a thing no less necessary for war than tanks, aeroplanes, and the "forbidden" poison gases.

The Third International was born of an indignant protest against social patriotism. But the revolutionary charge placed in it by the October Revolution is long ago expended. The Communist International now stands under the banner of the League of Nations, as does the Second International, only with a fresher store of cynicism. When the British Socialist, Sir Stafford Cripps, called the League of Nations an international union of brigands, which was more impolite than unjust, the London *Times* ironically asked: "In that case, how explain the adherence of the Soviet Union to the League of Nations?" It is not easy to answer. Thus the Moscow bureaucracy brings its powerful support to that social patriotism, to which the October

Revolution dealt a crushing blow.

Roy Howard tried to get a little illumination on this point also. What is the state of affairs—he asked Stalin—as to plans and intentions in regard to world revolution?

"We never had any such plans or intentions." But, well... "This is the result of a misunderstanding."

Howard:

> "A tragic misunderstanding?"

Stalin:

> "No, comic, or, if you please, tragi-comic." The quotation is verbatim. "What danger," Stalin continued, "can the surrounding states see in the ideas of the Soviet people if these states really sit firmly in the saddle?"

Yes, but suppose—the interviewer might ask—they do not sit so firm? Stalin adduced one more quieting argument:

> "The idea of exporting a revolution is nonsense. Every country if it wants one will produce its own revolution, and if it doesn't, there will be no revolution. Thus, for instance, our country wanted to make a revolution and made it..."

Again, we have quoted verbatim. From the theory of socialism in a single country, it is a natural transition to that of revolution in a single country. For what purpose, then, does the International exist?—the interviewer might have asked. But he evidently knew the limits of legitimate curiosity. The reassuring explanations of Stalin, which are read not only by capitalists but by workers, are full of holes. Before "our country" desired to make a revolution, we imported the idea of Marxism for other countries, and made use of foreign revolutionary experience. For decades we had our émigrés abroad who guided the struggle in Russia. We received moral and material aid from the workers' organizations of Europe and America. After our victory we organized, in 1919, the Communist International. We more than once announced the duty of the proletariat of countries in which the revolution had conquered to come to the aid of oppressed and insurrectionary classes, and that not only with ideas but if possible with arms. Nor did we limit ourselves to announcements. We in our own time aided the workers of Finland, Latvia, Estonia, and Georgia with armed force. We made an attempt to bring aid to the revolting Polish proletariat by the campaign of the Red Army against Warsaw. We sent organizers and commanders to the help of the Chinese in revolution. In 1926, we collected millions of rubles for the aid of the British strikers. At present, this all seems to have been a misunderstanding. A tragic one? No, it is comic. No wonder Stalin has declared that to live, in the Soviet Union, has become "gay". Even the Communist International has changed from a serious to a comic personage.

Stalin would have made a more convincing impression upon his interviewer if, instead of slandering the past, he had openly contrasted the policy of Thermidor to the policy of October.

"In the eyes of Lenin," he might have said, "the League of Nations was a machine for the preparation of a new imperialist war. We see in it an instrument of peace. Lenin spoke of the inevitability of revolutionary wars. We consider the idea of exporting revolution nonsense. Lenin denounced the union of the proletariat with the imperialist bourgeoisie as treason. We with all our power impel the international proletariat along this road. Lenin slashed the slogan of disarmament under capitalism as a deceit of the workers. We build our whole policy upon this slogan. Your tragi-comic misunderstand"—Stalin might have concluded—"lies in your taking us for the continuers of Bolshevism, when we are in fact its gravediggers."

### 3. The Red Army and its Doctrines

The old Russian soldier, brought up in the patriarchal conditions of the rural commune, was distinguished above all by a blind herd instinct. Suvorov, the generalissimo of Catherine II and Paul, was the unexcelled master of an army of feudal slaves. The great French revolution shelved forever the military act of the old Europe and of tzarist Russia. The empire, to be sure, still continued to add gigantic territorial conquests, but it won no further victories over the armies of civilized nations. A series of external defeats and inward disturbances was needed in order to transmute the national character in their fires. The Red Army could only have been formed on a new social and psychological basis. That long-suffering herd instinct and submissiveness to nature were replaced in the younger generations by a spirit of daring and the cult of technique. Together with the awakening of individuality went a swift rise of the cultural level. Illiterate recruits became fewer and fewer. The Red Army does not let anybody leave its ranks who cannot read and write. All sorts of athletic sports developed tumultuously in the Army and around it. Among the workers, officials and students in the badge of distinction for marksmanship enjoyed great popularity. In the winter months, skis gave the regiments a hitherto unknown mobility. Startling successes were achieved in the sphere of parachute jumping, gliding, and aviation. The arctic flights into the stratosphere are known to everybody. These high points speak for a whole mountain chain of achievements.

It is unnecessary to idealize the standard of the Red Army in organization or operation during the years of the civil war. For the young commanding staff, however, those were years of a great baptism. Rank-and-file soldiers of the tzar's army, underofficers and corporals, disclosed the talents of organizers and military leaders, and tempered their wills in a struggle of immense scope. These self-made men were more than once beaten, but in the long run they conquered. The better among them studied assiduously. Among the present higher chiefs, who went clear through the school of the civil war, the overwhelming majority has also graduated from academies or special courses. Among the senior officers, about half received a higher military education; the rest a cadet course. Military theory gave them the necessary discipline of thought, but did not destroy the audacity awakened by the dramatic operations of the civil war. This generation is now about 40 to 50 years old, the age of equilibrium of physical and spiritual forces, when a bold initiative relies upon experience and is not yet quenched by it.

The party, the Communist Youth, the trade unions—even regardless of how they fulfill their socialist mission—the administration of the nationalized industries, the co-operatives, the collective farms, the Soviet farms—even regardless of how they fulfill their economic tasks—are training innumerable cadres of young administrators, accustomed to operate with human and commodity masses, and to identify themselves with the state. They are the natural reservoir of the commanding staff. The high pre-service preparation of the student creates another independent reservoir. The students are grouped in special training battalions, which in case of mobilization can successfully develop into emergency schools of the commanding staff. To measure the scope of this source, it is sufficient to point out that the number of those graduated from the higher educational institutions has now reached 800,000 a year, the number of college and university students exceeds half-a-million, and that the general number of students in all the scholastic institutions is approaching 28,000,000.

In the sphere of economics, and especially industry, the social revolution has provided the enterprise of national defense with advantages of which the old Russia could not dream. Planning methods mean, in the essence of the matter, a continual mobilization of industry in the hands of the government, and make it possible to focus on the interests of defense even in building and equipping new factories. The correlation between the living and mechanical forces of the Red Army may be considered, by and large, as on a level with the best armies of the West. In the sphere of artillery re-equipment, decisive successes were obtained already in the course of the first five-year plan. Immense sums are being expended in the production of trucks and armored cars, tanks, and aeroplanes. There are at present about half-a-million tractors in this country. In 1936, 160,000 are to be put out, with a total horsepower of 8.5 million. The building of tanks is progressing at a parallel rate. The mobilization plans of the Red Army call for 30 to 45 tanks per kilometre of the active front. As a result of the Great War, the navy was reduced from 548,000 tons in 1917 to 82,000 in 1928. Here we had to begin almost from the beginning. In January 1936, Tukhachevsky announced at a session of the Central Executive Committee: "We are creating a powerful navy. We are concentrating our forces primarily upon the development of a submarine fleet." The Japanese naval staff is well-informed, we may assume, as to the achievements in this sphere. No less attention is now being given to the Baltic. Still, in the coming years, the navy can pretend only to an auxiliary role in the defence of the coastal front.

But the air fleet has advanced mightily. Over two years ago, a delegation of French aviation engineers was, in the words of the press, "astonished and delighted by the achievements in this sphere". They had an opportunity in particular to convince themselves that the Red Army is producing in increasing numbers heavy bombing planes for action on a radius of 1,200 to 1,500 kilometres. In case of a war in the Far East, the political and military centers of Japan would be subject to attack from the Soviet coast. According to data appearing in the press, the five-year plan of the Red Army for 1935 contemplated 62 air regiments capable of bringing simultaneously 5,000 aeroplanes into the line of fire. There is hardly a doubt that the plan was fulfilled, and probably more than fulfilled.

Aviation is closely bound up with a branch of industry, almost non-existent in tzarist Russia, but lately advancing by leaps and bounds —chemistry. It is no secret that the Soviet government—and, incidentally, the other governments of the world—does not believe for a second in the oft-repeated "prohibitions" of the use of poison gas. The work of the Italian civilizers in Abyssinia has again plainly shown what these humanitarian limitations of international brigandage are good for. We may assume that against any catastrophic surprises whatever in the sphere of military chemistry or military bacteriology, these most mysterious and sinister enterprises, the Red Army is as well-equipped as the armies of the West.

As to the quality of the articles of military manufacture,

there may be a legitimate doubt. We have noted, however, that instruments of production are better manufactured in the Soviet Union than objects of general use. Where the purchasers are influential groups of the ruling bureaucracy, the quantity of the product rises considerably above the average level, which is still very low. The most influential client is the war department. It is no surprise if the machinery of destruction is of better quality, not only than the objects of consumption, but also than the instruments of production. Military industry remains, however, a part of the whole industry and, although to a lesser degree, reflects its inadequacies. Voroshilov and Tukhachevsky lose no opportunity publicly to remind the industrialists: "We are not always fully satisfied with the quality of the products which you supply to the Red Army". In private sessions, the military leaders express themselves, we may assume, more categorically. The commissary supplies are, as a general rule, of lower quality than the munitions. The shoe is poorer than the machine gun. But also the aeroplane motor, notwithstanding indubitable progress, still considerably lags behind the best Western types. In the matter of military equipment as a whole, the old task is still there: to catch up as soon as possible to the standard of the future enemy.

It stands worse with agriculture. In Moscow, they often say that since the income from industry has already exceeded that from agriculture, the Soviet Union has ipso facto changed from an agrarian-industrial to an industrial-agrarian country. In reality, the new correlation of incomes is determined not so much by the growth of industry, significant as that is, as by the extraordinarily low level of agriculture. The unusual lenience of Soviet diplomacy for some years toward Japan was caused, among other things, by serious food-supply difficulties. The last three years, however, have brought considerable relief, and permitted in particular the creation of serious military food-supply bases in the Far East.

The sorest spot in the army, paradoxical as it may seem, is the horse. In the full blast of complete collectivization, about 55 per cent of the country's horses were killed. Moreover, in spite of motorization, a present-day army needs, as during the time of Napoleon, one horse every three soldiers. During the last year, however, things have taken a favourable turn in this matter: the number of horses in the country is again on the increase. In any case, even if war broke out in the coming months, a state with 170 million population will always be able to mobilize the necessary food resources and horses for the front—to be sure, at the expense of the rest of the population. But the popular masses of all countries in the case of war can, in general, hope for nothing but hunger, poison gas, and epidemics.

* * *

The great French Revolution created its army by amalgamating the new formations with the royal battalions of the line. The October Revolution dissolved the tzar's army wholly and without leaving a trace. The Red Army was built anew from the first brick. A twin of the Soviet regime, it shared its fate in great things and small. It owed its incomparable superiority over the tzar's army wholly to the great social revolution. It has not stood aside, however, from the processes of degeneration of the Soviet regime. On the contrary, these have found their most finished expression in the army. Before attempting to describe the possible role of the Red Army in a future military cataclysm, it is necessary to dwell a moment upon the evolution of its guiding ideas and structures.

The decree of the Soviet of People's Commissars of January 12, 1918, which laid the foundation for the regular armed forces, defined their objective in the following words:

> "With the transfer of power to the toiling and exploited classes, there has arisen the necessity to create a new army which shall be the bulwark of the Soviet power... and will serve as a support for the coming socialist revolutions in Europe."

In repeating on the 1st of May the "Socialist Oath"—still retained since 1918—the young Red Army soldier binds himself

> "before the eyes of the toiling classes of Russia and the whole world" in the struggle "for the cause of Socialism and the broth-

> erhood of nations, not to spare his strength nor even his life itself."

When Stalin now describes the international character of the revolution as a "comic misunderstanding" and "nonsense", he displays, besides all the rest, an inadequate respect for basic decrees of the Soviet power that are not annulled even to this day.

The army naturally was nourished by the same ideas as the party and the state. Its printed laws, journalism, oral agitation, were alike inspired by the international revolution as a practical task. Within the walls of the War Department, the programme of revolutionary internationalism not infrequently assumed an exaggerated character. The late S. Gussev, once head of the political administration in the army and subsequently a close ally of Stalin, wrote in 1921, in the official military journal:

> "We are preparing the class army of the proletariat... not only for defense against the bourgeois-landed counterrevolution, but also for revolutionary wars (both defensive and offensive) against the imperialist powers."

Moreover, Gussev directly blamed the then head of the War Department for inadequately preparing the Red Army for its international tasks. The author of these lines, answering Gussev in the press, called his attention to the fact that foreign military powers fulfill in a revolutionary process, not a fundamental, but an auxiliary role. Only in favourable circumstances can they hasten the denouement and facilitate the victory.

"Military intervention is like the forceps of the physician. Applied in season, it can lighten the birth pains; brought into operation prematurely, it can only cause a miscarriage." (5 December, 1921.)

We cannot, unfortunately, expound here with sufficient completeness the history of this not unimportant problem. We remark, however, that the present marshal, Tukhachevsky, addressed to the Communist International in 1921 a letter proposing to create under his presidency an "international general staff". That interesting letter was then published by Tukhachevsky in a volume of his articles under the expressive title "The War of the Classes". The talented, but somewhat too impetuous, commander ought to have known from printed explanations that

> "an international general staff could arise only on the basis of the national staff of *several* proletarian states; so long as that is impossible, an international staff would inevitably turn into a caricature."

If not Stalin himself—who in general avoids taking a definite position upon questions of principle, especially new ones—at least many of his future close associates stood in those years to the "left" of the leadership of the party and the army. There was no small amount of naive exaggeration, or, if you prefer, "comic misunderstanding", in their ideas. Is a great revolution possible without such things? We were waging a struggle against these left "caricatures" of internationalism long before it became necessary to turn our weapons against the no less extreme caricature involved in the theory of "socialism in a single country".

Contrary to the retrospective representations of it, the intellectual life of Bolshevism at the very heaviest period of the civil war was boiling like a spring. In all the corridors of the party and the state apparatus, including the army, discussion was raging about everything, and especially about military problems. The policy of the leaders underwent a free, and frequently a fierce, criticism. On the question of certain excessive military censorships, the then head of the War Department wrote in the leading military journal:

> "I willingly acknowledge that the censorship has made a mountain of errors, and I consider it very necessary to show that respected personage a more modest place. The censorship ought to defend military secrets... and it has no business interfering with anything else." (February 23, 1919.)

The question of an international general staff was only a small episode in an intellectual struggle, which, while kept within bounds of the discipline of action, led even to the formation of something in the nature of an oppositional faction within the army, at least within its upper strata. A school of "proletarian military doctrine" to which belonged or adhered Frunze, Tukhachevsky, Gussev, Voroshilov, and others, started from the a priori conviction that, not only in its political aims but in its structure, strategy and tactic, the Red Army could have nothing in common with the national armies of the capitalist countries. The new ruling class must have in all respects a distinct military system; it remained only to create it. During the civil war, the thing was limited, of course, chiefly to protests in principle against the bringing into service of the "generals"—former officers, that is, of the tzar's army—and back-kicking against the high command in its struggle with local improvisations and particular violations of discipline. The extreme apostles of the new word tried in the name of strategic principles, of "maneuverism" and "offensivism" pushed to that absolute, to reject even the centralized organization of the army, as inhibiting revolutionary initiative on future international fields of battle. In its essence, this was an attempt to extend the guerilla methods of the first period of the civil war into a permanent and universal system. A good many of the revolutionary commanders came out the more willingly for the new doctrine, since they did not want to study the old. The principal centre of these moods was Tzaritzyn (now Stalingrad), where Budenny, Voroshilov, and afterward Stalin, began their military work.

Only after the war ended was a more systematic attempt made to erect these innovations into a finished doctrine. The initiator was one of the outstanding commanders of the civil war, the late Frunze, a former political hard-labour prisoner, and he was supported by Voroshilov, and to some extent by Tukhachevsky. In essence, the proletarian military doctrine was wholly analogous to the doctrine of "proletarian culture", completely sharing its metaphysical schematism. In certain works left by the advocates of this tendency, this or that practical prescription, usually far from new, was arrived at deductively from the standard characteristics of the proletariat as an international and aggressive class—that is, from motionless psychological abstraction, and not from real conditions of time and place. Marxism, although acclaimed in every line, was in reality replaced by pure idealism. Notwithstanding the sincerity of these thought wanderings, it is not difficult to see in them the germ of the swiftly developing self-complacence of a bureaucracy which wanted to believe, and make others believe, that it was able in all spheres without special preparation and even without the material prerequisites to accomplish historic miracles.

The then head of the War Department answered Frunze in the press:

> "I also do not doubt that if a country with *a developed socialist economy* found itself compelled to wage war with a bourgeois country, the picture of the strategy of the socialist country would be wholly different. But this gives no basis for an attempt *today* to suck a 'proletarian strategy' out of our fingers.... By developing socialist, raising the cultural level of the masses... we will undoubtedly enrich the military art with new methods."

But for this it is necessary assiduously to learn from the advanced capitalist countries, and not to try to

> "infer a new strategy by speculative methods from the revolutionary nature of the proletariat." (April 1, 1922.)

Archimedes promised to move the Earth if they would give him a point of support. That was not badly said. However, if they offered him the needed point of support, it would have turned out that he had neither the lever nor the power to bring it into action. The victorious revolution gave us a new point of support, but in order to move the Earth it is still necessary to build the levers.

"The proletarian military doctrine" was rejected by the party, like its elder sister, "the doctrine of proletarian culture". However, in the sequel, at least so it appears, their destinies diverged. The banner of "proletarian culture" was raised by Stalin and Bukharin, to be sure without visible results, in the course of the seven-year period between the proclamation of "socialism in one country" and of the abolition of all classes (1924–31). The "proletarian military doctrine", on the contrary, notwithstanding that its former advocates soon stood at the helm of state, never had any resurrection. The external difference in the fates of these two so-closely-related doctrines is of profound significance in the evolution of Soviet society. "Proletarian culture" had to do with imponderable matters, and the bureaucracy was the more magnanimous about granting this moral compensation to the proletariat, the more rudely it pushed the proletariat from the seats of power. Military doctrine, on the contrary, goes to the quick, not only of the interests of defence, but of the interests of the ruling stratum. Here there was no place for ideological pamperings. The former opponents of the enlistment of the "generals" had themselves meantime become "generals". The prophets of an international general staff had quieted down under the canopy of the general staff of a "single country". The "war of the classes" was replaced by the doctrine of "collective security". The perspective of world revolution gave place to the deification of the status quo. In order to inspire confidence in possible allies, and not overirritate the enemies, the demand now was to differ as little as possible, no matter what the cost, from capitalist armies. Behind these changes of doctrine and repaintings of facade, social processes of historic import were taking place. The year 1935 was for the army a kind of two-fold state revolution—a revolution in relation to the militia system and to the commanding staff.

## 4. The Abolition of the Militia and the Restoration of Officers' Ranks

In what degree do the Soviet armed forces, at the end of the second decade of their existence, correspond to the type, which the Bolshevik party inscribed upon its banner?

The army of the proletarian dictatorship ought to have, according to the programme,

> "an overtly class character—that is, to be composed exclusively of the proletariat and the semi-proletariat layers of the peasantry close to it. Only in connection with the abolition of classes will such a class army convert itself into a national socialist militia."

Although postponing to a coming period the *all-national* character of the army, the party by no means rejected the *militia* system. On the contrary, according to a resolution of the 8th Congress (March 1919):

> "We are shifting the militia to a class basis and converting it into a Soviet militia." The aim of the military work was defined as the gradual creation of an army "as far as possible by extra-barrackroom methods— that is, in a set-up close to the labor conditions of the working class."

In the long run, all the divisions of the army were to coincide territorially with the factories, mines, villages, agricultural communes, and other organic groupings, "with a local commanding staff, with local stores of arms, and of all supplies". A regional, scholastic, industrial, and athletic union of the youth was to more than replace the corporative spirit instilled by the barracks, and inculcate conscious discipline without the elevation above the army of a professional officers' corps.

A militia, however, no matter how well corresponding to the nature of the socialist society, requires a high economic basis. Special circumstances are built up for a regular army. A territorial army, therefore, much more directly reflects the real condition of the country. The lower the level of culture and the sharper the distinction between village and city, the more imperfect and heterogeneous the militia. A lack of railroads, highways, and water routes, together with an absence of autoroads and a scarcity of automobiles, condemns the territorial army in the first critical weeks and months of war to extreme slowness of movement. In order to ensure a defense of the boundaries during mobilization, strategic transfers and concentrations, it is necessary, along with the territorial detachments, to have regular troops. The Red Army was created from the very beginning as a necessary compromise between the two systems, with the emphasis on the regular troops.

In 1924, the then head of the War Department wrote:

> "We must always have before our eyes two circumstances: If the

> very possibility of going over to the militia system was first created by the establishment of a Soviet structure, still the tempo of the change is determined by the general conditions of the culture of the country—technique, means of communications, literacy, etc. The political premises for a militia are firmly established with us, whereas the economic and cultural are extremely backward."

Granted the necessary material conditions, the territorial army would not only not stand second to the regular army, but far exceed it. The Soviet Union must pay dear for its defence, because it is not sufficiently rich for the cheaper militia system. There is nothing here to wonder at. It is exactly because of its poverty that the Soviet society has hung around its neck the very costly bureaucracy.

One and the same problem, the disproportion between economic base and social superstructure, comes up with remarkable regularity in absolutely all the spheres of social life, in the factory, the collective farm, the family, the school, in literature, and in the army. The basis of all relations is the contrast between a low level of productive forces, low even from a capitalist standpoint, and forms of property that are socialist in principle. The new social relations are raising up the culture. But the inadequate culture is dragging the social forms down. Soviet reality is an equilibrium between these two tendencies. In the army, thanks to the extreme definiteness of its structure, the resultant is measurable in sufficiently exact figures. The correlation between regular troops and militia can serve as a fair indication of the actual movement toward socialism.

Nature and history have provided the Soviet state with open frontiers 10,000 kilometres apart, with a sparse population, and bad roads. On the 15th of October, 1924, the old military leadership, then in its last month, once more urged that this not be forgotten:

> "In the next few years, the creation of a militia must of necessity have a preparatory character. Each successive step must follow from the carefully verified success of the preceding steps."

But with 1925 a new era began. The advocates of the former

proletarian military doctrine came to power. In its essence, the territorial army was deeply contradictory to that ideal of "offensivism" and "maneuverism" with which this school had opened its career. But they had now begun to forget about the world revolution. The new leaders hoped to avoid wars by "neutralizing" the bourgeoisie. In the course of the next few years, 74 per cent of the army was reorganized on a militia basis!

So long as Germany remained disarmed, and moreover "friendly", the calculations of the Moscow general staff in the matter of western boundaries were based on the military forces of the immediate neighbours: Rumania, Poland, Lithuania, Latvia, Esthonia, Finland, with the probably material support of the most powerful of the enemies, chiefly France. In that far-off epoch (which ended in 1933), France was not considered a providential "friend of peace". The surrounding states could put in the field together about 120 divisions of infantry, approximately 3,500,000 men. The mobilization plans of the Red Army tried to insure on the western boundary an army of the first class amounting to the same number. In the Far East, under all conditions in the theatre of war, it could be a question only of hundreds of thousands, and not millions. Each hundred fighters demands, in the course of a year, approximately 75 men to replace losses. Two years of war would withdraw from the country, leaving aside those who return from hospitals to active service, about 10 to 12 million men. The Red Army up to 1935 numbered in all 562,000 men—with the troops of the GPU, 620,000—with 40,000 officers. Moreover, at the beginning of 1935, 74 per cent, as we have already said, were in the territorial divisions, and only 26 per cent in the regular army. Could you ask a better proof that the socialist militia had conquered—if not by 100 per cent, at least by 74 per cent, and in any case "finally and irrevocably"?

However, all the above calculations, conditional enough in themselves, were left hanging in the air after Hitler came to power. Germany began feverishly to arm, and primarily against the Soviet Union. The prospect of a peaceful cohabitation with capitalism faded at once. The swift approach of military danger impelled the Soviet government, besides bringing up the numbers of the armed forces to 1,300,000, to change radically the structure of the Red Army. At the present time, it contains 77 per cent of regular, or so-called "kadrovy" divisions, and only 23 per cent of territorials! This shattering of the territorial divisions looks too much like a renunciation of the militia system—unless you forgot that an army is needed not for times of peace, but exactly for the moments of military danger. Thus, historic experience, starting from that sphere which is least of all tolerant of jokes, has ruthlessly revealed that only so much has been gained "finally and irrevocably" as is guaranteed by the productive foundation of society.

Nevertheless, the slide from 74 per cent to 23 per cent seems excessive. It was not brought to pass, we may assume, without a "friendly" pressure from the French general staff. It is still more likely that the bureaucracy seized upon a favourable pretext for this step, which was dictated to a considerable degree by political considerations. The divisions of a militia through their very character come into direct dependence upon the population. This is the chief advantage of the system from a socialist point of view. But this also is its danger from the point of view of the Kremlin. It is exactly because of this undesirable closeness of the army to the people that the military authorities of the advanced capitalist countries, where technically it would be easy to realize, reject the militia. The keen discontent in the Red Army during the first five-year plan undoubtedly supplied a serious motive for the subsequent abolition of the territorial divisions.

Our proposition would be unanswerably confirmed by an accurate diagram of the Red Army previous to and after the counter-reform. We have not such data, however, and if we had we should consider it impossible to use them publicly. But there is a fact, accessible to all, which permits of no two interpretations: at the same time that the Soviet government reduced the relative weight of the militia in the army to 51 per cent, it restored the Cossack troops, the sole militia formation in the tzar's army! Cavalry is always the privileged and most conservative part of an army. The Cossacks were always the most conservative part of the cavalry. During the war and the revolution, they served as a police force—first for the tzar, and then for Kerensky. Under the Soviet power, they remained perpetually Vendean. Collectivization—introduced among the Cossacks, moreover, with special measures of violence—has not yet, of course, changed their traditions and temper. Moreover, as an exceptional law, the Cossacks have been restored the right to possess their own horse. There is no lack, of course, of other indulgences. Is it possible to doubt that these riders of the steppes are again on the side of the privileged against the oppressed? Upon a background of unceasing repressions against oppositional tendencies among the workers' youth, the restoration of the cossack stripe and forelock is undoubtedly one of the clearest expressions of the Thermidor!

* * *

A still more deadly blow to the principles of the October Revolution was struck by the decree restoring the officers' corps in all its bourgeois magnificence. The commanding staff of the Red Army, with its inadequacies, but also with its inestimable merits, grew out of the revolution and the civil war. The youth, to whom independent political activity is closed, undoubtedly supply no small number of able representatives to the Red Army. On the other hand, the progressive degeneration of the state apparatus could not fail in its turn to reflect itself in the broad circles of the commanding staff. In one of the public conferences, Voroshilov, developing truisms in regard to the duty of commanders to be models to their men, thought it necessary just in that connection to make this confession:

> "Unfortunately, I cannot especially boast"; the lower ranks are growing while "often the commanding cadres lag behind." "Frequently the commanders are unable to answer in a suitable manner" new questions, etc.

A bitter confession from the most responsible—at least formally—leader of the army, a confession capable of evoking alarm but not surprise. What Voroshilov says about the commanders is true of all bureaucrats. Of course the orator himself does not entertain the thought that the ruling upper circles might be numbered among those who "lag behind". No wonder they are always and everywhere shouting at everybody, and angrily stamping their feet, and giving order to be "at your best". In simple fact, it is that uncontrolled corporation of "leaders" to whom Voroshilov himself belongs which is the chief cause of backwardness and routine, and of much else.

The army is a copy of society and suffers from all its diseases, usually at a higher temperature. The trade of war is too austere to get along with fictions and imitations. The army needs the fresh air of criticism. The commanding staff needs democratic control. The organizers of the Red Army were aware of this from the beginning, and considered it necessary to prepare for such a measure as the election of the commanding staff.

> "The growth of internal solidarity of the detachments, the development in the soldier of a critical attitude to himself and his commanders..." says the basic decision of the party on military questions, "will create favorable conditions in which the principle of electivity of the commanding personnel can receive wider and wider application."

Fifteen years after this decision was adopted—a span of time long enough, it would seem, for the maturing of inner solidarity and self-criticism —the ruling circles have taken the exactly opposite turn.

In September 1935, civilized humanity, friends and enemies alike, learned with surprise that the Red Army would now be crowned with an officers' hierarchy, beginning with lieutenant and ending with marshal. According to Tukhachevsky, the actual head of the War Department,

> "the introduction by the government of military titles will create a more stable basis for the development of commanding and technical cadres."

The explanation is consciously equivocal. The commanding cadres are reinforced above all by the confidence of the soldiers. For that very reason, the Red Army began by liquidating the officers' corp. The resurrection of hierarchical caste is not in the least demanded by the interests of military affairs. It is the commanding position, and not the rank, of the commander that is important. Engineers and physicians have no rank, but society finds the means of putting each in his needful place. The right to a commanding position is guaranteed by study, endowment, character, experience, which need continual and moreover individual appraisal. The rank of major adds nothing to the commander of a battalion. The elevation of the five senior commanders of the Red Army to the title of marshal, gives them neither new talents nor supplementary powers. It is not the army that really thus receives a "stable basis", but the officers' corps, and that at the price of aloofness from the army. The reform pursues a purely political aim: to give a new social weight to the officers. Molotov thus in essence defined the meaning of the decree: "to elevate the importance of the guiding cadres of our Army". The thing is not limited, either, to a mere introduction of titles. It is accompanied with an accelerated construction of quarters for the commanding staff. In 1936, 47,000 rooms are to be constructed, and 57 per cent more money is to be issued for salaries than during the preceding year. "To elevate the importance of the guiding cadres" means, at a cost of weakening the moral bonds of the army, to bind the officers closer together with the ruling circles.

It is worthy of note that the reformers did not consider it necessary to invent fresh titles for the resurrected ranks. On the contrary, they obviously wanted to keep step with the West. At the same time, they revealed their Achilles' heel in not daring to resurrect the title of general, which among the Russian people has too ironical a sound. In announcing the elevation to marshals of the five military dignitaries—choice of the five was made, to be it remarked, rather out of regard for personal loyalty to Stalin than for talents or services—the Soviet press did not forget to remind its readers of the tzar's army, its "caste and rank worship and obsequiousness". Why then such a slavish imitation of it? In creating new privileges, the bureaucracy employs at every step the arguments, which once served for the destruction of the old privileges. Insolence takes turns with cowardice, and is supplemented with increasing doses of hypocrisy.

However surprising at first glance the official resurrections of "caste and rank worship and obsequiousness", we must confess that the government had little freedom of choice left. The promotion of commanders on a basis of personal qualification can be realized only under conditions of free initiative and criticism in the army itself, and control over the army by the public opinion of the country. Severe discipline can get along excellently with a broad democracy and even directly rely upon it. No army, however, can be more democratic than the regime, which nourishes it. The source of bureaucratism, with its routine and swank, is not the special needs of military affairs, but the political needs of the ruling stratum. In the army, these needs only receive their most finished expression. The restoration of officers' castes 18 years after their revolutionary abolition testifies equally to the gulf which already separated the rules from the ruled, to the loss by the Soviet army of the chief qualities which gave it the name of "Red", and to the cynicism with which the bureaucracy erects these consequences of degeneration into law.

The bourgeois press has appraised this counterreform as it deserves. The French official paper, *La Temps,* wrote on 25 September, 1935:

> "This external transformation is one of the signs of a deep change which is now taking place through the Soviet Union. The regime, now definitely consolidated, is gradually becoming stabilized. Revolutionary habits and customs are giving place within the Soviet family and Soviet society to the feelings and customs, which continue to prevail within the so-called capitalist countries. The Soviets are becoming bourgeoized."

There is hardly a word to add to that judgment.

## 5. The Soviet Union in a War

Military danger is only one expression of the dependence of the Soviet Union upon the rest of the world, and consequently one argument against the utopian idea of an isolated socialist society. But it is only now that this ominous "argument" is brought forward.

To enumerate in advance all the factors of the coming dogfight of the nations would be a hopeless task. If such an apriori calculation were possible, conflicts of interest would always end in a peaceful bookkeeper's bargain. In the bloody equation of war, there are too many unknown quantities. In any case, there are on the side of the Soviet Union immense favorable factors, both inherited from the past and created by the new regime. The experience of intervention during the civil war proved once more that Russia's greatest advantage has been and remains her vast spaces. Foreign imperialism overthrew Soviet Hungary, though not, to be sure, without help from the lamentable government of Bela Kun, in a few days. Soviet Russia, cut off from the surrounding countries at the very start, struggled against intervention for three years. At certain moments, the territory of the revolution was reduced almost to that of the old Moscow principality. But even that proved sufficient to enable her to hold out, and in the long run triumph.

Russia's second greatest advantage is her human reservoir. Having grown almost 3,000,000 per year, the population of the Soviet Union has apparently now passed 170,000,000. A single recruiting class comprises about 1,300,000 men. The strictest sorting, both physical and political, would throw out not more than 400,000. The reserves, therefore, which may be theoretically estimated at 18 to 20 million, are practically unlimited.

But nature and man are only the raw materials of war. To so-called military "potential" depends primarily upon the economic strength of the state. In this sphere, the advantages of the Soviet Union by comparison with the old Russia are enormous. The planned economy has up to this time, as we have said, given its greatest advantages from the military point of view. The industrialization of the outlying regions, especially Siberia, has given a wholly new value to the steppe and forest spaces. Nevertheless, the Soviet Union still remains a backward country. The low productivity of labour, the inadequate quality of the products, the weakness of the means of transport, are only to a certain degree compensated by space and natural riches and the numbers of the population. In times of peace, the measuring of economic might between the two hostile social systems can be postponed —for a long time, although by no means forever—with the help of political devices, above all the monopoly of foreign trade. During a war the test is made directly upon the field of battle. Hence the danger.

Military defeats, although they customarily entail great political changes, do not always of themselves lead to a disturbance of the economic foundations of society. A social regime, which guarantees a higher development of riches and culture, cannot be overthrown by bayonets. On the contrary, the victors take over the institutions and customs of the conquered, if these are beyond them in evolution. Forms of property can be overthrown by military force only when they are sharply out of accord with the economic basis of the country. A defeat of Germany in a war against the Soviet Union would inevitably result in the crushing, not only of Hitler, but of the capitalist system. On the other hand, it is hardly to be doubted that a military defeat would also prove fatal, not only for the Soviet ruling stratum, but also for the social bases of the Soviet Union. The instability of the present structure in Germany is conditioned by the fact that its productive forces have long ago outgrown the forms of capitalist property. The instability of the Soviet regime, on the contrary, is due to the fact that its productive forces have far from grown up to the forms of socialist property. A military defeat threatens the social basis of the Soviet Union for the same reason that these bases require in peaceful times a bureaucracy and a monopoly of foreign trade—that is, because of their weakness.

Can we, however, expect that the Soviet Union will come out of the coming great war without defeat? To this frankly posed question, we will answer as frankly: If the war should remain only a war, the defeat of the Soviet Union would be inevitable. In a technical, economic, and military sense, imperialism in incomparably more strong. If it is not paralyzed by revolution in the West, imperialism will sweep away the regime, which issued from the October revolution.

It may be answered that "imperialism" is an abstraction, for it too is torn by contradictions. That is quite true, and were it not for those contradictions, the Soviet Union would long ago have disappeared from the scene. The diplomatic and military agreements of the Soviet Union are based in part upon them. However, it would be a fatal mistake not to see the limits beyond which those contradictions must subside. Just as the struggle of the bourgeois and petty bourgeois parties, from the most reactionary to the Social Democratic, subsides before the immediate threat of a proletarian revolution, so imperialist antagonisms will always find a compromise in order to block the military victory of the Soviet Union.

Diplomatic agreements, as a certain chancellor with some reason once remarked, are only "scraps of paper". It is nowhere written that they must survive even up to the outbreak of war. Not one of the treaties with the Soviet Union would survive the immediate threat of a social revolution in any part of Europe. Let the political crisis in Spain, to say nothing of France, enter a revolutionary phase, and the hope propounded by Lloyd George in savior-Hitler would irresistibly take possession of all bourgeois governments. On the other hand, if the unstable situation in Spain, France, Belgium, etc., should end in a triumph of the reaction, there would again remain not a trace of the Soviet pacts. And, finally, if the "scraps of paper" should preserve their validity during the first period of military operations, there is not a doubt that groupings of forces in the decisive phase of the war would be determined by factors of incomparably more powerful significance than the oaths of diplomats, perjurers as they are by profession.

The situation would be radically different, of course, if the bourgeois allies received material guarantees that the

Moscow government stands on the same side with them, not only of the war trenches, but of the class trenches, too. Availing themselves of the difficulties of the Soviet Union, which will be placed between two fires, the capitalist "friends of peace" will, of course, take all measures to drive a breach into the monopoly of foreign trade and the Soviet laws on property. The growing "defensist" movement among the Russian white émigrés in France and Czechoslovakia feeds wholly upon such calculations. And if you assume that the world struggle will be played out only on a military level, the Allies have a good chance of achieving their goal. Without the interference of revolution, the social bases of the Soviet Union must be crushed, not only in the case of defeat, but also in the case of victory.

More than two years ago, a programme announcement, *The Fourth International and War*, outlined this perspective in the following words:

> "Under the influence of the critical need of the state for articles of prime necessity, the individualistic tendencies of the peasant economy will receive a considerable reinforcement, and the centrifugal forces within the collective farms will increase with every month.... In the heated atmosphere of war, we may expect... the attracting of foreign allied capital, a breach in the monopoly of foreign trade, a weakening of state control of the trusts, a sharpening of competition between the trusts, conflicts between the trusts and the workers, etc.... In other words, in the case of a long war, if the world proletariat is passive, the inner social contradictions of the Soviet Union not only might, but must, lead to a bourgeois Bonapartist counterrevolution."

The events of the last two years have redoubled the force of this prognosis.

The preceding considerations, however, by no means lead to so-called "pessimistic" conclusions. If we do not want to shut our eyes to the immense material preponderance of the capitalist world, nor the inevitable treachery of the imperialist "allies", nor the inner contradictions of the Soviet regime, we are, on the one hand, in no degree inclined to overestimate the stability of the capitalist system, either in hostile or allied countries. Long before a war to exhaustion can measure the correlation of economic forces to the bottom, it will put to the test the relative stability of the regimes. All serious theoreticians of future slaughters of the people take into consideration the probability, and even the inevitability, of revolution among its results. The idea, again and again advanced in certain circles, of small "professional" armies, although little more real than the idea of individual heroes in the manner of David and Goliath, reveals in its very fantasticness the reality of the dread of an armed people. Hitler never misses a chance to reinforce his "love of peace" with a reference to the inevitability of a new Bolshevik storm in case of a war in the West. The power which is restraining for the time being the fury of war is not the League of Nations, not mutual security pacts, not pacifist referendums, but solely and only the self-protective fear of the ruling classes before the revolution.

Social regimes like all other phenomena must be estimated comparatively. Notwithstanding all its contradictions, the Soviet regime in the matter of stability still has immense advantages over the regimes of its probable enemies. The very possibility of a rule of the Nazis over the German people was created by the unbearable tenseness of social antagonisms in Germany. These antagonisms have not been removed, and not even weakened, but only suppressed, by the lid of fascism. A war will bring them to the surface. Hitler has far less chances than had Wilhelm II of carrying a war to victory. Only a timely revolution, by saving Germany from war, could save her from a new defeat.

The world press portrayed the recent bloody attack of Japanese officers upon the ministers of the government as the imprudent manifestation of a too flaming patriotism. In reality, these attacks, notwithstanding the difference of ideology, belong to the same historic type as the bombs of the Russian Nihilists against the tzarist bureaucracy. The population of Japan is suffocated under the combined yoke of Asiatic agrarianism and ultra modern capitalism. Korea, Manchukuo, China, at the first weakening of the military pincers, will rise against the Japanese tyranny. A war will bring the empire of the Mikado the greatest of social catastrophes.

The situation of Poland is but little better. The regime of Pilsudski, least fruitful of all regimes, proved incapable even of weakening the land slavery of the peasants. The western Ukraine (Galacia) is living under a heavy national oppression. The workers are shaking the country with continual strikes and rebellions. Trying to insure itself by a union with France and a friendship with Germany, the Polish bourgeoisie is incapable of accomplishing anything with its manoeuvres except to hasten the war and find in it a more certain death.

The danger of war and a defeat of the Soviet Union is a reality, but the revolution is also a reality. If the revolution does not prevent war, then war will help the revolution. Second births are commonly easier than first. In the new war, it will not be necessary to wait a whole two years and a half for the first insurrection. Once it is begun, moreover, the revolution will not this time stop half way. The fate of the Soviet Union will be decided in the long run not on the maps of the general staffs, but on the map of the class struggle. Only the European proletariat, implacably opposing its bourgeoisie, and in the same camp with them the "friends of peace", can protect the Soviet Union from destruction, or from an "allied" stab in the back. Even a military defeat of the Soviet Union would be only a short episode, in case of a victory of the proletariat in other countries. And on the other hand, no military victory can save the inheritance of the October Revolution, if imperialism holds out in the rest of the world.

The henchmen of the Soviet bureaucracy say that we "underestimate" the inner forces of the Soviet Union, the Red Army, etc., just as they have said that we "deny" the possibility of socialist construction in a single state. These arguments stand on such a low level that they do not even permit a fruitful exchange of opinions. Without the Red Army, the Soviet Union would be crushed and dismembered like China. Only her stubborn and heroic resistance to the future capitalist enemy can create favourable conditions for the development of the class struggle in the imperialist camp. The Red Army is thus a factor of immense significance. But this does not mean that it is the sole historic factor. Sufficient that it can give a mighty impulse to the revolution. Only the revolution can fulfill the chief task; to that the Red Army alone is unequal.

Nobody demands of the Soviet government international adventures, unreasonable acts, attempts to force by violence the course of world events. On the contrary, insofar as such attempts have been made by the bureaucracy in the past (Bulgaria, Esthonia, Canton, etc.), they have only played into the hands of the reaction, and they have met a timely condemnation from the Left Opposition. It is a question of the general direction of the Soviet state. The contradiction between its foreign policy and the interests of the world proletariat and the colonial peoples, finds its most ruinous expression in the subjection of the Communist International to the conservative bureaucracy with its new religion of inaction.

It is not under the banner of the status quo that the European worker and the colonial peoples can rise against imperialism, and against that war which must break out and overthrow the status quo almost as inevitably as a developed infant destroys the status quo of pregnancy. The toilers have not the slightest interest in defending existing boundaries, especially in Europe—either under the command of their bourgeoisies, or, still less, in a revolutionary insurrection against them. The decline of Europe is caused by the very fact that it is economically split up among almost 40 quasi-national states, which, with their customs, passports, money systems, and monstrous armies in defence of national particularism, have become a gigantic obstacle on the road of the economic and cultural development of mankind.

The task of the European proletariat is not the perpetuation of boundaries but, on the contrary, their revolutionary abolition, not the status quo, but a socialist United States of Europe!

## *Chapter 9*

# SOCIAL RELATIONS IN THE SOVIET UNION

In the Industries state ownership of the means of production prevails almost universally. In agriculture it prevails absolutely only in the Soviet farms, which comprise no more than 10 per cent of the tilled land. In the collective farms, co-operative or group ownership is combined in various proportions with state and private ownership. The land, although legally belonging to the state, has been transferred to the collectives for "perpetual" use, which differs little from group ownership. The tractors and elaborate machinery belong to the state; the smaller equipment belongs to the collectives. Each collective farmer moreover carries on individual agriculture. Finally, more than 10 per cent of the peasants remain individual farmers.

According to the census of 1934, 28.1 per cent of the population was workers and employees of state enterprises and institutions. Industrial and building-trades workers, not including their families, amounted in 1935 to 7.5 millions. The collective farms and co-operative crafts comprised, at the time of the census, 45.9 per cent of the population. Students, soldiers of the Red Army, pensioners, and other elements directly dependent upon the state, made up 3.4 per cent. Altogether, 74 per cent of the population belonged to the "socialist sector", and 95.8 per cent of the basic capital of the country fell to the share of this 74 per cent. Individual peasants and craftsmen still comprised, in 1934, 22.5 per cent, but they had possession of only a little more than 4 per cent of the national capital!

Since 1934 there has been no census; the next one will be in 1937. Undoubtedly, however, during the last two years the private enterprise sector has shrunk still more in favour of the "socialist". Individual peasants and craftsmen, according to the calculations of official economists, now constitute about 10 per cent of the population—that is, about 17 million people. Their economic importance has fallen very much lower than their numbers. The Secretary of the Central Committee, Andreyev, announced in April 1936: "The relative weight of socialist production in our country in 1936 ought to reach 98.5 per cent. That is to say, something like an insignificant 1.5 per cent still belongs to the non-socialist sector." These optimistic figures seem at first glance an unanswerable proof of the "final and irrevocable" victory of socialism. But woe to him who cannot see social reality behind arithmetic!

The figures themselves are arrived at with some stretching: it is sufficient to point out that the private allotments alongside the collective farms are entered under the "socialist" sector. However, that is not the crux of the question. The enormous and wholly indubitable statistical superiority of the state and collective forms of economy, important though it is for the future, does not remove another and no less important question: that of the strength of bourgeois tendencies within the "socialist" sector itself, and this not only in agriculture but in industry. The material level already attained is high enough to awaken increased demands in all, but wholly insufficient to satisfy them. Therefore, the very dynamic of economic progress involves an awakening of petty bourgeois appetites, not only among the peasants and representatives of "intellectual" labour, but also among the upper circles of the proletariat. A bare antithesis between individual proprietors and collective farmers, between private craftsmen and state industries, does not give the slightest idea of the explosive power of these appetites, which imbue the whole economy of the country, and express themselves, generally speaking, in the desire of each and every one to give as little as possible to society and receive as much as possible from it.

No less energy and ingenuity is being spent in solving money-grubbers' and consumers' problems than upon socialist construction in the proper sense of the word. Hence derives, in part, the extremely low productivity of social labour. While the state finds itself in continual struggle with the molecular action of these centrifugal forces, the ruling group itself forms the chief reservoir of legal and illegal personal accumulations. Masked as they are with new juridical norms, the petty bourgeois tendencies cannot, of course, be easily determined statistically. But their actual predominance in economic life is proven primarily by the "socialist" bureaucracy itself, that flagrant *contradictio in adjecto*, that monstrous and continually growing social distortion, which in turn becomes the source of malignant growths in society.

The new constitution—wholly founded, as we shall see, upon an identification of the bureaucracy with the state, and the state with the people—says: ."... the state property—that is, the possessions of the whole people". This identification is the fundamental sophism of the official doctrine. It is perfectly true that Marxists, beginning with Marx himself, have employed in relation to the workers' state the terms *state, national* and *socialist* property as simple synonyms. On a large historic scale, such a mode of speech involves no special inconveniences. But it becomes the source of crude mistakes, and of downright deceit, when applied to the first and still unassured stages of the development of a new society, and one moreover isolated and economically lagging behind the capitalist countries.

In order to become social, private property must as inevitably pass through the state stage as the caterpillar in order to become a butterfly must pass through the pupal stage. But the pupa is not a butterfly. Myriads of pupae perish without ever becoming butterflies. State property becomes the property of "the whole people" only to the degree that social privilege and differentiation disappear, and therewith the necessity of the state. In other words: state property is converted into socialist property in proportion as it ceases to be state property. And the contrary is true: the higher the Soviet state rises above the people, and the more fiercely it opposes itself as the guardian of property to the people as its squanderer, the more obviously does it testify against the socialist character of this state property.

"We are still far from the *complete* abolition of classes," confesses the official press, referring to the still existing differentiation of city and country, intellectual and physical labor. This purely academic acknowledgment has the advantage that it permits a concealment of the income of the bureaucracy under the honourable title of "intellectual" labour. The "friends"—to whom Plato is much dearer than the truth—also confine themselves to an academic admission of survivals of the old inequality. In reality, these much put-upon "survivals" are completely inadequate to explain the Soviet reality. If the differences between city and country have been mitigated in certain respects, in others they have been considerably deepened, thanks to the extraordinarily swift growth of cities and city culture—that is, of comforts for an urban minority. The social distance between physical and intellectual labor, notwithstanding the filling out of the scientific cadres by newcomers from below, has increased, not decreased, during recent years. The thousand-year-old caste barriers defining the life of every man on all sides—the polished urbanite and the uncouth muzhik, the wizard of science and the day laborer—have not just been preserved from the past in a more or less softened form, but have to a considerable degree been born anew, and are assuming a more and more defiant character.

The notorious slogan: "The cadres decide everything", characterizes the nature of Soviet society far more frankly than Stalin himself would wish. The cadres are in their very essence the organs of domination and command. A cult of "cadres" means above all a cult of bureaucracy, of officialdom, an aristocracy of technique. In the matter of playing up and developing cadres, as in other matters, the Soviet regime still finds itself compelled to solve problems, which the advanced bourgeoisie solved long ago in its own countries. But since the Soviet cadres come forward under a socialist banner, they demand an almost divine veneration and a continually rising salary. The development of "socialist" cadres is thus accompanied by a rebirth of bourgeois inequality.

From the point of view of property in the means of production, the differences between a marshal and a servant girl, the head of a trust and a day labourer, the son of a people's commissar and a homeless child, seem not to exist at all. Nevertheless, the former occupy lordly apartments, enjoy several summer homes in various parts of the country, have the best automobiles at their disposal, and have long ago forgotten how to shine their own shoes. The latter live in wooden barracks often without partitions, lead a half-hungry existence, and do not shine their own shoes only because they go barefoot. To the bureaucrat this difference does not seem worthy of attention. To the day labourer, however, it seems, not without reason, very essential.

Superficial "theoreticians" can comfort themselves, of course, that the distribution of wealth is a factor secondary to its production. The dialectic of interaction, however, retains here all its force. The destiny of the state-appropriated means of production will be decided in the long run according as these differences in personal existence evolve in one direction or the other. If a ship is declared collective property, but the passengers continue to be divided into first, second and third class, it is clear that, for the third-class passengers, differences in the conditions of life will have infinitely more importance than that juridical change in proprietorship. The first-class passengers, on the other hand, will propound, together with their coffee and cigars, the thought that collective ownership is everything and a comfortable cabin nothing at all. Antagonisms growing out of this may well explode the unstable collective.

The Soviet press relates with satisfaction how a little boy in the Moscow zoo, receiving to his question, "Whose is that elephant?" the answer: "The state's", made the immediate inference: "That means it's a little bit mine too." However, if the elephant were actually divided, the precious tusks would fall to the chosen, a few would regale themselves with elephantine hams, and the majority would get along with hooves and guts. The boys who are done out of their share hardly identify the state property with their own. The homeless consider "theirs" only that which they steal from the state. The little "socialist" in the zoological garden was probably the son of some eminent official accustomed to draw inferences from the formula: *"L'etat—c'est moi."*

If we translate socialist relations, for illustration, into the language of the market, we may represent the citizen as a stockholder in a company, which owns the wealth of the country. If the property belonged to all the people, that would presume an equal distribution of "shares", and consequently a right to the same dividend for all "shareholders". The citizens participate in the national enterprise, however, not only as "shareholders", but also as producers. On the lower stage of communism, which we have agreed to call socialism, payments for labour are still made according to bourgeois norms—that is, in dependence upon skill, intensity, etc. The theoretical income of each citizen is thus composed of two parts, a + b—that is, dividend + wages. The higher the technique and the more complete the organization of industry, the greater is the place occupied by a as against b, and the less is the influence of individual differences of labour upon standard of living. From the fact that wage differences in the Soviet Union are not less, but greater than in capitalist countries, it must be inferred that the shares of the Soviet citizen are not equally distributed, and that in his income the dividend as well as the wage payment is unequal. Whereas the unskilled labourer receives only b, the minimum payment which under similar conditions he would receive in a capitalist enterprise, the Stakhanovist or bureaucrat receives 2a + b, or 3a + b, etc., while b also in its turn may become 2b, 3b, etc. The differences in income are determined, in other words, not only by differences of individual productiveness, but also by a masked appropriation of the products of the labour of others. The privileged minority of shareholders is living at the expense of the deprived majority.

If you assume that the Soviet unskilled worker receives more than he would under a similar level of technique and culture in a capitalist enterprise—that is to say, that he is still a small shareholder—it is necessary to consider his wages as equal to a + b. The wages of the higher categories would be expressed with the formula: 3a + 2b, 10a + 15b, etc. This means that the unskilled worker has one share, the Stakhanovist three, the specialist ten. Moreover, their wages in the proper sense are related as 1:2:15. Hymns to the sacred socialist property sound under these conditions a good deal more convincing to the manager or the Stakhanovist, than to the rank-and-file worker or collective peasant. The rank-and-file workers, however, are the overwhelming majority of society. It was they, and not the new aristocracy, that socialism had in mind.

"The worker in our country is not a wage slave and is not the seller of a commodity called labor power. He is a free workman." *(Pravda)* For the present period this unctuous formula is unpermissible bragging. The transfer of the factories to the state changed the situation of the worker only juridically. In reality, he is compelled to live in want and work a definite number of hours for a definite wage. Those hopes which the worker formerly had placed in the party and the trade unions, he transferred after the revolution to the state created by him. But the useful functioning of this implement turned out to be limited by the level of technique and culture. In order to raise this level, the new state resorted to the old methods of pressure upon the muscles and nerves of the worker. There grew up a corps of slave drivers. The management of industry became superbureaucratic. The workers lost all influence whatever upon the management of the factory. With piecework payment, hard conditions of material existence, lack of free movement, with terrible police repression penetrating the life of every factory, it is hard indeed for the worker to feel himself a "free workman". In the bureaucracy he sees the manager, in the state, the employer. Free labour is incompatible with the existence of a bureaucratic state.

With the necessary changes, what has been said above relates also to the country. According to the official theory, collective farm property is a special form of socialist property. *Pravda* writes that the collective farms "are in essence already of the same type as the state enterprises and are consequently socialistic", but immediately adds that the guarantee of the socialist development of agriculture lies in the circumstance that "the Bolshevik Party administers the collective farms". *Pravda* refers us, that is, from economics to politics. This means in essence that socialist relations are not as yet embodied in the real relations among men, but dwell in the benevolent heart of the authorities. The workers will do very well if they keep a watchful eye on that heart. In reality the collective farms stand halfway between individual and state economy, and the petty bourgeois tendencies within them are admirably helped along by the swiftly growing private allotments or personal economies conducted by their members.

Notwithstanding the fact that individual tilled land amounts to only four million hectares, as against one hundred and eight million collective hectares—that is, less than 4 per cent—thanks to the intensive and especially the truck-garden cultivation of this land, it furnishes the peasant family with the most important objects of consumption. The main body of horned cattle, sheep and pigs is the property of the collective farmers, and not of the collectives. The peasants often convert their subsidiary farms into the essential ones, letting the unprofitable collectives take second place. On the other hand, those collectives, which pay highly for the working day, are rising to a higher social level and creating a category of well-to-do farmers. The centrifugal tendencies are not yet dying, but on the contrary are growing stronger. In any case, the collectives have succeeded so far in transforming only the juridical forms of economic relations in the country—in particular the methods of distributing income but they have left almost without change the old hut and vegetable garden, the barnyard chores, the whole rhythm of heavy muzhik labour. To a considerable degree they have left also the old attitude to the state. The state no longer, to be sure, serves the landlords or the bourgeoisie, but it takes away too much from the villages for the benefit of the cities, and it retains too many greedy bureaucrats.

For the census to be taken on 6 January,1937, the following list of social categories has been drawn up: worker; clerical worker; collective farmer; individual farmer; individual craftsman; member of the liberal professions; minister of religion; other non-labouring elements. According to the official commentary, this census list fails to include any other social characteristics only because there are no classes in the Soviet Union. In reality the list is constructed with the direct intention of concealing the privileged upper strata, and the more deprived lower depths. The real divisions of Soviet society, which should and might easily be revealed with the help of an honest census, are as follows: heads of the bureaucracy, specialists, etc., living in bourgeois conditions; medium and lower strata, on the level of the petty bourgeoisie; worker and collective farm aristocracy—approximately on the same level; medium working mass; medium, stratum of collective farmers; individual peasants and craftsmen; lower worker and peasant strata passing over into the *lumpenproletariat;* homeless children, prostitutes, etc.

When the new constitution announces that in the Soviet Union "abolition of the exploitation of man by man" has been attained, it is not telling the truth. The new social differentiation has created conditions for the revival of the exploitation of man in its most barbarous form—that of buying him into slavery for personal service. In the lists for the new census personal servants are not mentioned at all. They are, evidently, to be dissolved in the general group of "workers". There are, however, plenty of questions about this: Does the socialist citizen have servants, and just how many (maid, cook, nurse, governess, chauffeur)? Does he have an automobile at his personal disposal? How many rooms does he occupy? etc. Not a word in these lists about the scale of earnings! If the rule were revived that exploitation of the labour of others deprives one of political rights, it would turn out, somewhat unexpectedly, that the cream of the ruling group are outside the bounds of the Soviet constitution. Fortunately, they have established a complete equality of rights ... for servant and master! Two opposite tendencies are growing up out of the depth of the Soviet regime. To the extent that, in contrast to a decaying capitalism, it develops the productive forces, it is preparing the economic basis of socialism. To the extent that, for the benefit of an upper stratum, it carries to more and more extreme expression bourgeois norms of distribution, it is preparing a capitalist restoration. This contrast between forms of property and norms of distribution cannot grow indefinitely. Either the bourgeois norm must in one form or another spread to the means of production, or the norms of distribution must be brought into correspondence with the socialist property system.

The bureaucracy dreads the exposure of this alternative. Everywhere and all the time in the press, in speeches, in statistics, in the novels of its litterateurs, in the verses of its poets, and, finally, in the text of the new constitution—it painstakingly conceals the real relations both in town and country with abstractions from the socialist dictionary. That is why the official ideology is all so lifeless, talentless and false.

### 1. State Capitalism?

We often seek salvation from unfamiliar phenomena in familiar terms. An attempt has been made to conceal the enigma of the Soviet regime by calling it "state capitalism". This term has the advantage that nobody knows exactly what it means. The term "state capitalism" originally arose to designate all the phenomena, which arise when a bourgeois state takes direct charge of the means of transport or of industrial enterprises. The very necessity of such measures is one of the signs that the productive forces have outgrown capitalism and are bringing it to a partial self-negation in practice. But the outworn system, along with its elements of self-negation, continues to exist as a capitalist system.

Theoretically, to be sure, it is possible to conceive a situation in which the bourgeoisie as a whole constitutes itself a stock company, which, by means of its state, administers the whole national economy. The economic laws of such a regime would present no mysteries. A single capitalist, as is well known, receives in the form of profit, not that part of the surplus value, which is directly created by the workers of his own enterprise, but a share of the combined surplus value created throughout the country proportionate to the amount of his own capital. Under an integral "state capitalism", this law of the equal rate of profit would be realized, not by devious routes—that is, competition among different capitals—but immediately and directly through state bookkeeping. Such a regime never existed, however, and, because of profound contradictions among the proprietors themselves, never will exist—the more so since, in its quality of universal repository of capitalist property, the state would be too tempting an object for social revolution.

During the war, and especially during the experiments in fascist economy, the term "state capitalism" has often been understood to mean a system of state interference and regulation. The French employ a much more suitable term for this *etatism.* There are undoubtedly points of contact between state capitalism and "state-ism", but taken as systems they are opposite rather than identical. State capitalism means the substitution of state property for private property, and for that very reason remains partial in character. State-ism, no matter where in Italy, Mussolini, in Germany, Hitler, in America, Roosevelt, or in France, Leon Blum—means state intervention on the basis of private property, and with the goal of preserving it. Whatever be the programmes of the government, stateism inevitably leads to a transfer of the damages of the decaying system from strong shoulders to weak. It "rescues" the small proprietor from complete ruin only to the extent that his existence is necessary for the preservation of big property. The planned measures of stateism are dictated not by the demands of a development of the productive forces, but by a concern for the preservation of private property at the expense of the productive forces, which are in revolt against it. State-ism means applying brakes to the development of technique, supporting unviable enterprises, perpetuating parasitic social strata. In a word, state-ism is completely reactionary in character.

The words of Mussolini: "Three-fourths of Italian economy, industrial and agricultural, is in the hands of the state" (26 May, 1934), are not to be taken literally. The fascist state is not an owner of enterprises, but only an intermediary between their owners. These two things are not identical. *"Popolo d'Italia"* says on this subject: "The corporative state directs and integrates the economy, but does not run it *("dirige e porta alla unita l'economia, ma non fa l'economia, non gestisce")*, which, with a monopoly of production, would be nothing but collectivism." (11 June, 1986.) Toward the peasants and small proprietors in general, the fascist bureaucracy takes the attitude of a threatening lord and master. Toward the capitalist magnates, that of a first plenipotentiary. "The corporative state," correctly writes the Italian Marxist, Feroci, "is nothing but the sales clerk of monopoly capital.... Mussolini takes upon the state the whole risk of the enterprises, leaving to the industrialists the profits of exploitation." And Hitler in this respect follows in the steps of Mussolini. The limits of the planning principle, as well as its real content, are determined by the class dependence of the fascist state. It is not a question of increasing the power of man over nature in the interests of society, but of exploiting society in the interests of the few. "If I desired," boasts Mussolini, "to establish in Italy—which really has not happened —state capitalism or state socialism, I should possess today all the necessary and adequate objective conditions." All except one: *the expropriation of the class of capitalists*. In order to realize this condition, fascism would have to go over to the other side of the barricades—"which really has not happened" to quote the hasty assurance of Mussolini, and, of course, will not happen. To expropriate the capitalists would require other forces, other cadres and other leaders.

The first concentration of the means of production in the hands of the state to occur in history was achieved by the proletariat with the method of social revolution, and not by capitalists with the method of state trustification. Our brief analysis is sufficient to show how absurd are the attempts to identify capitalist state-ism with the Soviet system. The former is reactionary, the latter progressive.

## 2. Is the bureaucracy a ruling class?

Classes are characterized by their position in the social system of economy, and primarily by their relation to the means of production. In civilized societies, property relations are validated by laws. The nationalization of the land, the means of industrial production, transport and exchange, together with the monopoly of foreign trade, constitute the basis of the Soviet social structure. Through these relations, established by the proletarian revolution, the nature of the Soviet Union as a proletarian state is for us basically defined.

In its intermediary and regulating function, its concern to maintain social ranks, and its exploitation of the state apparatus for personal goals, the Soviet bureaucracy is similar to every other bureaucracy, especially the fascist. But it is also in a vast way different. In no other regime has a bureaucracy ever achieved such a degree of independence from the dominating class. In bourgeois society, the bureaucracy represents the interests of a possessing and educated class, which has at its disposal innumerable means of everyday control over its administration of affairs. The Soviet bureaucracy has risen above a class, which is hardly emerging from destitution and darkness, and has no tradition of dominion or command. Whereas the fascists, when they find themselves in power, are united with the big bourgeoisie by bonds of common interest, friendship, marriage, etc., the Soviet bureaucracy takes on bourgeois customs without having beside it a national bourgeoisie. In this sense we cannot deny that it is something more than a bureaucracy. It is in the full sense of the word the sole privileged and commanding stratum in the Soviet society.

Another difference is no less important. The Soviet bureaucracy has expropriated the proletariat politically in order by methods of its own to defend the social conquests. But the very fact of its appropriation of political power in a country where the principal means of production are in the hands of the state, creates a new and hitherto unknown relation between the bureaucracy and the riches of the nation. The means of production belong to the state. But the state, so to speak, "belongs" to the bureaucracy. If these as yet wholly new relations should solidify, become the norm and be legalized, whether with or without resistance from the workers, they would, in the long run, lead to a complete liquidation of the social conquests of the proletarian revolution. But to speak of that now is at least premature. The proletariat has not yet said its last word. The bureaucracy has not yet created social supports for its dominion in the form of special types of property. It is compelled to defend state property as the source of its power and its income. In this aspect of its activity it still remains a weapon of proletarian dictatorship.

The attempt to represent the Soviet bureaucracy as a class of "state capitalists" will obviously not withstand criticism. The bureaucracy has neither stocks nor bonds. It is recruited, supplemented and renewed in the manner of an administrative hierarchy, independently of any special property relations of its own. The individual bureaucrat cannot transmit to his heirs his rights in the exploitation of the state apparatus. The bureaucracy enjoys its privileges under the form of an abuse of power It conceals its income; it pretends that as a special social group it does not even exist. Its appropriation of a vast share of the national income has the character of social parasitism. All this makes the position of the commanding Soviet stratum in the highest degree contradictory, equivocal and undignified, notwithstanding the completeness of its power and the smoke screen of flattery that conceals it.

Bourgeois society has in the course of its history displaced many political regimes and bureaucratic castes, without changing its social foundations. It has preserved itself against the restoration of feudal and guild relations by the superiority of its productive methods. The state power has been able either to co-operate with capitalist development, or put brakes on it. But in general the productive forces, upon a basis of private property and competition, have been working out their own destiny. In contrast to this, the property relations, which issued from the socialist revolution are indivisibly bound up with the new state as their repository. The predominance of socialist over petty bourgeois tendencies is guaranteed, not by the automatism of the economy—we are still far from that—

but by political measures taken by the dictatorship. The character of the economy as a whole thus depends upon the character of the state power.

A collapse of the Soviet regime would lead inevitably to the collapse of the planned economy, and thus to the abolition of state property. The bond of compulsion between the trusts and the factories within them would fall away. The more successful enterprises would succeed in coming out on the road of independence. They might convert or they might find some themselves into stock companies, other transitional form of property— one, for example, in which the workers should participate in the profits. The collective farms would disintegrate at the same time, and far more easily. The fall of the present bureaucratic dictatorship, if it were not replaced by a new socialist power, would thus mean a return to capitalist relations with a catastrophic decline of industry and culture.

But if a socialist government is still absolutely necessary for the preservation and development of the planned economy, the question is all the more important, upon whom the present Soviet government relies, and in what measure the socialist character of its policy is guaranteed. At the 11th Party Congress in March 1922, Lenin, in practically bidding farewell to the party, addressed these words to the commanding group: "History knows transformations of all sorts. To rely upon conviction, devotion and other excellent spiritual qualities— that is not to be taken seriously in politics". Being determines consciousness. During the last fifteen years, the government has changed its social composition even more deeply than its ideas. Since of all the strata of Soviet society the bureaucracy has best solved its own social problem, and is fully content with the existing situation, it has ceased to offer any subjective guarantee whatever of the socialist direction of its policy. It continues to preserve state property only to the extent that it fears the proletariat. This saving fear is nourished and supported by the illegal party of Bolshevik-Leninists, which is the most conscious expression of the socialist tendencies opposing that bourgeois reaction with which the Thermidorian bureaucracy is completely saturated. As a conscious political force the bureaucracy has betrayed the revolution. But a victorious revolution is fortunately not only a programme and a banner, not only political institutions, but also a system of social relations. To betray it is not enough. You have to overthrow it. The October Revolution has been betrayed by the ruling stratum, but not yet overthrown. It has a great power of resistance, coinciding with the established property relations, with the living force of the proletariat, the consciousness of its best elements, the impasse of world capitalism, and the inevitability of world revolution.

**3. The question of the character of the Soviet Union not yet decided by history**

In order better to understand the character of the present Soviet Union, let us make two different hypotheses about its future. Let us assume first that the Soviet bureaucracy is overthrown by a revolutionary party having all the attributes of the old Bolshevism, enriched moreover by the world experience of the recent period. Such a party would begin with the restoration of democracy in the trade unions and the Soviets. It would be able to, and would have to, restore freedom of Soviet parties. Together with the masses, and at their head, it would carry out a ruthless purgation of the state apparatus. It would abolish ranks and decorations, all kinds of privileges, and would limit inequality in the payment of labour to the life necessities of the economy and the state apparatus. It would give the youth free opportunity to think independently, learn, criticize and grow. It would introduce profound changes in the distribution of the national income in correspondence with the interests and will of the worker and peasant masses. But so far as concerns property relations, the new power would not have to resort to revolutionary measures. It would retain and further develop the experiment of planned economy. After the political revolution—that is, the deposing of the bureaucracy—the proletariat would have to introduce in the economy a series of very important reforms, but not another social revolution.

If—to adopt a second hypothesis—a bourgeois party were

to overthrow the ruling Soviet caste, it would find no small number of ready servants among the present bureaucrats, administrators, technicians, directors, party secretaries and privileged upper circles in general. A purgation of the state apparatus would, of course, be necessary in this case too. But a bourgeois restoration would probably have to clean out fewer people than a revolutionary party. The chief task of the new power would be to restore private property in the means of production. First of all, it would be necessary to create conditions for the development of strong farmers from the weak collective farms, and for converting the strong collectives into producers' cooperatives of the bourgeois type into agricultural stock companies. In the sphere of industry, denationalization would begin with the light industries and those producing food. The planning principle would be converted for the transitional period into a series of compromises between state power and individual "corporations"—potential proprietors, that is, among the Soviet captains of industry, the émigré former proprietors and foreign capitalists. Notwithstanding that the Soviet bureaucracy has gone far toward preparing a bourgeois restoration, the new regime would have to introduce in the matter of forms of property and methods of industry not a reform, but a social revolution.

Let us assume to take a third variant—that neither a revolutionary nor a counter-revolutionary party seizes power. The bureaucracy continues at the head of the state. Even under these conditions social relations will not jell. We cannot count upon the bureaucracy's peacefully and voluntarily renouncing itself in behalf of socialist equality. If at the present time, notwithstanding the too obvious inconveniences of such an operation, it has considered it possible to introduce ranks and decorations, it must inevitably in future stages seek supports for itself in property relations. One may argue that the big bureaucrat cares little what are the prevailing forms of property, provided only they guarantee him the necessary income. This argument ignores not only the instability of the bureaucrat's own rights, but also the question of his descendants. The new cult of the family has not fallen out of the clouds. Privileges have only half their worth, if they cannot be transmitted to one's children. But the right of testament is inseparable from the right of property. It is not enough to be the director of a trust; it is necessary to be a stockholder. The victory of the bureaucracy in this decisive sphere would mean its conversion into a new possessing class. On the other hand, the victory of the proletariat over the bureaucracy would insure a revival of the socialist revolution. The third variant consequently brings us back to the two first, with which, in the interests of clarity and simplicity, we set out.

* * *

To define the Soviet regime as transitional, or intermediate, means to abandon such finished social categories as *capitalism* (and therewith "state capitalism") and also *socialism.* But besides being completely inadequate in itself, such a definition is capable of producing the mistaken idea that from the present Soviet regime only a transition to socialism is possible. In reality a backslide to capitalism is wholly possible. A more complete definition will of necessity be complicated and ponderous.

The Soviet Union is a contradictory society halfway between capitalism and socialism, in which: (a) the productive forces are still far from adequate to give the state property a socialist character; (b) the tendency toward primitive accumulation created by want breaks out through innumerable pores of the planned economy; (c) norms of distribution preserving a bourgeois character lie at the basis of a new differentiation of society; (d) the economic growth, while slowly bettering the situation of the toilers, promotes a swift formation of privileged strata; (e) exploiting the social antagonisms, a bureaucracy has converted itself into an uncontrolled caste alien to socialism; (f) the social revolution, betrayed by the ruling party, still exists in property relations and in the consciousness of the toiling masses; (g) a further development of the accumulating contradictions can as well lead to socialism as back to capitalism; (h) on the road to capitalism the counterrevolution would have to break the resistance of the workers; (i) on the road to socialism the workers would have to overthrow the bureaucracy. In the last analysis, the question will be decided by a struggle of living social forces, both on the national and the world arena.

Doctrinaires will doubtless not be satisfied with this hypothetical definition. They would like categorical formulae: yes—yes, and no— no. Sociological problems would certainly be simpler, if social phenomena had always a finished character. There is nothing more dangerous, however, than to throw out of reality, for the sake of logical completeness, elements, which today violate your scheme and tomorrow may wholly overturn it. In our analysis, we have above all avoided doing violence to dynamic social formations, which have had no precedent and have no analogies. The scientific task, as well as the political, is not to give a finished definition to an unfinished process, but to follow all its stages, separate its progressive from its reactionary tendencies, expose their mutual relations, foresee possible variants of development, and find in this foresight a basis for action.

## *Chapter 10*

# THE SOVIET UNION IN THE MIRROR OF THE NEW CONSTITUTION

### 1. Work "According to Ability" and Personal Property

On the 11th of June 1936, the Central Executive Committee approved the draft of a new Soviet Constitution, which, according to Stalin's declaration, repeated daily by the whole press, will be "the most democratic in the world". To be sure, the manner in which the constitution was drawn up is enough to cause doubts as to this. Neither in the press nor at any meetings was a word ever spoken about this great reform. Moreover, as early as 1 March, 1936, Stalin declared to the American interviewer, Roy Howard: "We will doubtless adopt our new constitution at the end of this year." Thus Stalin knew with complete accuracy just when this new constitution, about which the people at that moment knew nothing at all, would be adopted. It is impossible not to conclude that "the most democratic constitution in the world" was worked out and introduced in a not quite perfectly democratic manner. To be sure, in June the draft was submitted to the "consideration" of the people of the Soviet Union. It would be vain, however, to seek in this whole sixth part of the globe one Communist who would dare to criticize a creation of the Central Committee, or one non-party citizen who would reject a proposal from the ruling party. The discussion reduced itself to sending resolutions of gratitude to Stalin for the "happy life". The content and style of these greetings had been thoroughly worked out under the old constitution.

The first section, entitled "Social Structure", concludes with these words: "In the Soviet Union, the principle of socialism is realized: *From each according to his abilities to each according to his work.*" This inwardly contradictory, not to say nonsensical, formula has entered, believe it or not, from speeches and journalistic articles into the carefully deliberated text of the fundamental state law. It bears witness not only to a complete lowering of theoretical level in the lawgivers, but also to the lie with which, as a mirror of the ruling stratum, the new constitution is imbued. It is not difficult to guess the origin of the new "principle". To characterize the Communist society, Marx employed the famous formula: "From each according to his abilities, to each according to his needs." The two parts of this formula are inseparable. "From each according to his abilities," in the Communist, not the capitalist, sense, means: Work has now ceased to be an obligation, and has become an individual need; society has no further use for any compulsion. Only sick and abnormal persons will refuse to work. Working "according to their ability"—that is, in accord with their physical and psychic powers, without any violence to themselves—the members of the commune will, thanks to a high technique, sufficiently fill up the stores of society so that society can generously endow each and all "according to their needs", without humiliating control. This two-sided but indivisible formula of communism thus assumes abundance, equality, an all-sided development of personality, and a high cultural discipline.

The Soviet state in all its relations is far closer to a backward capitalism than to communism. It cannot yet even think of endowing each "according to his needs". But for this very reason it cannot permit its citizens to work "according to their abilities". It finds itself obliged to keep in force the system of piecework payment, the principle of which may be expressed thus: "Get out of everybody as much as you can, and give him in exchange as little as possible". To be sure, nobody in the Soviet Union works above his "abilities" in the absolute sense of the word— that is, above his physical and psychic potential. But this is true also of capitalism. The most brutal as well as the most refined methods of exploitation run into limits set by nature. Even a mule under the whip works "according to his ability", but from that it does not follow that the whip is a social principle for mules. Wage labour does not cease even under the Soviet regime to wear the humiliating label of slavery. Payment "according to work"— in reality, payment to the advantage of "intellectual" at the expense of physical, and especially unskilled, work—is a source of injustice, oppression and compulsions for the majority, privileges and a "happy life" for the few.

Instead of frankly acknowledging that bourgeois norms of labour and distribution still prevail in the Soviet Union, the authors of the constitution have cut this integral Communist principle in two halves, postponed the second half to an indefinite future, declared the first half already realized, mechanically hitched on to it the capitalist norm of piecework payment, named the whole thing "principle of Socialism", and upon this falsification erected the structure of their constitution!

Of greatest practical significance in the economic sphere is undoubtedly Article X, which in contrast to most of the articles has quite clearly the task of guaranteeing, against invasion from the bureaucracy itself, the personal property of the citizens in their articles of domestic economy, consumption, comfort and daily life. With the exception of "domestic economy", property of this kind, purged of the psychology of greed and envy which clings to it, will not only be preserved under communism but will receive an unheard of development. It is subject to doubt, to be sure, whether a man of high culture would want to burden himself with a rubbish of luxuries. But he would not renounce any one of the conquests of comfort. The first task of communism is to guarantee the comforts of life to all. In the Soviet Union, however, the question of personal property still wears a petty bourgeois and not a communist aspect. The personal property of the peasants and the not well-off city people is the target of outrageous arbitrary acts on the part of the bureaucracy, which on its lower steps frequently assures by such means its own relative comfort. A growth of the prosperity of the country now makes it possible to renounce these seizures of personal property, and even impels the government to protect personal accumulations as a stimulus to increase the productivity of labour. At the same time—and this is of no small importance a protection by law of the hut, cow and home-furnishings of the peasant, worker or clerical worker, also legalizes the town house of the bureaucrat, his summer home, his automobile and all the other "objects of personal consumption and comfort", appropriated by him on the basis of the "socialist" principle: "From each according to his abilities, to each according to his work." The bureaucrat's automobile will certainly be protected by the new fundamental law more effectively than the peasant's wagon.

## 2. The Soviets and democracy

In the political sphere, the distinction of the new constitution from the old is its return from the Soviet system of election according to class and industrial groups, to the system of bourgeois democracy based upon the so-called "universal, equal and direct" vote of an atomized population. This is a matter, to put it briefly, of juridically liquidating the dictatorship of the proletariat. Where there are no capitalists, there is also no proletariat—say the creators of the new constitution—and consequently the state itself from being proletarian becomes national. This argument, with all its superficial lure, is either nineteen years late or many years in advance of its time. In expropriating the capitalists, the proletariat did actually enter upon its own liquidation as a class. But from liquidation in principle to actual dissolution in society is a road more prolonged, the longer the new state is compelled to carry out the rudimentary work of capitalism. The Soviet proletariat still exists as n class deeply distinct from the peasantry, the technical intelligentsia and the bureaucracy—and moreover as the sole class interested right up to the end in the victory of socialism. The new constitution wants to dissolve this class in "the nation" politically, long before it is economically dissolved in society.

To be sure, the reformers decided after some waverings to call the state, as formerly, *Soviet*. But that is only a crude political ruse dictated by the same considerations out of regard for which Napoleon's empire continued to be called a republic. Soviets in their essence are organs of class rule, and cannot be anything else. The democratically elected institutions of local self-administration are municipalities, dumas, zemstvos, anything you will, but not soviets. A general state Legislative Assembly on the basis of democratic formulas is a belated parliament (or rather its caricature), but by no means the highest organ of the Soviets. In trying to cover themselves with the historic authority of the Soviet system, the reformers merely show that the fundamentally new administration, which they are giving to, the state life dare not as yet come out under its own name.

Of itself, an equalization of the political rights of workers and peasants might not destroy the social nature of the state, if the influence of the proletariat upon the country were sufficiently guaranteed by the general state of economy and culture. The development of socialism certainly ought to proceed in that direction. But if the proletariat, while remaining a minority of the population, is really ceasing to need political ascendancy in order to guarantee a socialist course of social life, that means that the very need of state compulsion is reducing itself to nothing, giving place to cultural discipline.

The abolition of elective inequalities ought in that case to be preceded by a distinct and evident weakening of the compulsive functions of the state. Of this, however, there is not a word said either in the new constitution or, what is more important, in life.

To be sure, the new charter "guarantees" to the citizens the so-called "freedoms" of speech, press, assemblage and street processions. But each of these guarantees has the form either of a heavy muzzle or of shackles upon the hands and feet. Freedom of the press means a continuation of the fierce advance-censorship whose chains are held by the Secretariat of a Central Committee whom nobody has elected. Freedom of Byzantine flattery is thus, of course, fully "guaranteed". Meanwhile, the innumerable articles, speeches, and letters of Lenin, ending in his "testament", will continue under the new constitution to be locked up merely because they rub the new leaders the wrong way. That being the case with Lenin, it is unnecessary to speak about other authors. The crude and ignorant command of science, literature and art will be wholly preserved. "Freedom of assemblage" will mean, as formerly, the obligation of certain groups of the population to appear at meetings summoned by the authorities for the adoption of resolutions prepared in advance. Under the new constitution as under the old, hundreds of foreign communists, trusting in the Soviet "right of asylum", will remain in prisons and concentration camps for crimes against the dogma of infallibility. In the matter of "freedom", everything will remain as of old. Even the Soviet press does not try to sow any illusions about that. On the contrary, the chief goal of the new constitutional reform is declared to be a "further reinforcement of the dictatorship". Whose dictatorship, and over whom?

As we have already heard, the ground for political equality was prepared by the abolition of class contradictions. It is no longer to be a class but a "people's" dictatorship. But when the bearer of dictatorship becomes the people, freed from class contradictions that can only mean the dissolution of the dictatorship in a socialist society—and, above all, the liquidation of the bureaucracy. Thus teaches the Marxian doctrine. Perhaps it has been mistaken? But the very authors of the constitution refer, although very cautiously, to the program of the party written by Lenin. Here is what the program really says: ."... Deprivation of political rights, and al1 other limitations of freedom whatsoever, are necessary exclusively in the form of temporary measures.... In proportion as the objective possibility of the exploitation of man by man disappears, the necessity of these temporary measures will also disappear." Abandonment of the "deprivation of political rights" is thus inseparably bound with the abolition of "all limitations of freedom whatsoever". The arrival at a socialist society is characterized not only by the fact that the peasants are put on an equality with the workers, and that political rights are restored to the small percentage of citizens of bourgeois origin, but above all by the fact that real freedom is established for the whole 100 per cent of the population. With the liquidation of classes, not only the bureaucracy dies away, and not only the dictatorship, but the state itself. Let some imprudent person, however, try to utter even a hint in this direction: the G.P.U. will find adequate grounds in the new constitution to send him to one of the innumerable concentration camps. Classes are abolished. Of Soviets there remains only the name. But the bureaucracy is still there. The equality of the rights of workers and peasants means, in reality, an equal lack of rights before the bureaucracy.

No less significant is the introduction of the secret ballot. If you take it on faith that the new political equality corresponds to an achieved social equality, then there remains a puzzling question: In that case why must voting henceforth be protected by secrecy? Whom exactly does the population of a socialist country fear, and from whose attempts must it be defended? The old Soviet constitution saw in open voting, as in the limitation of elective rights, a weapon of the revolutionary class against bourgeois and petty bourgeois enemies. We cannot assume that now the secret ballot is being introduced for the convenience of a counterrevolutionary minority. It is a question, evidently, of defending the rights of the people. But who is feared by a socialist people, which have recently thrown off a tzar, a nobility and a bourgeoisie? The sycophants do not even give a thought to this question. Yet there is more in it than in all the writings of the Barbusses, the Louis Fischers, the Durantys, the Webbs, and the like of them.

In a capitalist society, the secret ballot is meant to defend the exploited from the terror of the exploiters. If the bourgeoisie finally adopted such a reform, obviously under pressure from the masses, it was only because it became interested in protecting its state at least partially from the demoralization introduced by itself. But in a socialist society there can be, it would seem, no terror of the exploiters. From whom is it necessary to defend the Soviet citizens? The answer is clear: from the bureaucracy. Stalin was frank enough to recognize this. To the question: Why are secret elections necessary? he answered verbatim: "Because *we* intend to give the Soviet people full freedom to vote for those whom they want to elect." Thus humanity learns from an authoritative source that today the "Soviet people" cannot yet vote for those whom they want to elect. It would be hasty to conclude from this that the new constitution will really tender them this opportunity in the future. Just now, however, we are occupied with another side of this problem. Who, exactly, is this "we" who can give or not give the people a free ballot? It is that same bureaucracy in whose name Stalin speaks and acts. This exposure of his applies to the ruling party exactly as it does to the state, for Stalin himself occupies the post of General Secretary of the Party with the help of a system which does not permit the members to elect those whom they want. The words "*we* intend to give the Soviet people" freedom of voting are incomparably more important than the old and new constitution taken together, for in this incautious phrase lies the actual constitution of the Soviet Union as it has been drawn up, not upon paper, but in the struggle of living forces.

### 3. Democracy and the party

The promise to give the Soviet people freedom to vote "for those whom they want to elect" is rather a poetic figure than a political formula. The Soviet people will have the right to choose their "representatives" only from among candidates whom the central and local leaders present to them under the flag of the party. To be sure, during the first period of the Soviet era the Bolshevik party also exercised a monopoly. But to identify these two phenomena would be to take appearance for reality. The prohibition of opposition parties was a temporary measure dictated by conditions of civil war, blockade, intervention and famine. The ruling party, representing in that period a genuine organization of the proletarian vanguard, was living a full-blooded inner life. A struggle of groups and factions to a certain degree replaced the struggle of parties. At present, when socialism has conquered "finally and irrevocably", the formation of factions is punished with concentration camp or firing squad. The prohibition of other parties, from being a temporary evil, has been erected into a principle. The right to occupy themselves with political questions has even been withdrawn from the Communist Youth, and that at the very moment of publication of the new constitution. Moreover, the citizens and citizenesses enjoy the franchise from the age of 18, but the age limit for Communist Youth existing until 1986 (23 years) is now wholly abolished. Politics is thus once for all declared the monopoly of an uncontrolled bureaucracy.

To a question from an American interviewer as to the role of the party in the new constitution, Stalin answered: "Once there are no classes, once the barriers between classes are disappearing ["there are no classes, the barriers between classes—which are not! —are disappearing"— L.T.], there remains only something in the nature of a not at all fundamental difference between various little strata of the socialist society. There can be no nourishing soil for the creation of parties struggling among themselves. Where there are not several classes, there cannot be several parties, for a party is part of a class. Every word is a mistake and some of them two! It appears from this that classes are homogeneous; that the boundaries of classes are outlined sharply and once for all; that the consciousness of a class strictly corresponds to its place in society. The Marxist teaching of the class nature of the party is thus turned into a caricature. The dynamic of political consciousness is excluded from the historical process in the interests of administrative order. In reality classes are heterogeneous; they are torn by inner antagonisms, and arrive at the solution of common problems no otherwise than through an inner struggle of tendencies, groups and parties. It is possible, with certain qualifications, to concede that "a party is part of a class". But since a class has many "parts"—some look forward and some back—one and the same class may create several parties. For the same reason one party may rest upon parts of different classes. An example of only one party corresponding to one class is not to be found in the whole course of political history—provided, of course, you do not take the police appearance for the reality.

In its social structure, the proletariat is the least heterogeneous class of capitalist society. Nevertheless, the presence of such "little strata" as the workers' aristocracy and the workers' bureaucracy is sufficient to give rise to opportunistic parties, which are converted by the course of things into one of the weapons of bourgeois domination. Whether from the standpoint of Stalinist sociology, the difference between the workers' aristocracy and the proletarian mass is "fundamental" or only "something in the nature of" matters not at all. It is from this difference that the necessity arose in its time for breaking with the Social Democracy and creating the Third International.

Even if in the Soviet society "there are no classes", nevertheless this society is at least incomparably more heterogeneous and complicated than the proletariat of capitalist countries, and consequently can furnish adequate nourishing soil for several parties. In making this imprudent excursion into the field of theory, Stalin proved a good deal more than he wanted to. From his reasonings it follows not only that there can be no *different* parties in the Soviet Union, but that there cannot even be *one* party. For where there are no classes, there is in general no place for politics. Nevertheless, from this law Stalin draws a "sociological" conclusion in favour of the party of which he is the General Secretary.

Bukharin tries to approach the problem from another side. In the Soviet Union, he says, the question where to go—whether back to capitalism or forward to socialism—is no longer subject to discussion. Therefore, "partisans of the hostile liquidated classes organized in parties cannot be permitted". To say nothing of the fact that in a country of triumphant socialism partisans of capitalism would be merely ludicrous Don Quixotes incapable of creating a party, the existing political differences are far from comprised in the alternative: to socialism or to capitalism. There are other questions: How go toward socialism, with what tempo, etc. The choice of the road is no less important than the choice of the goal. Who is going to choose the road? If the nourishing soil for political parties has really disappeared, then there is no reason to forbid them. On the contrary, it is time, in accordance with the party program, to abolish "all limitations of freedom whatsoever".

In trying to dispel the natural doubts of his American interviewer, Stalin advanced a new consideration: "Lists of nominees will be presented not only by the Communist Party, but also by all kinds of nonparty social organizations. And we have hundreds of them.... Each one of the little strata [of Soviet society] can have its special interests and reflect [express?] them through the existing innumerable social organizations." This sophism is no better than the others. The Soviet "social" organizations—trade union, co-operative, cultural, etc. do not in the least represent the interests of different "little strata", for they all have one and the same hierarchical structure. Even in those cases where they apparently represent mass organizations, as in the trade unions and co-operatives, the active role in them is played exclusively by representatives of the upper privileged groups, and the last word remains with the "party"—that is, the bureaucracy. The constitution merely refers the elector from Pontius to Pilate.

The mechanics of this are expressed with complete precision in the very text of the fundamental law. Article 126, which is the axis of the constitution as a political system, "guarantees the right" to all male and female citizens to group themselves in trade unions, co-operatives, youth, sport, defensive, cultural, technical and scientific organizations. As to the party—that is, the concentration of power—there it is not a question of the right of all, but of the privilege of the minority. .".. The most active and conscious [so considered, that is, from above—L.T.] citizens from the ranks of the working class and other strata of the toiling masses, are united in the Communist Party ... *which constitutes the guiding nucleus of all organizations, both social and governmental."* This astoundingly candid formula, introduced into the text of the constitution itself, reveals the whole fictitiousness of the political role of those "social organizations"—subordinate branches of the bureaucratic firm.

But if there is not to be a struggle of parties, perhaps the different factions within the one party can reveal themselves at these democratic elections? To the question of a French journalist as to the groupings of the ruling party, Molotov answered: "In the party ... attempts have been made to create special factions ... but it is already several years since the situation in this matter has fundamentally changed, and the Communist Party is actually a unit." This is proven best of all by the continuous purgations and the concentration camps. After the commentary of Molotov, the mechanics of democracy are completely clear. "What remains of the October Revolution," asks Victor Serge, "if every worker who permits himself to make a demand, or express a critical judgment, is subject to imprisonment? Oh, after that you can establish as many secret ballots as you please!" It is true: even Hitler did not infringe upon the secret ballot.

The reformers have dragged in theoretical arguments about the mutual relations of classes and parties by the hair. It is not a question of sociology, but of material interests. The ruling party, which enjoys a monopoly in the Soviet Union, is the political machine of the bureaucracy, which in reality has something to lose and nothing more to gain. It wishes to preserve the "nourishing soil" for itself alone.

* * *

In a country where the lava of revolution has not yet cooled, privileges burn those who possess them as a stolen gold watch burns an amateur thief. The ruling Soviet stratum has learned to fear the masses with a perfectly bourgeois fear. Stalin gives the growing special privileges of the upper circles a "theoretical" justification with the help of the Communist International, and defends the Soviet aristocracy from popular discontent with the help of concentration camps. In order that this mechanism should keep on working, Stalin is compelled from time to time to take the side of "the people" against the bureaucracy—of course, with its tacit consent. He finds it useful to resort to the secret ballot in order at least partially to purge the state apparatus of the corruptions, which are devouring it.

As early as 1928, Rakovsky wrote, discussing a number of

cases of bureaucratic gangsterism which were coming to the surface: "The most characteristic and most dangerous thing in this spreading wave of scandals is the passiveness of the masses, the Communist masses even more than the nonparty ... Owing to fear of those in power, or simply owing to political indifference, they have passed these things by without protest, or have limited themselves to mere grumbling." During the eight years, which have passed since that time, the situation has become incomparably worse. The decay of the political machine, exposing itself at every step, has begun to threaten the very existence of the state no longer now as an instrument for the socialist transformation of society, but as a source of power, income and privileges to the ruling stratum. Stalin was compelled to give a glimpse of this motive to the reform. "We have not a few institutions," he told Roy Howard, "which work badly.... The secret ballot in the Soviet Union will be a whip in the hands of the population against badly working organs of power." A remarkable confession! After the bureaucracy has created a socialist society with its own hands, it feels the need ... of a whip! That is one of the motives of the constitutional reform. There is another no less important.

In abolishing the soviets, the new constitution dissolves the workers in the general mass of the population. Politically the soviets, to be sure, long ago lost their significance. But with the growth of new social antagonisms and the awakening of a new generation, they might again come to life. Most of all, of course, are to be feared the city soviets with the increasing participation of fresh and demanding communist youth. In the cities the contrast between luxury and want is too clear to the eyes. The first concern of the Soviet aristocracy is to get rid of worker and Red Army soviets. With the discontent of the scattered rural population it is much easier to deal. The collectivized peasants can even with some success be used against the city workers. This is not the first time that a bureaucratic reaction has relied upon the country in its struggle against the city.

Whatever in the new constitution is principled and significant, and really elevates it high above the most democratic constitutions of bourgeois countries, is merely a watered-down paraphrase of the fundamental documents of the October Revolution. Whatever has to do with estimating the economic conquests, distorts reality with false perspective and braggadocio. And finally whatever concerns freedom and democracy is saturated through and through with the spirit of usurpation and cynicism.

Representing, as it does, an immense step back from socialist to bourgeois principles, the new constitution, cut and sewed to the measure of the ruling group, follows the same historic course as the abandonment of world revolution in favor of the League of Nations, the restoration of the bourgeois family, the substitution of the standing army for the militia, the resurrection of ranks and decorations, and the growth of inequality. By juridically reinforcing the absolutism of an "extra-class" bureaucracy, the new constitution creates the political premises for the birth of a new possessing class.

## Chapter 11

# WHITHER THE SOVIET UNION?

### 1. Bonapartism as a regime of crisis

The question we previously raised in the name of the reader: "How could the ruling clique, with its innumerable mistakes, concentrate unlimited power in its hands?"—or, in other words: "How explain the contradiction between the intellectual poverty of the Thermidorians and their material might?"—now permits a more concrete and categorical answer. The Soviet society is not harmonious. What is a sin for one class or stratum is a virtue for another. From the point of view of socialist forms of society, the policy of the bureaucracy is striking in its contradictions and inconsistencies. But the same policy appears very consistent from the standpoint of strengthening the power of the new commanding stratum.

The state support of the kulak (1923–28) contained a mortal danger for the socialist future. But then, with the help of the petty bourgeoisie the bureaucracy succeeded in binding the proletarian vanguard hand and foot, and suppressing the Bolshevik Opposition. This "mistake" from the point of view of socialism was a pure gain from the point of view of the bureaucracy. When the kulak began directly to threaten the bureaucracy itself, it turned its weapons against the kulak. The panic of aggression against the kulak, spreading also to the middle peasant, was no less costly to the economy than a foreign invasion. But the bureaucracy had defended its positions. Having barely succeeded in exterminating its former ally, it began with all its power to develop a new aristocracy. Thus undermining socialism? Of course but at the same time strengthening the commanding caste. The Soviet bureaucracy is like all ruling classes in that it is ready to shut its eyes to the crudest mistakes of its leaders in the sphere of general politics, provided in return they show an unconditional fidelity in the defence of its privileges. The more alarmed becomes the mood of the new lords of the situation, the higher the value they set upon ruthlessness against the least threat to their so justly earned rights. It is from this point of view that the caste of parvenus selects its leaders. Therein lies the secret of Stalin's success.

The growth of power and independence in a bureaucracy, however, is not unlimited. There are historical factors stronger than marshals, and even than general secretaries. A rationalization of economy is unthinkable without accurate accounts. Accounts are irreconciliable with the caprices of a bureaucracy. Concern for the restoration of a stable ruble, which means a ruble independent of the "leaders", is imposed upon the bureaucracy by the fact that their autocratic rule is coming into greater and greater contradiction with the development of the productive forces of the country —just as absolute monarchy became in its time irreconcilable with the development of the bourgeois market. Money accounting, however, cannot fail to give a more open character to the struggle of the different strata for the distribution of the national income. The question of the wage-scale, almost a matter of indifference during the epoch of the food-card system, is now decisive for the workers, and with it the question of the trade unions. The designation of trade union officials from above is destined to meet more and more resistance. More than that, under piecework payment the worker is directly interested in a correct ordering of the factory management. The Stakhanovists are complaining more and more loudly of the faults of organization in production. Bureaucratic nepotism in the matter of appointing directors, engineers, etc., is becoming more and more intolerable. The co-operatives and the state trade are coming much more than formerly into dependence upon the buyer. The collective farms and the individual collective farmers are learning to translate their dealings with the state into the language of figures. They are growing unwilling to endure submissively the naming from above of leaders whose sole merit is frequently their closeness to the local bureaucratic clique. And, finally, the ruble promises to cast a light into that most mysterious region: the legal and illegal incomes of the bureaucracy. Thus, in a politically strangled country, money circulation becomes an important lever for the mobilization of oppositional forces, and foretells the beginning of the end of "enlightened" absolutism.

While the growth of industry and the bringing of agriculture into the sphere of state planning vastly complicates the tasks of leadership, bringing to the front the problem of quality, bureaucratism destroys the creative initiative and the feeling of responsibility without which there is not, and cannot be, qualitative progress. The ulcers of bureaucratism are perhaps not 80 obvious in the big industries, but they are devouring, together with the co-operatives' the light and food-producing industries, the collective farms, the small local industries—that is, all those branches of economy which stand nearest to the people.

The progressive role of the Soviet bureaucracy coincides with the period devoted to introducing into the Soviet Union the most important elements of capitalist technique.

The rough work of borrowing, imitating, transplanting and grafting, was accomplished on the bases laid down by the revolution. There was, thus far, no question of any new word in the sphere of technique, science or art. It is possible to build gigantic factories according to a ready-made Western pattern by bureaucratic command—although, to be sure, at triple the normal cost. But the farther you go, the more the economy runs into the problem of quality, which slips out of the hands of a bureaucracy like a shadow. The Soviet products are as though branded with the gray label of indifference. Under a nationalized economy, *quality* demands a democracy of producers and consumers, freedom of criticism and initiative —conditions incompatible with a totalitarian regime of fear, lies and flattery.

Behind the question of quality stands a more complicated

and grandiose problem, which may be comprised in the concept of *independent, technical* and *cultural creation*. The ancient philosopher said that strife is the father of all things. No new values can be created where a free conflict of ideas is impossible. To be sure, a revolutionary dictatorship means by its very essence strict limitations of freedom. But for that very reason epochs of revolution have never been directly favourable to cultural creation: they have only cleared the arena for it. The dictatorship of the proletariat opens a wider scope to human genius the more it ceases to be a dictatorship. The socialist culture will flourish only in proportion to the dying away of the state. In that simple and unshakable historic law is contained the death sentence of the present political regime in the Soviet Union. Soviet democracy is not the demand of an abstract policy, still less an abstract moral. It has become a life-and-death need of the country.

If the new state had no other interests than the interests of society, the dying away of the function of compulsion would gradually acquire a painless character. But the state is not pure spirit. Specific functions have created specific organs. The bureaucracy taken as a whole is concerned not so much with its function as with the tribute which this function brings in. The commanding caste tries to strengthen and perpetuate the organs of compulsion. To make sure of its power and income, it spares nothing and nobody. The more the course of development goes against it, the more ruthless it becomes toward the advanced elements of the population. Like the Catholic Church it has put forward the dogma of infallibility in the period of its decline, but it has raised it to a height of which the Roman pope never dreamed.

The increasingly insistent deification of Stalin is, with all its elements of caricature, a necessary element of the regime. The bureaucracy has need of an inviolable superarbiter, a first consul if not an emperor, and it raises upon its shoulders him who best responds to its claim for lordship. That "strength of character" of the leader, which so enraptures the literary dilettantes of the West, is in reality the sum total of the collective pressure of a caste, which will stop at nothing in defence of its position. Each one of them at his post is thinking: *l'etat c'est moi.* In Stalin each one easily finds himself. But Stalin also finds in each one a small part of his own spirit. Stalin is the personification of the bureaucracy. That is the substance of his political personality.

Caesarism, or its bourgeois form, Bonapartism, enters the scene in those moments of history when the sharp struggle of two camps raises the state power, so to speak, above the nation, and guarantees it, in appearance, a complete independence of classes in reality, only the freedom necessary for a defence of the privileged. The Stalin regime, rising above a politically atomized society, resting upon a police and officers' corps, and allowing of no control whatever, is obviously a variation of Bonapartism—a Bonapartism of a new type not before seen in history.

Caesarism arose upon the basis of a slave society shaken by inward strife. Bonapartism is one of the political weapons of the capitalist regime in its critical period. Stalinism is a variety of the same system, but upon the basis of a workers' state torn by the antagonism between an organized and armed Soviet aristocracy and the unarmed toiling masses.

As history testifies, Bonapartism gets along admirably with a universal, and even a secret, ballot. The democratic ritual of Bonapartism is the *plebiscite.* From time to time, the question is presented to the citizens: *for* or *against* the leader? And the voter feels the barrel of a revolver between his shoulders. Since the time of Napoleon III, who now seems a provincial dilettante, this technique has received an extraordinary development. The new Soviet constitution which establishes *Bonapartism on a plebiscite basis* is the veritable crown of the system.

In the last analysis, Soviet Bonapartism owes its birth to the belatedness of the world revolution. But in the capitalist countries the same cause gave rise to fascism. We thus arrive at the conclusion, unexpected at first glance, but in reality inevitable, that the crushing of Soviet democracy by an all-powerful bureaucracy and the extermination of bourgeois democracy by fascism were produced by one and the same cause: the dilatoriness of the world proletariat in solving the problems set for it by history. Stalinism and fascism, in spite of a deep difference in social foundations, are symmetrical phenomena. In many of their features they show a deadly similarity. A victorious revolutionary movement in Europe would immediately shake not only fascism, but Soviet Bonapartism. In turning its back to the international revolution, the Stalinist bureaucracy was, from its own point of view, right. It was merely obeying the voice of self-preservation.

### 2. The struggle of the bureaucracy with "the class enemy"

From the first days of the Soviet regime the counterweight to bureaucratism was the party. If the bureaucracy managed the state, still the party controlled the bureaucracy. Keenly vigilant lest inequality transcend the limits of what was necessary, the party was always in a state of open or disguised struggle with the bureaucracy. The historic role of Stalin's faction was to destroy this duplication, subjecting the party to its own officialdom and merging the latter in the officialdom of the state. Thus was created the present totalitarian regime. It was his doing the bureaucracy this not unimportant service that guaranteed Stalin's victory.

During the first ten years of its struggle, the Left Opposition did not abandon the programme of ideological conquest of the party for that of conquest of power against the party. Its slogan was: reform, not revolution. The bureaucracy, however, even in those times, was ready for any revolution in order to defend itself against a democratic reform. In 1927, when the struggle reached an especially bitter stage, Stalin declared at a session of the Central Committee, addressing himself to the Opposition: "Those cadres can be removed only by civil war!" What was a threat in Stalin's words became, thanks to a series of defeats of the European proletariat, a historic fact. The road of reform was turned into a road of revolution.

The continual purgations of the party and the Soviet organizations have the object of preventing the discontent of the masses from finding a coherent political expression. But repressions do not kill thought; they merely drive it underground. Wide circles of communists as well as nonparty citizens, keep up two systems of thought, one official and one secret. Spying and talebearing are corroding social relations throughout. The bureaucracy unfailingly represents its enemies as the enemies of socialism. With the help of judicial forgeries, which have become the normal thing, it imputes to them any crime it finds convenient. Under threat of the firing squad, it extracts confessions dictated by itself from the weak, and then makes these confessions the basis for accusations against the more sturdy.

"It would be unpardonably stupid and criminal," teaches *Pravda* of 5 June, 1936,—commenting upon the "most democratic constitution in the world,"—notwithstanding the abolition of classes to assume that "class forces hostile to socialism are reconciled to their defeat.... The struggle goes on." Who are these "hostile class forces"? *Pravda* answers: "Relics of counterrevolutionary groups, White Guards of all colors, *especially* the Trotskyist-Zinovievist." After the inevitable reference to "spy work, conspiracies and terrorist activity" (by Trotskyist-Zinovievists!), the organ of Stalin gives this promise: "We will in the future too beat down and exterminate with a firm hand the enemies of the people, the Trotskyist reptiles and furies, no matter how skillfully they disguise themselves." Such threats, daily repeated in the Soviet press, are but accompaniments to the work of the G.P.U. A certain Petrov, member of the party since 1918, participant in the civil war, subsequently a Soviet agricultural expert and member of the Right Opposition, who escaped from exile in 1936, writing in a liberal émigré paper, now characterizes the so-called Trotskyists as follows: "The lefts? Psychologically, the last revolutionists, genuine and fervent. No gray bargaining, no compromises. Most admirable people. But idiotic ideas ... a world conflagration and such like raving." We will leave aside the question of their "ideas". This moral and political appraisal of the left from their enemy on the right, speaks for itself. It is these "last revolutionists, genuine, fervent", that the colonels and generals of the G.P.U. are arraigning for ... counterrevolutionary activity in the interests of imperialism.

The hysteria of the bureaucratic hatred against the Bolshevik Opposition acquires an especially sharp political meaning in connection with the removal of limitations upon people of bourgeois origin. The conciliatory decrees in relation to their employment, work and education are based upon the consideration that the resistance of the former ruling classes dies away in proportion as the stability of the new order becomes clear. "There is now no need of these limitations," explained Molotov at a session of the Central Executive Committee in January 1936. At the same moment, however, it was revealed that the most malicious "class enemies" are recruited from among those who struggled throughout their whole lives for socialism, starting with the closest co-workers of Lenin, such as Zinoviev and Kamenev. In distinction from the bourgeoisie, the "Trotskyists", according to *Pravda,* become more desperate, "the more clearly the features of a nonclass socialist society are drawn". The delirious character of this philosophy, arising from the necessity of covering up new relations with old formulas, cannot, of course, conceal a real shift in the social antagonisms. On the one hand, the creation of a caste of "gentry" opens broad opportunities for careers to the more ambitious offspring of the bourgeoisie: there is no risk in giving them equal rights. On the other hand, the same phenomenon produces a sharp and extremely dangerous discontent in the masses, and especially the worker youths. Hence, the exterminating campaign against "furies and reptiles". The sword of the dictatorship, which used to fell those who wanted to restore the privileges of the bourgeoisie, is now directed against those who revolt against the privileges of the bureaucracy. The blows fall not upon the class enemies of the proletariat, but upon the proletarian vanguard. Corresponding to this basic change in its functions, the political police, formerly recruited from especially devoted and self-sacrificing Bolsheviks, are now composed of the most demoralized part of the bureaucracy.

In their persecution of revolutionists, the Thermidorians

pour out all their hatred upon those who remind them of the past, and make them dread the future. The prisons, the remote corners of Siberia and Central Asia, the fast multiplying concentration camps, contain the flower of the Bolshevik Party, the most sturdy and true. Even in the solitary confinement prisons of Siberia the Oppositionists are still persecuted with searches, postal blockades and hunger. In exile wives are forcibly separated from their husbands, with one sole purpose: to break their resistance and extract a recantation. But even those who recant are not saved. At the first suspicion or hint from some informer against them, they are subjected to redoubled punishment. Help given to exiles even by their relatives is prosecuted as a crime. Mutual aid is punished as a conspiracy.

The sole means of self-defence in these conditions is the hunger strike. The G.P.U. answers this with forcible feeding or with an offer of freedom to die. During these years hundreds of Oppositionists, both Russian and foreign, have been shot, or have died of hunger strikes, or have resorted to suicide. Within the last twelve years, the authorities have scores of times announced to the world the final rooting out of the opposition. But during the "purgations" in the last month of 1935 and the first half of 1936, hundreds of thousands of members of the part! were again expelled, among them several tens of thousands of "Trotskyists". The most active were immediately arrested and thrown into prisons and concentration camps. As to the rest, Stalin, through *Pravda*, openly advised the local organs not to give them work. In a country where the sole employer is the state, this means death by slow starvation. The old principle: who does not work shall not eat, has been replaced with a new one: who does not obey shall not eat. Exactly how many Bolsheviks have been expelled, arrested, exiled, exterminated, since 1923, when the era of Bonapartism opened, we shall find out when we go through the archives of Stalin's political police. How many of them remain in the underground will become known when the shipwreck of the bureaucracy begins.

How much significance can twenty or thirty thousand

Oppositionists have for a party of two million? On such a question a mere juxtaposition of figures means nothing. Ten revolutionists in a regiment are enough to bring it over, in a red-hot political atmosphere, to the side of the people. Not for nothing does the staff mortally fear tiny underground circles, or even single individuals. This reactionary general-staff fear, which imbues the Stalinist bureaucracy throughout, explains the mad character of its persecutions and its poisonous slanders.

Victor Serge, who lived through all the stages of the repression in the Soviet Union, has brought startling news to western Europe from those who are undergoing torture for their loyalty to the revolution and hostility to its gravediggers. "I exaggerate nothing," he writes. "I weigh every word. I can back up every one of my statements with tragic proof and with names. Among this mass of martyrs and Protestants, for the most part silent, one heroic minority is nearer to me than all the others, precious for its energy, its penetration, its stoicism, its devotion to the Bolshevism of the great epoch. Thousands of these Communists of the first hour, comrades of Lenin and Trotsky, builders of the Soviet Republic when Soviets still existed, are opposing the principles of socialism to the inner degeneration of the regime, are defending as best they can (and all they can is to agree to all possible sacrifices) the rights of the working class.... I bring you news of those who are locked up there. They will hold out, whatever is necessary, to the end. Even if they do not live to see a new revolutionary dawn ... the revolutionists of the West can count upon them. The flame will be kept burning, even if only in prisons. In the same way they are counting upon you. You must—we must—defend them in order to defend workers' democracy in the world, in order to revive the liberating image of the dictatorship of the proletariat, and some day restore to the Soviet Union its moral greatness and the confidence of the workers."

### 3. The inevitability of a new revolution

Discussing the dying away of the state, Lenin wrote that

the custom of observing the rules of social life can lose all need of compulsion *if* there is nothing which provokes indignation, protest and revolt, and thus creates the necessity for repression." The essence of the matter lies in that *if*. The present regime in the Soviet Union provokes protest at every step, a protest the more burning in that it is repressed. The bureaucracy is not only a machine of compulsion but also a constant source of provocation. The very existence of a greedy, lying and cynical caste of rulers inevitably creates a hidden indignation. The improvement of the material situation of the workers does not reconcile them with the authorities; on the contrary, by increasing their self-respect and freeing their thought for general problems of politics, it prepares the way for an open conflict with the bureaucracy.

The unremovable "leaders" love to issue statements about the necessity of "studying", of "acquiring technique", "cultural self-education", and other admirable things. But the ruling layer itself is ignorant and little cultured; it studies nothing seriously, is disloyal and rude in social contacts. Its pretension to patronize all spheres of social life, to take command not only of co-operative shops but of musical compositions, is the more intolerable for that. The Soviet population cannot rise to a higher level of culture without freeing itself from this humiliating subjection to a caste of usurpers.

Will the bureaucrat devour the workers' state, or will the working class clean up the bureaucrat? Thus stands the question upon whose decision hangs the fate of the Soviet Union. The vast majority of the Soviet workers are even now hostile to the bureaucracy. The peasant masses hate them with their healthy plebian hatred. If in contrast to the peasants the workers have almost never come out on the road of open struggle, thus condemning the protesting villages to confusion and impotence, this is not only because of the repressions. The workers fear lest, in throwing out the bureaucracy, they will open the way for a capitalist restoration. The mutual relations between state and class are much more complicated than they are represented by the vulgar "democrats". Without a planned economy the Soviet Union would be thrown back for decades. In that sense the bureaucracy continues to fulfill a necessary function. But it fulfills it in such a way as to prepare an explosion of the whole system, which may completely sweep out the results of the revolution. The workers are realists. Without deceiving themselves with regard to the ruling caste at least with regard to its lower tiers, which stand near to them—they see in it the watchman for the time being of a certain part of their own conquests. They will inevitably drive out the dishonest, impudent and unreliable watchman as soon as they see another possibility. For this it is necessary that in the West or the East another revolutionary dawn arise.

The cessation of visible political struggle is portrayed by the friends and agents of the Kremlin as a "stabilization" of the regime. In reality it signalizes only a temporary stabilization of the bureaucracy. With popular discontent driven deep, the younger generation feels with special pain the yoke of this "enlightened absolutism" in which there is so much more absolutism than enlightenment. The increasingly ominous vigilance of the bureaucracy against any ray of living thought, and the unbearable tensity of the hymns of praise addressed to a blessed providence in the person of the "leader", testify alike to a growing separation between the state and society. They testify to a steady intensifying of inner contradictions, a pressure against the walls of the state, which seeks a way out and must inevitably find one.

In a true appraisal of the situation, the not infrequent terrorist acts against representatives of power have a very high significance. The most notorious of these was the murder of Kirov, a clever and unscrupulous Leningrad dictator, a typical representative of his corporation. In themselves, terrorist acts are least of all capable of overthrowing a Bonapartist oligarchy. Although the individual bureaucrat dreads the revolver. The bureaucracy as a whole is able to exploit an act of terror for the justification of its own violences, and incidentally to implicate in the murder its own political enemies (the affair of Zinoviev, Kamenev and the others). *[Translator's note: The reference here is to the January 1935 trial and not the August 1936 trial, the lines having been written prior to the latter.]* Individual terror is a weapon of impatient or despairing individuals, belonging most frequently to the younger generation of the bureaucracy itself. But, as was the case in tzarist times, political murders are unmistakable symptoms of a stormy atmosphere, and foretell the beginning of an open political crisis.

In introducing the new constitution, the bureaucracy shows that it feels this danger and is taking preventive measures. However, it has happened more than once that a bureaucratic dictatorship, seeking salvation in "liberal" reforms, has only weakened itself. While exposing Bonapartism, the new constitution creates at the same time a semi-legal cover for the struggle against it. The rivalry of bureaucratic cliques at the elections may become the beginning of a broader political struggle. The whip against "badly working organs of power" may be turned into a whip against Bonapartism. All indications agree that the further course of development must inevitably lead to a clash between the culturally developed forces of the people and the bureaucratic oligarchy. There is no peaceful outcome for this crisis. No devil ever yet voluntarily cut off his own claws. The Soviet bureaucracy will not give up its positions without a fight. The development leads obviously to the road of revolution.

With energetic pressure from the popular mass, and the disintegration inevitable in such circumstances of the government apparatus, the resistance of those in power may prove much weaker than now appears. But as to this only hypotheses are possible. In any case, the bureaucracy can be removed only by a revolutionary force. And, as always, there will be fewer victims the more bold and decisive is the attack. To prepare this and stand at the head of the masses in a favorable historic situation—that is the task of the Soviet section of the Fourth International. Today it is still weak and driven underground. But the illegal existence of a party is not nonexistence. It is only a difficult form of existence. Repressions can prove fully effective against a class that is disappearing from the scene this was fully proven by the revolutionary dictatorship of 1917 to 1923 —but violences against a revolutionary vanguard cannot save a caste, which, if the Soviet Union is destined in general to further development, has outlived itself.

The revolution, which the bureaucracy is preparing against itself, will not be social, like the October Revolution of 1917. It is not a question this time of changing the economic foundations of society, of replacing certain forms of property with other forms. History has known elsewhere not only social revolutions, which substituted the bourgeois for the feudal regime, but also political revolutions, which, without destroying the economic foundations of society, swept out an old ruling upper crust (1880 and 1848 in France, February 1917 in Russia, etc.). The overthrow of the Bonapartist caste will, of course, have deep social consequences, but in itself it will be confined within the limits of political revolution.

This is the first time in history that a state resulting from a workers' revolution has existed. The stages through which it must go are nowhere written down. It is true that the theoreticians and creators of the Soviet Union hoped that the completely transparent and flexible Soviet system would permit the state peacefully to transform itself, dissolve, and die away, in correspondence with the stages of the economic and cultural evolution of society. Here again, however, life proved more complicated than theory anticipated. The proletariat of a backward country was fated to accomplish the first socialist revolution. For this historic privilege, it must, according to all evidences, pay with a second supplementary revolution —against bureaucratic absolutism. The programme of the new revolution depends to a great extent upon the moment when it breaks out, upon the level, which the country has then attained, and to a great degree upon the international situation. The fundamental elements of the programme are already clear, and have been given throughout the course of this book as an objective inference from an analysis of the contradictions of the Soviet regime.

It is not a question of substituting one ruling clique for another, but of changing the very methods of administering the economy and guiding the culture of the country.

Bureaucratic autocracy must give place to Soviet democracy. A restoration of the right of criticism, and a genuine freedom of elections, are necessary conditions for the further development of the country. This assumes a revival of freedom of Soviet parties, beginning with the party of Bolsheviks, and a resurrection of the trade unions. The bringing of democracy into industry means a radical revision of plans in the interests of the toilers. Free discussion of economic problems will decrease the overhead expense of bureaucratic mistakes and zigzags. Expensive playthings palaces of the Soviets, new theaters, show-off subways—will be crowded out in favour of workers' dwellings. "Bourgeois norms of distribution" will be confined within the limits of strict necessity, and, in step with the growth of social wealth, will give way to socialist equality. Ranks will be immediately abolished. The tinsel of decorations will go into the melting pot. The youth will receive the opportunity to breathe freely, criticize, make mistakes, and grow up. Science and art will be freed of their chains. And, finally, foreign policy will return to the traditions of revolutionary internationalism.

More than ever the fate of the October Revolution is bound now with the fate of Europe and of the whole world. The problems of the Soviet Union are now being decided on the Spanish peninsula, in France, in Belgium. At the moment when this book appears the situation will be incomparably more clear than today, when civil war is in progress under the walls of Madrid. If the Soviet bureaucracy succeeds, with its treacherous policy of "people's fronts", in insuring the victory of reaction in Spain and France—and the Communist International is doing all it can in that direction—the Soviet Union will find itself on the edge of ruin. A bourgeois counter-revolution rather than an insurrection of the workers against the bureaucracy will be on the order of the day. If, in spite of the united sabotage of reformists and "Communist" leaders, the proletariat of Western Europe finds the road to power, a new chapter will open in the history of the Soviet Union. The first victory of a revolution in Europe would pass like an electric shock through the Soviet masses, straighten them up, raise their spirit of independence, awaken the traditions of 1905 and 1917, undermine the position of the Bonapartist bureaucracy, and acquire for the Fourth International no less significance than the October Revolution possessed for the Third. Only in that way can the first Workers' State be saved for the socialist future.

## *Appendix*

# "SOCIALISM IN ONE COUNTRY"

THE REACTIONARY TENDENCIES of autarchy are a defense reflex of senile capitalism to the task with which history confronts it, that of freeing its economy from the fetters of private property and the national state, and organizing it in a planned manner throughout the Earth.

In Lenin's "Declaration of the Rights of the Toiling and Exploited People"—presented by the Soviet of People's Commissars for the approval of the Constituent Assembly during its brief hours of life—the "fundamental task" of the new regime was thus defined: "The establishment of a socialist organization of society and the victory of socialism in all countries". The international character of the revolution was thus written into the basic document of the new regime. No one at that time would have dared present the problem otherwise! In April 1924, three months after the death of Lenin, Stalin wrote, his brochure of compilations called *The Foundations of Leninism*:

> "For the overthrow of the bourgeoisie, the efforts of one country are enough—to this the history of our own revolution testifies. For the final victory of socialism, for the organization of socialist production, the efforts of one country, especially a peasant country like ours, are not enough—for this we must have the efforts of the proletarians of several advanced countries."

These lines need no comment. The edition in which they were printed, however, has been withdrawn from circulation.

The large-scale defeats of the European proletariat, and the first very modest economic successes of the Soviet Union, suggested to Stalin, in the autumn of 1924, the idea that the historic mission of the Soviet bureaucracy was to build socialism in a single country. Around this question there developed a discussion, which to many superficial minds seemed academic or scholastic, but which in reality reflected the incipient degeneration of the Third International and prepared the way for the Fourth.

Petrov, the former communist, now a White émigré, whom we have already quoted [in previous chapters of the book], tells from his own memories how fiercely the younger generation of administrators opposed the doctrine of the dependence of the Soviet Union upon the international revolution. "How is it possible that we in our own country can not contrive to build a happy life?" If Marx has it otherwise, that means that "we are no Marxists, we are Russian Bolsheviks—that's what!" To these recollections of disputes in the middle of the twenties, Petrov adds: "Today I can not but think that the theory of building socialism in one country was not a mere Stalinist invention." Completely true! It expressed unmistakably the mood of the bureaucracy. When speaking of the victory of socialism, they meant their own victory.

In justifying his break with the Marxist tradition of internationalism, Stalin was incautious enough to remark that Marx and Engels were not unacquainted with the law of uneven development of capitalism supposedly discovered by Lenin. In a catalogue of intellectual curiosities, that remark ought really to occupy a foremost place. Unevenness of development permeates the whole history of mankind, and especially the history of capitalism. A young Russian historian and economist, Solntez, a man of exceptional gifts and moral qualities tortured to death in the prisons of the Soviet bureaucracy for membership in the Left Opposition, offered in 1926 a superlative theoretical study of the law of uneven development in Marx. It could not, of course, be printed in the Soviet Union. Also under the ban, although for reasons of an opposite nature, is the work of the long dead and forgotten German Social-Democrat, Vollmar, who as early as 1878 developed the perspective of an "isolated socialist state"—

not for Russia, but for Germany— containing references to this "law" of uneven development which is supposed to have been unknown until Lenin.

> "Socialism unconditionally assumes economically developed relations," wrote Georg Vollmar, "and if the question were limited to them alone, socialism ought to be strongest where the economic development is highest. But the thing does not stand that way at all. England is undoubtedly the most developed country economically, yet we see that socialism plays there a very secondary role, while in economically less developed Germany socialism has already such power that the entire old society no longer feels stable."

Referring to the multitude of historic factors, which determine the course of events, Vollmar continued:

> "It is clear that with an interrelation of such innumerable forces the development of any general human movement could not, and can not, be identical in the matter of time and form even in two countries, to say nothing of all.... Socialism obeys the same law.... The assumption of a simultaneous victory of socialism in all cultured countries is absolutely ruled out, as is also, and for the same reasons, the assumption that all the rest of the civilized states will immediately and inevitably imitate the example of a socialistically organized state...."
>
> Thus—Vollmar concludes—"we arrive at the isolated socialist state, concerning which I trust I have proven that it is, although not the only possibility, nevertheless the greatest possibility."

In this work, written when Lenin was eight years old, the law of uneven development receives a far more correct interpretation that that to be found among the Soviet epigones, beginning with the autumn of 1924. We must remark, incidentally, that in this part of his investigation Vollmar, a very second-rate theoretician, is only paraphrasing the thoughts of Engels —to whom, we are told, the law of unevenness of capitalist development remained "unknown".

"The isolated socialist state" has long ceased to be a hypothesis, and became a fact—in Russia to be sure, not in Germany. But this very fact of isolation is also a precise expression of the relative strength of world capitalism, the relative weakness of socialism. From an isolated "socialist" state to a socialist society once for all done with the state remains a long historic road, and this road exactly coincides with the road of international revolution.

Beatrice and Sidney Webb on their part assure us that Marx and Engels did not believe in the possibility of building an isolated socialist society only because neither of them "had ever dreamt" of such a powerful weapon as the monopoly of foreign trade. One can hardly read these lines from the aged authors without embarrassment. The taking over by the state of commercial banks and companies, railroads, mercantile marine, is as necessary a measure of the socialist revolution as the nationalization of the means of production, including the means employed in the export branches of industry. The monopoly of foreign trade is nothing but a concentration in the hands of the state of the material instruments of export and import. To say that Marx and Engels "never dreamt" of the monopoly of foreign trade is to say that they never dreamt of the socialist revolution. To complete the picture, we may note that in the work of the above-quoted Vollmar, the monopoly of foreign trade is presented, quite correctly, as one of the most important instruments of the "isolated socialist state". Marx and Engels must then have learned about this secret from Vollmar, had he himself not learned it earlier from them.

The "theory" of socialism in one country—a "theory" never expounded, by the way, or given any foundation, by Stalin himself—comes down to the sufficiently sterile and unhistoric notion that, thanks to the natural riches of the country, a socialist society can be built within the geographic confines of the Soviet Union. With the same success you might affirm that socialism could triumph if the population of the earth were a twelfth of what it is. In reality, however, the purpose of this new theory was to introduce into the social consciousness a far more concrete system of ideas, namely: the revolution is wholly completed; social contradictions will steadily soften; the kulak will gradually grow into socialism;

the development as a whole, regardless of events in the external world, will preserve a peaceful and planned character. Bukharin, in attempting to give some foundation to the theory, declared it unshakably proven that

> "we shall not perish owing to class differences within our country and our technical backwardness, that we can build socialism even on this pauper technical basis, that this growth of socialism will be many times slower, that we will crawl with a tortoise tempo, and that nevertheless we are building this socialism, and we will build it."

We remark the formula: "Build socialism even on a pauper technical basis", and we recall once more the genial intuition of the young Marx: with a low technical basis "only want will be generalized, and with want the struggle for necessities begins again, and all the old crap must revive".

In April 1926, at a Plenum of the Central Committee, the following amendment to the theory of the tortoise tempo was introduced by the Left Opposition:

> "It would be a fundamental error to think that in a capitalist environment we can go towards socialism at an arbitrary tempo. Our further approach to socialism will be ensured only on condition that the distance separating our industry from the advanced capitalist industry shall not increase, but clearly and palpably decrease."

Stalin with good reason declared this amendment a "masked" attack upon the theory of socialism in one country, and categorically rejected the very inclination to link up the tempo of domestic construction with the conditions of international development. Here is what he said verbatim, according to the stenographic report of the Plenum:

> "Whoever drags in here an international factor does not understand the very form of the question. He is either confused in the matter because he does not understand it, or he is consciously trying to confuse the question."

The amendment of the Opposition was rejected.

But the illusion of a socialism to be built at a tortoise tempo, on a pauper basis in an environment of powerful enemies, did not long withstand the blows of criticism. In November of the same year the 15th Party Conference, without a word of preparation in the press, acknowledged that it would be necessary "in a relatively [?] minimal historical period to catch up to and then surpass the level of industrial development of the advanced capitalist countries." The Left Opposition at any rate was here "surpassed". But in advancing this slogan—catch up to and surpass the whole world "in a minimal period"—yesterday's theorists of the tortoise tempo had fallen captive to that same international factor of which the Soviet bureaucracy had such a superstitious fear. Thus in the course of eight months the first and purest version of the Stalinist theory was liquidated.

Socialism must inevitably "surpass" capitalism in all spheres—wrote the Left Opposition in a document illegally distributed in March 1927—

> but at present the question is not of the relation of socialism to capitalism in general, but of the economic development of the Soviet Union in relation to Germany, England and the United States. What is to be understood by the phrase 'minimal historic period'? A whole series of future five-year plans will leave us far from the level of the advanced countries of the West. What will be happening in the capitalist world during this time?
> [...]

If you admit the possibility of its flourishing anew for a period of decades, then the talk of socialism in our backward country is pitiable tripe. Then it will be necessary to say that we were mistaken in our appraisal of the whole epoch as an epoch of capitalist decay. Then the Soviet Republic will prove to have been the second experiment in proletarian dictatorship since the Paris Commune, broader and more fruitful, but only an experiment.... Is there, however, any serious ground for such a decisive reconsideration of our whole epoch, and of the meaning of the October revolution as a link in an international revolution? No!

[...]

In finishing to a more or less complete extent their period of reconstruction [after the war]... the capitalist countries are reviving, and reviving in an incomparably sharper form, all the old pre-war contradictions, domestic and international. This is the basis of the proletarian revolution. It is a fact that we are building socialism. A greater fact, however, and not a less—since the whole in general is greater that the part—is the preparation of a European and world revolution. The part can conquer only together with the whole.

[...]

The European proletariat needs a far shorter period for its take-off to the seizure of power than we need to catch up technically with Europe and America.... We must, meanwhile, systematically narrow the distance separating our productivity of labor from that of the rest of the world. The more we advance, the less danger there is of possible intervention by low prices, and consequently by armies... The higher we raise the standard of living of the workers and peasants, the more truly shall we hasten the proletarian revolution in Europe, the sooner will that revolution enrich us with world technique, and the more truly and genuine will our socialist construction advance as a part of European and world construction."

This document, like the others, remained without answer—unless you consider expulsions from the party and arrests an answer to it.

After the abandonment of the idea of a tortoise tempo, it became necessary to renounce the idea bound up with it of the kulak's growing into socialism. The administrative extermination of kulakism, however, gave the theory of socialism in one country new nourishment. Once classes are "fundamentally" abolished, this means that socialism is "fundamentally" achieved (1931). In essence, this formula restored the conception of a socialist society built upon a "pauper basis". It was in those days, as we remember, that an official journalist explained that the absence of milk for babies is due to a lack of cows and not the shortcomings of the socialist system.

A concern for the productivity of labour, however, prevented any long resting upon these sedative formulae of

1931, which had to serve as moral compensation for the devastations effected by complete collectivization.

> "Some think," Stalin unexpectedly announced in connection with the Stakhanov movement, "that socialism can be strengthened by way of a certain material equalization of people on the basis of a pauper life. That is not true. [...] In reality, socialism can conquer only on the basis of a high productivity of labor, higher than under capitalism."

Completely correct!

However, at the very same time the new programme of the Communist Youth—adopted in April 1936 at the same congress which withdrew from the Communist Youth its last remnant of political rights—defined the socialist character of the Soviet Union in the following categoric terms: "The whole national economy of the country has become socialist." Nobody bothers to reconcile these contradictory conceptions. Each one is put into circulation in accord with the demands of the moment. It does not matter, for no one dares to criticize.

The spokesman at the congress explained the very necessity of the new program for the Communist Youth in the following words:

> "The old program contains a deeply mistaken anti-Leninist assertion to the effect that Russia 'can arrive at socialism only through a world proletarian revolution'. This point of the program is basically wrong. It reflects Trotskyist views."—that same views that Stalin was still defending in April 1924.

Aside from that, it remains unexplained how a programme written in 1921 by Bukharin, and carefully gone over by the Politburo with the participation of Lenin, could turn out after fifteen years to be "Trotskyist", and have to be revised to an exactly opposite effect! But logical arguments are powerless where it is a question of interests. Having won their independence from the proletariat of their own country, the bureaucracy cannot recognize the dependence of the Soviet Union upon the world proletariat. The law of uneven development brought it about that the contradiction between the technique and property relations of capitalism shattered the weakest link in the world chain. Backward Russian capitalism was the first to pay for the bankruptcy of world capitalism. The law of uneven development is supplemented throughout the whole course of history by the law of combined development. The collapse of the bourgeoisie in Russia led to the proletarian dictatorship —that is, to a backward country's leaping ahead of the advanced countries. However, the establishment of socialist forms of property in the backward country came up against the inadequate level of technique and culture. Itself born of the contradictions between his world productive forces and capitalist forms of property, the October Revolution produced in its turn a contradiction between low national productive forces and socialist forms of property.

To be sure, the isolation of the Soviet Union did not have those immediate dangerous consequences, which might have been feared. The capitalist world was too disorganized and paralyzed to unfold to the full extent its potential power. The "breathing spell" proved longer than a critical optimism had dared to hope. However, isolation and the impossibility of using the resources of world economy even upon capitalistic bases (the amount of foreign trade has decreased from 1913 four to five times) entailed, along with enormous expenditures upon military defence, an extremely disadvantageous allocation of productive forces, and a slow raising of the standard of living of the masses. But a more maligned product of isolation and backwardness has been the octopus of bureaucratism.

The juridical and political standards set up by the revolution exercised a progressive action upon the backward economy, but upon the other hand they themselves felt the lowering influence of that backwardness. The longer the Soviet Union remains in a capitalist environment, the deeper runs the degeneration of the social fabric. A prolonged isolation would inevitably end not in national communism, but in a restoration of capitalism.

If a bourgeoisie cannot peacefully grow into a socialist democracy, it is likewise true that a socialist state cannot peacefully merge with a world capitalist system. On the historic order of the day stands not the peaceful socialist development of "one country", but a long series of world disturbances: wars and revolutions. Disturbances are inevitable also in the domestic life of the Soviet Union. If the bureaucracy was compelled in its struggle for a planned economy to dekulakize the kulak, the working class will be compelled in its struggle for socialism to debureaucratize the bureaucracy.

On the tomb of the latter will be inscribed the epitaph: "Here lies the theory of socialism in one country."

### 1. The "Friends" of the Soviet Union

For the first time a powerful government provides a stimulus abroad not to the respectable right, but to the left and extreme left press. The sympathies of the popular masses for the great revolution are being very skillfully canalized and sluiced into the mill of the Soviet bureaucracy. The "sympathizing" Western press is imperceptibly losing the right to publish anything, which might aggrieve the ruling stratum of the Soviet Union. Books undesirable to the Kremlin are maliciously unmentioned. Noisy and mediocre apologists are published in many languages. We have avoided quoting throughout this work the specific productions of the official "friends", preferring the crude originals to the stylized foreign paraphrases. However, the literature of the "friends", including that of the Communist International, the most crass and vulgar part of it, presents in cubic meters an impressive magnitude, and plays not the last role in politics. We must devote a few concluding pages to it.

At present the chief contribution to the treasury of thought is declared to be the Webbs' book, *Soviet Communism*. Instead of relating what has been achieved and in what direction the achieved is developing, the authors expound for twelve hundred pages what is contemplated, indicated in the bureaus, or expounded in the laws. Their conclusion is: When the projects, plans and laws are carried out, then communism will be realized in the Soviet Union. Such is the content of this depressing book, which rehashes the reports of Moscow bureaus and the anniversary articles of the Moscow press.

Friendship for the Soviet bureaucracy is not friendship for the proletarian revolution, but, on the contrary, insurance against it. The Webbs are, to be sure, ready to acknowledge that the communist system will sometime or other spread to the rest of the world.

> "But how, when, where, with what modifications, and whether through violent revolution, or by peaceful penetration, or even by conscious imitation, are questions we cannot answer."

This diplomatic refusal to answer—or, in reality, this unequivocal answer —is in the highest degree characteristic of the "friends", and tells the actual price of their friendship. If everybody had thus answered the question of revolution before 1917, when it was infinitely harder to answer, there would have been no Soviet state in the world, and the British "friends" would have had to expand their fund of friendly emotion upon other objects.

The Webbs speak as of something, which goes without saying about the vanity of hoping for a European revolution in the near future, and they gather from that a comforting proof of the correctness of the theory of socialism in one country. With the authority of people for whom the October Revolution was a complete, and moreover an unpleasant, surprise, they give us lessons in the necessity of building a socialist society within the limits of the Soviet Union in the absence of other perspectives. It is difficult to refrain from an impolite movement of the shoulders! In reality, our dispute with the Webbs is not as to the necessity of building factories in the Soviet Union and employing mineral fertilizers on the collective farms, but as to whether it is necessary to prepare a revolution in Great Britain and how it shall be done. Upon that question the learned sociologues answer: "We do not know." They consider the very question, of course, in conflict with "science".

Lenin was passionately hostile to the conservative bourgeois who imagines himself a socialist, and, in particular, to the British Fabians. By the biographical glossary attached to his *Works*, it is not difficult to find out that his attitude to the Webbs throughout his whole active life remained one of unaltered fierce hostility. In 1907 he first wrote of the Webbs as "obtuse eulogists of English philistinism", who try to represent Chartism, the revolutionary epoch of the English labour movement, as mere childishness. Without Chartism, however, there would have been no Paris Commune. Without both, there would have been no October Revolution. The Webbs found in the Soviet Union only an administrative mechanism and a bureaucratic plan. They found neither Chartism nor Communism nor the October Revolution. A revolution remains for them today, as before, an alien and hostile matter, if not indeed "mere childishness".

In his polemics against opportunists, Lenin did not trouble himself, as is well known, with the manners of the salon. But his abusive epithets ("lackeys of the bourgeoisie", "traitors", "boot-lick souls") expressed during many years a carefully weighed appraisal of the Webbs and the evangels of Fabianism—that is, of traditional respectability and worship for what exists. There can be no talk of any sudden change in the views of the Webbs during recent years. These same people who during the war support their bourgeoisie, and who accepted later at the hands of the King the title of Lord Passfield, have renounced nothing, and changed not at all, in adhering to Communism in a single, and moreover a foreign, country. Sidney Webb was Colonial Minister—that is, chief jailkeeper of British imperialism—in the very period of his life when he was drawing near to the Soviet bureaucracy, receiving material from its bureaus, and on that basis working upon this two-volume compilation.

As late as 1923, the Webbs saw no great difference between Bolshevism and Tzarism (see, for example, *The Decay of Capitalist Civilization*, 1923). Now, however, they have fully reorganized the "democracy" of the Stalin regime. It is needless to seek any contradiction here. The Fabians were indignant when the revolutionary proletariat withdrew freedom of activity from "educated" society, but they think it quite in the order of things when a bureaucracy withdraws freedom of activity from the proletariat. Has not this always been the function of the laborite's workers' bureaucracy? The Webbs swear, for example, that criticism in the Soviet Union is completely free. A sense of humour is not to be expected of these people. They refer with complete seriousness to that notorious "self-criticism" which is enacted as a part of one's official duties, and the direction of which, as well as its limits, can always be accurately foretold.

Naivete? Neither Engels nor Lenin considered Sidney Webb naive. Respectability rather. After all, it is a question of an established regime and of hospitable hosts. The Webbs are extremely disapproving in their attitude to a Marxian criticism of what exists. They consider themselves called to preserve the heritage of the October Revolution from the Left Opposition. For the sake of completeness we observe that in its day the Labour Government in which Lord Passfield (Sidney Webb) held a portfolio refused the author of this work a visa to enter Great Britain. Thus Sidney Webb, who in those very days was working on his book upon the Soviet Union, is theoretically defending the Soviet Union from being undermined, but practically he is defending the Empire of His Majesty. In justice be it said that in both cases he remains true to himself.

* * *

For many of the petty bourgeoisie who master neither pen nor brush, an officially registered "friendship" for the Soviet Union is a kind of certificate of higher spiritual interests. Membership in Freemason lodges or pacifist clubs has much in common with membership in the society of "Friends of the Soviet Union", for it makes it possible to live two lives at once: an everyday life in a circle of commonplace interests, and a holiday life evaluating to the soul. From time to time the "friends" visit Moscow. They note down in their memory tractors, crèches, Pioneers, parades, parachute girls—in a word, everything except the new aristocracy. The best of them close their eyes to this out of a feeling of hostility toward capitalist reaction. Andre Gide frankly acknowledges this:

> "The stupid and dishonest attack against the Soviet Union has brought it about that we now defend it with a certain obstinacy."

But the stupidity and dishonesty of one's enemies is no justification for one's own blindness. The working masses, at any rate, have need of clearsighted friends.

The epidemic sympathy of bourgeois radicals and socialist bourgeois for the ruling stratum of the Soviet Union has causes that are not unimportant. In the circle of professional politicians, notwithstanding all differences of programme, there is always a predominance of those friendly to such "progress" as is already achieved or can easily be achieved. There are incomparably more reformers in the world than revolutionists, more accommodationists than irreconciables. Only in exceptional historic periods, when the masses come into movement, do the revolutionists emerge from their isolation, and the reformers become more like fish out of water.

In the milieu of the present Soviet bureaucracy, there is not a person who did not, prior to April 1917, and even considerably later, regards the idea of a proletarian dictatorship in Russia as fantastic. (At that time this "fantasy" was called... Trotskyism.) The older generation of the foreign "friends" for decades regarded as *Realpolitiker* to Russian Mensheviks, who stood for a "people's front" with the liberals and rejected the idea of dictatorship as arrant madness. To recognize a dictatorship when it is already achieved and even bureaucratically befouled —that is a different matter. That is a matter exactly to the minds of these "friends". They now not only pay their respects to the Soviet state, but even defined it against its enemies—not so much, to be sure, against those who yearn for the past, as against those who are preparing the future. Where these "friends" are active preparing, as in the case of the French, Belgian, English and other reformists, it is convenient to them to conceal their solidarity with the bourgeoisie under a concern for the defense of the Soviet Union. Where, on the other hand, they have unwillingly become defeatists, as in the case of the German and Austrian social patriots of yesterday, they hope that the alliance of France with the Soviet Union may help them settle with Hitler or Schussnigg. Leon Blum, who was an enemy of Bolshevism in its heroic epoch, and opened the pages of *Le Populaire* for the express purpose of publicly baiting the October Revolution, would now not print a line exposing the real crimes of the Soviet bureaucracy. Just as the Biblical Moses, thirsting to see the face of Jehovah, was permitted to make his bow only to the rearward parts of the divine anatomy, so the honorable reformists, worshipers of the accomplished fact, are capable of knowing and acknowledging in a revolution only its meaty bureaucratic posterior.

The present communist "leaders" belong in essence to the same type. After a long series of monkey jumps and grimaces, they have suddenly discovered the enormous advantages of opportunism, and have seized upon it with the freshness proper to that ignorance which has always distinguished them. Their slavish and not always disinterested kowtowing to the upper circles in the Kremlin alone renders them absolutely incapable of revolutionary initiative. They answer critical arguments no otherwise than with snarling and barking; and, moreover, under the whip of the boss they wag their tails. This most unattractive aggregation, which in the hour of danger will scatter to the four winds, considers us flagrant "counterrevolutionists". What of it? History, in spite of its austere character, cannot get along without an occasional farce.

The more honest or open-eyed of the "friends", at least when speaking tete-a-tete, concede that there is a spot on the Soviet sun. But substituting a fatalistic for a dialectic analysis, they console themselves with the thought that "a certain" bureaucratic degeneration in the given conditions was historically inevitable. Even so! The resistance to this degeneration also has not fallen from the sky. A necessity has two ends: the reactionary and the progressive. History teaches that persons and parties which drag at the opposite ends of a necessity turn out in the long run on opposite sides of the barricade.

The final argument of the "friends" is that reactionaries will seize upon any criticism of the Soviet regime. That is indubitable! We may assume that they will try to get something for themselves out of the present book. When was it ever otherwise? The *Communist Manifesto* spoke scornfully of the fact that the feudal reaction tried to use against liberalism the arrows of socialist criticism. That did not prevent revolutionary socialism from following its road. It will not prevent us either. The press of the Communist International, it is true, goes so far as to assert that our criticism is preparing military intervention against the Soviets. This obviously means that the capitalist governments, learning from our works of the degeneration of the Soviet bureaucracy, will immediately equip a punitive expedition to avenge the trampled principles of October! The polemists of the Communist International are not armed with rapiers but wagon tongues, or some still less nimble instrument. In reality a Marxist criticism, which calls things by their real names, can only increase the conservative credit of the Soviet diplomacy in the eyes of the bourgeoisie.

It is otherwise with the working class and its sincere champions among the intelligentsia. Here our work will cause doubts and evoke distrust —not of revolutionaries, but of its usurpers. But that is the very goal we have set ourselves. The motor force of progress is truth and not lies.